ISLAM FOR NON-MUSLIMS

Islam for Non-Muslims

F Khan

MD Publications Pvt Ltd
New Delhi
www.mdppl.com

Published by :

MD Publications Pvt Ltd
"MD House", 11, Darya Ganj,
New Delhi - 110 002
Phone : +91-11- 45355555
E-mail : contact@mdppl.com
Website: www.mdppl.com

ISBN : 978-81-7533-353-6

Published and Printed by Mr. Pranav Gupta on behalf of **MD Publications Pvt Ltd** at Repro India Limited.

PREFACE

The word "Muslim" means one who submits to the will of God. This is done by declaring that "there is no god except one God and Muhammad is the messenger of God." In a broader sense, anyone who willingly submits to the will of God is a Muslim. Thus, all the prophets preceding the prophet Muhammad are considered Muslims. The Quran specifically mentions Abraham who lived long before Moses and Christ that, "he was not a Jew or a Christian but a Muslim," because, he had submitted to the will of God. Thus there are Muslims who are not submitting at all to the will of God and there are Muslims who are doing their best to live an Islamic life. One cannot judge Islam by looking at those individuals who have a Muslim name but in their actions, they are not living or behaving as Muslims. The extent of being a Muslim can be according to the degree to which one is submitting to the will of God, in his beliefs and his actions.

Islam, the root of which is Silm and Salam means peace. One of the beautiful names of God is that He is the Peace. It means more than that: submission to the One God, and to live in peace with the Creator, within one's self, with other people and with the environment. Thus, Islam is a total system of living. A Muslim is supposed to live in peace and harmony with all these segments; hence, a Muslim is any person anywhere in the world whose obedience, allegiance, and loyalty are to God, the Lord of the Universe.

Muslims believe that Islam is a total and a complete way of life. It encompasses all aspect of life. As such, the teachings of Islam do not separate religion from politics. As a matter of fact, state and religion are under the obedience of Allah through the teachings of Islam. Hence, economic and social transactions, as we educational and political systems are also of the teachings of Islam.

The Prophet and his successors in Islam have conceded to every non-Muslim community, from among subjects of the Islamic state, a judicial autonomy, not only for personal status, but also for all the affairs of life - civil, penal, and others. The safeguard of the rights of non-Muslims, in the Islamic territory, goes even to the extent of giving them the liberty of practising customs entirely opposed to those of Islam. The Islamic law makes a certain distinction among different non-Muslim communities, insofar as their relations with individual Muslims are concerned. It divides non-Muslims into what we might call "developed" and "primitive," or those who believe in the One God and follow Divine laws revealed to the founder of their religions, and those who do not do that (such idolators, atheists, pagans, animists, etc.).

I am very thankful to Mr. Pranav Gupta, Director of MD Publications Pvt Ltd, New Delhi, for his kind cooperation and support for this book.

F Khan

Contents

1

The Status of Non-Muslims in Islam

It is natural that one should make a distinction, and even discrimination, between the near and the distant and between the relative and the stranger. With intellectual and moral evolution there is a tendency in human society to facilitate the assimilation of the foreigner. If a society were to group itself solely on the basis of blood relationships, naturalization would be out of the question for ever. The same is true if the basis were the colour of skin, which cannot be concealed. Language as a factor of social unity requires long years for a veritable assimilation. Place of birth is even less perceptible in a stranger, and ever since man had crossed the horizon of city-states, not much importance has been attached to this last factor. However, one would remark that in all these various conceptions of social unity, the basis is a mere accident of nature, and belongs more to the animal instinct than to the rationality of man. It is common knowledge that Islam has rejected all these notions of nationality and selected only the identity of ideas - a thing which depends on the choice of man and not the accidents and hazards of birth - as the basic tie of society and the factor of union. Naturalization and assimilation in such a society is not only easy and accessible to all human races in their entirety, but it is also closer to reason and more practical, showing how to live one's life in peace and tranquility.

If a believer in God or a capitalist is considered as a stranger in communist countries, a black-skinned in such white countries as practice social segregation, or a non-Italian in Italy, it should not be surprising if a non-Muslim should be considered as a stranger in the land of Islam. Conceptions, or rather angles of view, differ, yet everybody makes some distinction or other between those who belong to his own group and those who do not.

As in other political or social systems, Islam also makes a distinction between its "relatives" and "strangers," but there are two characteristics peculiar to it:(1) the facility to cross this barrier by subscribing to its ideology, and (2) but little inequality between the two categories regarding the affairs of this world. We shall try to throw some light on this last aspect of the question.

DIVINE ORIGIN OF DUTIES

One should not forget the great practical importance attached to the fact that Muslims obey their system of law as something of Divine origin, and not merely the will of the majority of the leaders of the country. In this latter case, the minority enters on a struggle so that its own conceptions may prevail. In the democracies of our time, not only do the majorities often change from election to election but are also constituted or disintegrated by all sorts of commutations and combinations, and the party in power tries to upset the policy pursued by its predecessors, causing, among other changes, the modification of laws. Without entering here into the question of the adaptability of Islamic laws to the exigencies of social evolution, one might deem it as an incontestable truth that there is greater stability in the Muslim law - due to the Divine origin - than in any other secular legislation of the world with the following result:

The Islamic law ordains justice to, and observation of certain rules regarding the non-Muslims. These therefore feel no apprehension in the face of political quarrels and parliamentary elections of the country of their residence, with regard to the Islamic laws in force. The ruler or parliament cannot modify them.

BASIC NOTIONS

The believers and nonbeliever's cannot be equals, the former will go to Paradise, and the latter to hell, but all this concerns the Hereafter. As to the life in this world, Muslim jurists like ad-Dabusi and others have at all times revealed the greatest equality compatible with their system between "relatives" and"strangers," as we shall presently see.

There is the question of religious tolerance. The Qur'an (2:256) prescribes that there should be no compulsion in religion. The residing subjects as well as the temporary sojourners have an assurance regarding their safety and the liberty of their conscience.

There is the question of hospitality and asylum, regarding which the theoretical position is strengthened by the practice of more than a thousand years. There is the well-known verse of the Qur'an (9:6): "And if anyone of the pagans seeketh thy asylum (O Muhammad), then give him asylum . . . and afterwards convey him to his place of safety . . ." The victims of racial, religious, political and other persecutions have always found refuge and shelter in the land of Islam.

[What a touching and even stupefying teaching is the command that a Muslim should collaborate even with the enemy in the state of war! Says the Holy Qur'an (5:2) " . . . and let not the hatred of a people who have stopped your going to the Inviolable Mosque (of the Ka'bah) incite you to transgress; but help ye one another unto charity and piety. Help not one another unto sin and transgression. Lo! God is severe in punishment." Mutual help is not to be restricted among Muslims alone, but with entire humanity without restriction of religion and race!-Editor]

PRACTICE OF THE PROPHET

When the Prophet Mohammed settled down in Medina, he found there complete anarchy, the region having never known before either a State or a king to unite the tribes torn by internecine feuds. In just a few weeks, he succeeded in rallying all the inhabitants of the region into order. He constituted a city state, in which Muslims, Jews, pagan Arabs and also probably a small number of Christians, all entered into a statal organism by means of a social contract.

The constitutional law of this first 'Muslim' State - which was the confederacy as a sequence of the multiplicity of the population groups - has come down to us in toto, and we read therein not only in clause 25: "to Muslims their religion, and to Jews their religion," or, "that there would be benevolence and justice," but even the unexpected passage in the same clause 25: "the Jews . . . are a community (in alliance) with - according Ibn Hisham and in the version of Abu-'Ubaid, a community (forming part) of - the believers (i.e., Muslims)."

The very fact that, at the time of the constitution of this city-state, the autonomous Jewish villages acceded of their free will to the confederal State, and recognized Muhammad as their supreme political head, implies in our opinion that the non-Muslim subjects possessed the right of votes in the election of the head of the Muslim State, at least in so far as the political life of the country was concerned.

Military defence was, according to the document in question, the duty of all elements of the population, including the Jews. This implies their participation in the consultation, and in the execution of the plans adopted. In fact section 37 laid down: "the Jews would bear their expenses and the Muslims theirs, and there will be mutual succour between them in case an aggressor attacks the parties to this Document." Further section 45 says that war and peace will be indivisible for the parties to the Document.

Some months after the establishment of this City-State, we see the Prophet Muhammad concluding treaties of defensive alliance and mutual aid with the pagan Arabs of the neighbourhood of Medina. Some of them embraced Islam about ten years afterwards. During all those long years, mutual confidence was most complete, as the following incidents will show.

In the year 2 AH, the pagans of Mecca sent a diplomatic mission to Abyssinia, in order to demand of the Negus the "extradition" of Meccan Muslims who had taken refuge in his country. To counteract their machinations, the Prophet also sent, in his turn, an ambassador for interceding with the Negus in favour of the Muslims who had sought asylum in his country due to religious persecution by their co-citizens. This ambassador of Islam was 'Amr ibn Umaiyah ad-Damri, "who had not yet embraced Islam." In fact, he belonged to one of the Allied tribes of the neighbourhood of Medina just referred to.

At a time when there were constant wars on extensive frontiers of the Islamic territory, military service was very far from being an easy means of earning a livelihood; the risks to life and to the economic situation of the combatants were very real. Even if the exemption of the non-Muslim subjects from this service was motivated by the suspicions in regard to their trustworthiness, all non-Muslims who had accepted Muslim domination and did not seek its overthrow in collusion with foreigners welcomed this exemption from military service. They could thus pursue in tranquillity their avocations and prosper, while the Muslims would be engaged in military duties with all the attendant risks. So, the non-Muslims paid little supplementary tax, the jizyah - of which the women, children and the poor from among them were exempt - which was neither heavy nor unjust. In the time of the Prophet, the jizyah amounted to ten dirhams annually, which represented the expenses of an average family for ten days. Moreover, if a non-Muslim subject participated in military service during some expedition in a year, he was exempted from the jizyah for the year in question. Some typical cases will show the real character of this tax.

In the beginning of Islam, this tax did not exist in the Muslim State, in either Medina or elsewhere. It was towards the year 9 AH that the Qur'an ordained it. That it was a question of expediency, and not a matter of dogmatic duty in Islam, is sufficiently shown by the following incidents. It is reported (by Ibn Sa'd on the authority of Zuhri) that at the moment of the death of his son, Ibrahim, the Prophet Mohammed declared: "Had he survived, I would have exempted all the Copts from the jizyah, as a mark of esteem for Ibrahim's mother. (Who was a Coptic girl). Or again, (cf. Suyuti Husn al-Mahadarah, ch. Khalij Amir al-Mu'minin), when a non-Muslim Egyptian laid before the Muslim government the project of re-digging the ancient canal from Fustat (Cairo) down to the Red Sea, thus facilitating the maritime transport of Egyptian food stuffs to Medina - the famous Nahr Amir al-Mu'minin - the caliph "Umar rewarded him by exempting him from jizyah during his entire life. There are jurists who opine that one should also take into consideration the international repercussions affecting Muslim interests, in view of the fact that Islam has penetrated countries which are under non-Muslim domination; and the jizyah territory would inevitably produce a reaction on Muslims in Christian and other countries.

There is another saying of the Prophet which was pronounced on his death bed and which directs the transfer of the Jewish and Christian populations of the Hijaz to other regions; its context has not been mentioned in the traditions, but it is evident that it concerned certain populations of this region on account of their political behaviour, and that it was not a general prohibition against the members of these two communities. It may be noticed that, in the time of the caliphs, there were non-Muslim slaves, male and female, belonging to Muslims and living along with their masters, at Mecca, Medina, etc. A celebrated case of free non-Muslims is that of the Christian doctor, whose consultation rooms were just below the minaret of the mosque of the Ka'bah (Mecca). He lived there in the time of "Umar ibn 'Abd al-'Aziz or soon after him (cf. Ibn Sa'd, V. 365 - Da'wud ibn 'Abdur Rahman. In fact Da'wud was a pious Muslim, yet his physician father remained a Christian). Ibn Sa'd also records the case of a Christian, Jufainah, who taught reading and writing to school children in Medina.

We may also recall the direction of the Prophet on his death bed: "Observe scrupulously the protection accorded by me to non-Muslim subjects. Another saying of the Prophet reported by Abu Da'wud is: "whoever oppresses non-Muslim subjects, shall find me to be their advocate on the day of Resurrection (against the oppressing Muslims)."

The directions as well as the practice of the Prophet constitute the highest law for Muslims. As to the assimilation of these laws into the life of Muslims and practice of later times, a study of history could profitability be pursued? We shall referr to a few facts here.

LATER PRACTICE

A governor of the Caliph 'Umar selected a non-Muslim secretary. Learning the news, the Caliph issued an order to have him replaced by a Muslim. This refers to a time when the province in question had not yet been purified, and a war was still in progress. This is understandable in view of the importance of the post and the natural mistrust of the inhabitants of the newly conquered country. Moreover this governor was an illiterate person. In order to better comprehend the attitude of 'Umar, let us recall another incident of the same great caliph (reported by al-Baladhuri, Ansab): "One day he wrote to his governor of Syria: Send us a Greek, who could put in order the accounts of our revenues." He put a Christian at the head of this administration, in Medina.

The same Caliph often consulted non-Muslims on military, economical and administrative questions.

One would not reproach Muslims for preserving the post of the imam (the leader of the prayer-service in the mosque) exclusively for their co-religionists. Islam has desired the coordination of all aspects of life, spiritual as well as temporal. Hence, the fact that the leading of the prayer-service in the mosque is a duty and privilege of the head of state that is also head of the religion. If one takes into consideration this state of things, one will understand easily why a non-Muslim subject cannot be elected head of a Muslim State.

But this exception does on no account imply the exclusion of non-Muslim subjects from the political and administrative life of the country. Ever since the time of the caliphs, non-Muslims have been seen holding the rank of ministers in Muslim States. A parallel practice has not been witnessed in the more important secular democracies of the world, where Muslim subjects are not lacking. That this practice of the caliphs is not contrary to the teaching of Islam, is borne witness to by classical authors, and Shafi'ite jurists (like al-Mawardi) and Hanbalite one's (like Abu Ya'la al-Farra') have not hesitated to support the view that the caliph may lawfully nominate non-Muslim subjects as ministers and members of executive councils. We have already spoken of a non-Muslim ambassador sent by the Prophet himself to Abyssinia.

SOCIAL AUTONOMY

Perhaps the most characteristic feature of Islam, in its attitude regarding the non-Muslims, is the award of social and judicial autonomy. In a long passage of the Qur'an, we read:

"If then they have recourse unto thee (O Muhammad), Judge between them or disclaim jurisdiction; if thou disclaimest jurisdiction, then they cannot harm thee at all; but if thou judgest, Judge between them with equity; lo! God loveth the equitable. How can they come unto thee for judgment when they have the Torah, wherein is contained the judgment of God? Yet even after that they turn away; such folk are not believers. Lo! We did reveal the Torah, wherein is guidance and a light, by which the prophets who surrendered (unto God) judged the Jews, and the rabbis and the priests judged by such of God's Scripture as they were bidden to observe, and thereunto they were witnesses; so fear not mankind, but fear Me, and barter not My revelations for a little gain; whoso judgeth not by that which God hath revealed: such are disbelievers.

And We prescribed for them therein the life for the life, and the eye for the eye, and the nose for the notes, and the ear for the ear, and the tooth for the tooth, and for wounds retaliation; but whoso forgoeth it (by way of charity) it shall be expiation for him; whoso judgeth not by that which God hath revealed: such are wrong doers. And we caused Jesus, son of Mary, to follow in their footsteps, confirming that which was revealed before it in the Torah - guidance and an admonition unto those who are God-fearing. Let the people of the Gospel judge by that which God hath revealed therein; whoso judgeth not by that which God hath revealed; such are evil-livers. And unto thee (O Muhammad) have We revealed the Scripture with the Truth, confirming whatever Scripture was sent before it, and a watcher over it: so judge between them by that which God hath revealed, and follow not their desires away from the truth which hath come unto thee: for each We have appointed a Divine law (Shari'ah) and a traced-out way; had God willed, He could have made you one community, but He may try you by that which He hath given you (He hath made you as you are); so vie one with the other in Good works; unto God ye will all return, and He will then inform you of that wherein ye differ." [Qur'an 5:42-48]

It is on the basis of this amendment, that the Prophet and his successors in Islam have conceded to every non-Muslim community, from among subjects of the Islamic state, a judicial autonomy, not only for personal status, but also for all the affairs of life - civil, penal, and others. In the time of the Orthodox Caliphs, for instance, we find evidence of contemporary Christians (for text cf. infra 497) attesting to the fact that the Muslim government had delegated in favour of Christian priests, many temporal judicial powers. In the time of the 'Abbasid caliphs, we find the Christian patriarch and the Jewish hakham, among the highest dignitaries of state, connected directly with the Caliph.

In the time of the Prophet, the Jews of Medina had their Bait al-Midras (both a synagogue and educational institute). In the treaty with the Christians of Najaran (Yaman), the Prophet gave the guarantee not only for the security of the person and property of the inhabitants, but had also expressly left the nomination of bishops and priests to the Christian community itself.

There is a tendency among a large number of people to imitate and ape their governors and chiefs in the outer conduct of life such as dress, coiffure, etiquette, etc. The result is a superficial assimilation, which brings no advantage to the ruling community, but which causes a moral damage to the classes which imitate in a servile manner. In an Islamic State, non-Muslims constitute a protected community (dhimmi). Therefore it is the duty of the government to protect the legitimate interests of these "strangers." Hence that we see, during the 'Abbasid caliphate that, far from seeking the assimilation of "strangers" by force, the government discouraged all imitation of one by the other: Muslims, Christians, Jews, Magians and others conserved by their own modes of dress, their social manners and their distinctive individualities. Only a total assimilation, for religious conversion, was sought, and not a confusion of communities. This is proof enough that the measure had nothing to do with the religious exigencies of Islam - and in the time of the Prophet there was absolutely no trace of it - but a condition of life, suiting the social conceptions of the epoch: and its essential purpose was to recognize, at the very first sight, the religious community of each and every individual. The intention was to protect in this way the culture of everyone, so that its intrinsic values and defects should come more into relief. In passing, it may be repeated that the conception of nationality in Islam is based neither on an ethnic source nor on the place of birth, but on the identity of ideology, i.e., of religion.

The person, property and honour of every individual, whether indigenous or heterogenous, are fully protected in the Islamic territory. The Sharh al-Hidayah, which is a legal manual of current use, employs, for instance, the characteristic expression: "Defamation is prohibited, be it concerning the Muslim or a Protected (non-Muslim)." Another jurist of great authority, the author of al-Bahr ar-Rai'iq says: "even the bones of the dead among the Protected (non-Muslims) have the right to be respected, even as the bones of Muslims. It is not allowed to profane them, because if the ill treatment of a Protected (non-Muslim) is forbidden in his life-time, on account of the protection which he enjoys, the protection of his bones against every profanation is equally obligatory after his death." The jurists are unanimous in declaring that, if a Muslim violates a non-Muslim woman, he will receive the same punishment as is prescribed against the violation of Muslim women.

In the time of the caliph 'Umar, certain Muslims had usurped a piece of land belonging to a Jew, and had constructed a mosque on the site. Learning the news, the caliph ordered the demolition of the mosque and the restoration of the land to the Jews. Prof. Cardahi (a Christian of Lebanon, in a series of lectures on Private International Law of Islam, delivered at The Hague, 1933) writes, "this house of the to Bait al-Yahudi, still exists and is well-known." Another classical example, cited by Ibn Kathir and others is that of the Grand Mosque of Damascus. An Umaiyad caliph had occupied the church to enlarge the Mosque. Later when the complaint was brought before caliph 'Umar ibn 'Abd al-'Aziz, he ordered that part of the mosque to be built on the usurped piece of ground be demolished and the church restored there. But the Christians themselves preferred a monetary compensation and the matter was thus amicably be settled.

Let us cite the circular of the caliph "'Umar ibn 'Abd al-'Aziz, (preserved by Ibn Sa'd, V. 280), which is eloquent testimony:

"With the name of God, the Most Merciful, the All Merciful, from the Servant of God, Commander of the Faithful, 'Umar (ibn 'abd al-'Aziz) to (the governor) 'Adi ibn Artat and to the believing Muslims in his company: Peace be with you. Whereafter I send you praise of God, beside Whom there is no God. Thereafter: Pay attention to the condition of the Protected (non-Muslims), treat them tenderly. If any of them reaches old age and has no resources, it is you who should spend on him. If he has contractual brethren, demand these latter to spend on him. Apply retaliation if anybody commits tort against him. This is as if you have a slave, who reaches old age, you should spend on him telling his death or liberate him. I have learned that you accept tithe on the import of wine and make it enter the Treasury belonging to God. I warn you never to let it enter the Treasury belonging to God, however small the amount maybe, unless it be a legally pure property. Peace be with you."

Another letter of the same caliph (cf. Ibn Sa'd, V. 253) says:

"Purify the registers from the charge of obligation (i.e., taxes levied unjustly); and study old files (also). If any injustice has been committed regarding a Muslim or a non-Muslim, restore him his right. If any such person should have died, remit his rights to his heirs."

It is common knowledge that the Muslim jurists recognize the right of preemption in regard to neighbours. If anybody sells his immovable property, the neighbour has the prior right over a stranger. This right is recognized in favour of non-Muslims as well.

The safeguard of the rights of non-Muslims, in the Islamic territory, goes even to the extent of giving them the liberty of practising customs entirely opposed to those of Islam. For instance the consumption of alcoholic drinks is forbidden to Muslims, yet the non-Muslim inhabitants of the country have full liberty not only of consumption, but also of manufacture, importation and sale of the same. The same is true for games of chance, marriage with close relatives, the contract entailing interest, etc. In olden times, this did not affect Muslims, and abuses with their repercussions were rare. Modern jurists have restricted the liberty insofar as international commerce is concerned. As attempts to restrict alcoholic consumption will be ineffectual if they should not be applicable to the whole population, the consent of the representatives of non-Muslims has facilitated the task for jurists, who in principle would not intervene in the practices of different communities differing in points of religion.

The Islamic law makes a certain distinction among different non-Muslim communities, insofar as their relations with individual Muslims are concerned. It divides non-Muslims into what we might call "developed" and "primitive," or those who believe in the One God and follow Divine laws revealed to the founder of their religions, and those who do not do that (such idolators, atheists, pagans, animists, etc.). All are tolerated as subjects and enjoy protection with regard to the liberty of conscience and life, yet a Muslim in his private life treats them differently: a Muslim has the right to marry a "developed" non-Muslim woman, but not a "primitive" one. So is it too that a Muslim may not only marry a Christian or a Jewish girl, but also give her the liberty to conserve her religion. She may go to church or to synagogue, she may drink wine, etc. It is forbidden for a Muslim to marry a woman who does not believe in God or an idolatress or a polytheist. A Muslim woman cannot be the wife of non-Muslim to whatever category he may belong (Q. 60:10). Again, a Muslim cannot eat the flesh of animals slaughtered by members of the "primitive" communities.

CONVERSION

The Islamic law expressly recognizes for non-Muslims the liberty to preserve their beliefs; and while it forbids categorically all recourse to compulsion for converting others to Islam, it maintains rigorous discipline among its own adherents. The basis of the Islamic "nationality" is religious and not ethnic, linguistic nor regional. Hence apostasy has naturally been considered political treason. It is true that this crime is punished by penalties, but the necessity scarcely as history has proved. Not only at the time when the Muslims reigned supreme from the Pacific to the Atlantic Oceans, but even in our own age of political as well as material and intellectual weakness among Muslims, apostasy of Muslims is surprisingly non-existent. This is true not only of regions where there is the semblance of a Muslim State, but even elsewhere, under the colonial powers that have made all humanly possible efforts to convert Muslims to other religions. Islam is gaining ground today, even among Western peoples, from Finland to Norway to Italy, from Canada to Argentina. And all this in spite of the absence of any organized missionary activity.

HOLY WAR

It refers to the notion commonly held of the holy war. The entire life of a Muslim, be it concerning spiritual affairs or temporal ones, is a discipline regulated by Divine law. If a Muslim celebrates even his service of prayer without conviction (for ostentation, for instance), it is not a spiritual act of devotion, but a crime against God, a worship of the self punishable in the Hereafter. On the contrary, if a Muslim takes his meals for the purpose of having the needed strength to perform his obligations regarding God, even if he cohabits with his wife, as an act of obedience to the Divine law which orders him that, these acts of need and pleasure constitute saintly acts, acts of devotion, meriting all the Divine rewards promised for piety, as a saying of the Prophet indicates.

Such being the concept of life, a just struggle cannot be anything except a holy act. All war is forbidden in Islam, if it is not waged for a just cause, ordained by the Divine law. The life of the Prophet provides reference to only three kinds of wars: defensive, punitive and preventive. In a celebrated correspondence with the Emperor Heraclius of Byzantium, in connection with the assassination of a Muslim ambassador in the Byzantine territory, the Prophet proposed three alternatives: "Embrace Islam - if not, then pay the jizyah tribute. . . if not, then do not interfere between thy subjects and Islam if these former desire to embrace Islam or pay the jizyah" (cf. Abu 'Ubaid, Kitab al-Amwal, s. 5 5). To establish liberty of conscience in the world was the aim and object of the struggle of the Prophet Muhammad, and who may have a greater authority in Islam than he? This is the "holy war" of the Muslims, the one which is undertaken not for the purposes of exploitation, but in a spirit of sacrifice, its sole object being to make the Word of God prevail. All else is illegal. There is absolutely no question of waging war for compelling people to embrace Islam - that would be an unholy war.

RIGHT OF NON-MUSLIMS IN ISLAMIC STATE

CONCEPT OF ISLAMIC STATE

"An Islamic state is essentially an ideological state, and is thus radically different from a national state." This statement made by Mawdudi lays the basic foundation for the political, economical, social, and religious system of all Islamic countries which impose the Islamic law. This ideological system intentionally discriminates between people according to their religious affiliations. Mawdudi, a prominent Pakistani Muslim scholar, summarizes the basic differences between Islamic and secular states as follows:

1. An Islamic state is ideological. People who reside in it are divided into Muslims, who believe in its ideology and non-Muslims who do not believe.
2. Responsibility for policy and administration of such a state "should rest primarily with those who believe in the Islamic ideology." Non-Muslims, therefore, cannot be asked to undertake or be entrusted with the responsibility of policymaking.
3. An Islamic state is bound to distinguish (i.e. discriminates) between Muslims and non-Muslims. However the Islamic law "Shari`a" guarantees to non-Muslims "certain specifically stated rights beyond which they are not permitted to meddle in the affairs of the state because they do not subscribe to its ideology." Once they embrace the Islamic faith, they "become equal participants in all matters concerning the state and the government."

The above view is the representative of the Hanifites, one of the four Islamic schools of jurisprudence. The other three schools are the Malikites, the Hanbilites (the strictest and the most fundamentalist of all), and the Shafi'ites. All four schools agree dogmatically on the basic creeds of Islam but differ in their interpretations of Islamic law which is derived from four sources:

a. *Qur'an* (read or recites): The sacred book of Muslim community containing direct quotes from Allah as allegedly dictated by Gabriel.
b. *Hadith* (narrative): The collections of Islamic traditions including sayings and deeds of Muhammad as heard by his contemporaries, first, second, and third hand.
c. *Al-Qiyas* (analogy or comparison): The legal decision drawn by Islamic Jurists based on precedent cases.

d. *Ijma'* (consensus): The interpretations of Islamic laws handed down by the consensus of reputed Muslim scholars in a certain country.

Textual laws prescribed in the Qur'an are few. The door is left wide open for prominent scholars versed in the Qur'an, the Hadith, and other Islamic discipline to present their Fatwa (legal opinion) as we shall see later.

CLASSIFICATION OF NON-MUSLIMS

In his article, "The Ordinances of the People of the Covenant and the Minorities in an Islamic State," Sheikh Najih Ibrahim Ibn Abdullah remarks that legists classify non-Muslims or infidels into two categories: Dar-ul-Harb or the household of War, which refers to non-Muslims who are not bound by a peace treaty, or covenant, and whose blood and property are not protected by the law of vendetta or retaliation; and Dar-us-Salam or the household of Peace, which refers to those who fall into three classifications:

1. Zimmis (those in custody) are non-Muslim subjects who live in Muslim countries and agree to pay the Jizya (tribute) in exchange for protection and safety, and to be subject to Islamic law. These enjoy a permanent covenant.
2. People of the Hudna (truce) are those who sign a peace treaty with Muslims after being defeated in war. They agree to reside in their own land, yet to be subject to the legal jurisprudence of Islam like Zimmis, provided they do not wage war against Muslims.
3. Musta'min (protected one) is persons who come to an Islamic country as messengers, merchants, visitors, or student wanting to learn about Islam. A Musta'min should not wage war against Muslims and he is not obliged to pay Jizya, but he would be urged to embrace Islam. If a Musta'min does not accept Islam, he is allowed to return safely to his own country. Muslims are forbidden to hurt him in any way. When he is back in his own homeland, he is treated as one who belongs to the Household of War.

ISLAMIC LAW AND ZIMMIS

Muslim Muftis (legal authorities) agree that the contract of the Zimmis should be offered primarily to the People of the Book that is, Christians and Jews, then to the Magis or Zoroastrians. However, they disagree on whether any contract should be signed with other groups such as communists or atheists. The Hanbalites and the Shafi'ites believe that no contract should be made with the ungodly or those who do not believe in the supreme God. Hanifites and Malikites affirm that the Jizya may be accepted from all infidels regardless of their beliefs and faith in God. Abu Hanifa, however, did not want pagan Arabs to have this option because they are the people of the Prophet. They must be given only two options: accept Islam or be killed.

THE JIZYA (TRIBUTE)

Jizya literally means penalty. It is a protection tax levied on non-Muslims living under Islamic regimes, confirming their legal status. Mawdudi states that "the acceptance of the Jizya establishes the sanctity of their lives and property, and thereafter neither the Islamic state, nor the Muslim public have any right to violate their property, honor or liberty." Paying the Jizya is a symbol of humiliation and submission because Zimmis are not regarded as citizens of the Islamic state although they are, in most cases, natives to the country.

Such an attitude alienates the Zimmis from being an essential part of the community. How can a Zimmi feel at home in his own land, among his own people, and with his own government, when he knows that the Jizya, which he pays, is a symbol of humiliation and submission? In his book The Islamic Law Pertaining to non-Muslims, Sheikh 'Abdulla Mustafa Al-Muraghi indicates that the. Jizya can only be exempted from the Zimmi who becomes a Muslim or dies. The Shafi'i reiterates that the Jizya is not automatically put aside when the Zimmi embraces Islam. Exemption from the Jizya has become an incentive to encourage Zimmis to relinquish their faith and embrace Islam.

Sheik Najih Ibrahim Ibn Abdulla summarizes the purpose of the Jizya. He says, quoting Ibn Qayyim al-Jawziyya, that the Jizya is enacted:

"...to spare the blood (of the Zimmis), to be a symbol of humiliation of the infidels and as an insult and punishment to them, and as the Shafi`ites indicate, the Jizya is offered in exchange for residing in an Islamic country." Thus Ibn Qayyim adds, "Since the entire religion belongs to God, it aims at humiliating ungodliness and its followers, and insulting them. Imposing the Jizya on the followers of ungodliness and oppressing them is required by God's religion. The Qur'anic text hints at this meaning when it says: `until they give the tribute by force with humiliation.' (Qur'an 9:29). What contradicts this is leaving the infidels to enjoy their might and practice their religion as they wish so that they would have power and authority."

ZIMMIS AND RELIGIOUS PRACTICES

Muslims believe that the Zimmis are Mushrikun (polytheists) for they see the belief in the Trinity as belief in three gods. Islam is the only true religion, they claim. Therefore, to protect Muslims from corruption, especially against the unforgivable sin of shirk (polytheism), its practice is forbidden among Muslims, because it is considered the greatest abomination. When Christians practice it publicly, it becomes an enticement and exhortation to apostasy. It is significant here to notice that according to Muraghi, Zimmis and infidels are polytheists and therefore, must have the same treatment.

According to Muslim jurists, the following legal ordinances must be enforced on Zimmis (Christians and Jews alike) who reside among Muslims:

1. Zimmis are not allowed to build new churches, temples, or synagogues. They are allowed to renovate old churches or houses of worship provided they do not allow adding any new construction. "Old churches" are those which existed prior to Islamic conquests and are included in a peace accord by Muslims. Construction of any church, temple, or synagogue in the Arab Peninsula (Saudi Arabia) is prohibited. It is the land of the Prophet and

only Islam should prevail there. Yet, Muslims, if they wish, are permitted to demolish all non-Muslim houses of worship in any land they conquer.

2. Zimmis are not allowed to pray or read their sacred books out loud at home or in churches, lest Muslims hear their prayers.
3. Zimmis are not allowed to print their religious books or sell them in public places and markets. They are allowed to publish and sell them among their own people, in their churches and temples.
4. Zimmis are not allowed to install the cross on their houses or churches since it is a symbol of infidelity.
5. Zimmis are not permitted to broadcast or display their ceremonial religious rituals on radio or television or to use the media or to publish any picture of their religious ceremonies in newspaper and magazines.
6. Zimmis are not allowed to congregate in the streets during their religious festivals; rather, each must quietly make his way to his church or temple.
7. Zimmis are not allowed to join the army unless there is indispensable need for them in which case they are not allowed to assume leadership positions but are considered mercenaries.

Mawdudi, who is a Hanifite, expresses a more generous opinion toward Christians. He said:

"In their own towns and cities they are allowed to do so (practice their religion) with the fullest freedom. In purely Muslim areas, however, an Islamic government has full discretion to put such restrictions on their practices as it deems necessary."

APOSTASY IN ISLAM

Apostasy means rejection of the religion of Islam either by action or the word of the mouth. "The act of apostasy, thus, put an end to one's adherence to Islam." when one rejects the fundamental creeds of Islam, he rejects the faith, and this is an act of apostasy such an act is a grave sin in Islam. The Qur'an indicates,

"How shall Allah guide those who reject faith after they accepted it and bore witness that the Apostle was true and the clear sign had come unto them? But Allah guides not the people of unjust of such the reward is that on them rests the curse of Allah, of His angels and of all mankind in that will they dwell; nor will their penalty be lightened, nor respite be their lot, except for those that repent after that and make amends; for verily Allah is Oft-forging, Most Merciful (Qur'an 3:86-89).

Officially, Islamic law requires Muslims not to force Zimmis to embrace Islam. It is the duty of every Muslim, they hold, to manifest the virtues of Islam so that those who are non-Muslims will convert willingly after discovering its greatness and truth. Once a person becomes a Muslim, he cannot recant. If he does, he will be warned first, and then he will be given three days to reconsider and repent. If he persists in his apostasy, his wife is required to divorce him, his property is confiscated, and his children are taken away from him. He is not allowed to remarry. Instead, he should be taken to court and sentenced to death. If he repents, he may return to his wife and children or remarry. According to the Hanifites an apostate female is not allowed to get married. She must spend time in meditation in order to return to Islam. If she does not repent or recant, she will not be sentenced to death, but she is to be persecuted, beaten and jailed until she dies. Other schools of Sharia demand her death. The above punishment is prescribed in a Hadith recorded by the Bukhari: "It is reported by `Abaas ... that the messenger of Allah ... said, `Whosoever changes his religion (from Islam to any other faith), kill him."

In his book Shari'ah: The Islamic Law, Doi remarks, "The punishment by death in the case of Apostasy has been unanimously agreed upon by all the four schools of Islamic jurisprudence."

A non-Muslim wishing to become a Muslim is encouraged to do so and anyone, even a father or a mother, who attempts to stop him, may be punished. However, anyone who makes an effort to proselytize a Muslim to any other faith may face punishment.

CIVIC LAWS

Zimmis and Muslims are subject to the same civic laws. They are to be treated alike in matters of honor, theft, adultery, murder, and damaging property. They have to be punished in accordance with the Islamic law regardless of their religious affiliation. Zimmis and Muslims alike are subject to Islamic laws in matters of civic business, financial transactions such as sales, leases, firms, and establishment of companies, farms, securities, mortgages, and contracts. For instance, theft is punishable by cutting off the thief's hand whether he is a Muslim or a Christian. But when it comes to privileges, the Zimmis do not enjoy the same treatment. For instance, Zimmis are not issued licenses to carry weapons.

MARRIAGE AND CHILDREN

A Muslim male can marry a Zimmi girl, but a Zimmi man is not allowed to marry a Muslim girl. If a woman embraces Islam and wants to get married, her non-Muslim father does not have the authority to give her away to her bridegroom. She must be given away by a Muslim guardian.

If one parent is a Muslim, children must be raised as Muslims. If the father is a Zimmi and his wife converts to Islam, she must get a divorce; then she will have the right of custody of her child. Some fundamentalist schools indicate that a Muslim husband has the right to confine his Zimmi wife to her home and restrain her from going to her own house of worship.

CAPITAL PUNISHMENT

The Hanifites believe that both Zimmis and Muslims must suffer the same Penalty for similar crimes. If a Muslim kills a Zimmi intentionally, he must be killed in return. The same applies to a Christian who kills a Muslim. But other schools of Law have different interpretations of Islamic law. The Shafi'ites declare that a Muslim who assassinates a Zimmi must not be killed, because it is not reasonable to equate a Muslim with a polytheist (Mushrik). In such a case, blood price must be paid. The penalty depends on the school of law adopted by the particular Islamic country where the crime or offense is committed. This illustrates the implication of different interpretations of the Islamic law based on the Hadith.

Each school attempts to document its legal opinion by referring to the Hadith or to an incident experienced by the Prophet or the "rightly guided" Caliphs.

THE WITNESS OF ZIMMIS

Zimmis cannot testify against Muslims. They can only testify against other Zimmis or Musta'min. Their oaths are not considered valid in an Islamic court. According to the Shari'a, a Zimmi is not even qualified to be under oath. Muraghi states bluntly, "The testimony of a Zimmi is not accepted because Allah - may He be exalted - said: 'God will not let the infidels (*kafir*) have an upper hand over the believers'." A Zimmi, regarded as an infidel, cannot testify against any Muslim regardless of his moral credibility. If a Zimmi has falsely accused another Zimmi and was once punished, his credibility and integrity is tarnished and his testimony is no longer acceptable. One serious implication of this is that if one Muslim has committed a serious offense against another, witnessed by Zimmis only, the court will have difficulty deciding the case since the testimonies of Zimmis are not acceptable. Yet, this same Zimmi whose integrity is blemished, if he converts to Islam, will have his testimony accepted against the Zimmis and Muslims alike, because according to the Shari'a, "By embracing Islam he has gained a new credibility which would enable him to witness..." All he has to do is to utter the Islamic confession of faith before witnesses, and that will elevate him from being an outcast to being a respected Muslim enjoying all the privileges of a devout Muslim.

PERSONAL LAW

On personal matters of marriages, divorces, and inheritance, Zimmis are allowed to appeal to their own religious courts. Each Christian denomination has the right and authority to determine the outcome of each case. Zimmis are free to practice their own social and religious rites at home and in church without interference from the state, even in such matters as drinking wine, rearing pigs, and eating pork, as long as they do not sell them to Muslims. Zimmis are generally denied the right to appeal to an Islamic court in family matters, marriage, divorce, and inheritance. However, in the event a Muslim judge agrees to take such a case, the court must apply Islamic law.

POLITICAL RIGHTS AND DUTIES

The Islamic state is an ideological state, thus the head of the state inevitably must be a Muslim, because he is bound by the Shari'a to conduct and administer the state in accordance with the Qur'an and the Sunna. The function of his advisory council is to assist him in implementing the Islamic principles and adhering to them. Anyone who does not embrace Islamic ideology cannot be the head of state or a member of the council.

Mawdudi, aware of the requirements of modern society, seems to be more tolerant toward Zimmis. He says,

"In regard to a parliament or a legislature of the modern type which is considerably different from the advisory council in its traditional sense, this rule could be relaxed to allow non-Muslims to be members provided that it has been fully ensured in the constitution that no law which is repugnant to the Qur'an and the Sunna should be enacted, that the Qur'an and the Sunna should be the chief source of public law, and that the head of the state should necessarily be a Muslim."

Under these circumstances, the sphere of influence of non-Muslim minorities would be limited to matters relating to general problems of the country or to the interest of the minorities. Their participation should not damage the fundamental requirement of Islam. Mawdudi adds,

"It is possible to form a separate representative assembly for all non-Muslim groups in tbe capacity of a central agency.

The membership and the voting rights of such an assembly will be confined to non-Muslims and they would be given the fullest freedom within its frame-work."

These views do not receive the approval of most other schools of the Shari'a which hold that non-Muslims are not allowed to assume any position which might bestow on them any authority over any Muslim. A position of sovereignty demands the implementation of Islamic ideology. It is alleged that a non-Muslim (regardless of his ability, sincerity, and loyalty to his country) cannot and would not work faithfully to achieve the ideological and political goals of Islam.

BUSINESS WORLD

The political arena and the official public sectors are not the only area in which non-Muslims are not allowed to assume a position of authority. A Muslim employee who works in a company inquires in a letter "if it is permissible for a Muslim owner (of a company) to confer authority on a Christian over other Muslims? (Al-Muslim Weekly; Vol. 8; issue No. 418; Friday 2, 5, 1993).

Basically, the command of non-Muslims over Muslims in not admissible, because God Almighty said: 'Allah will not give access to the infidels (i.e. Christians) to have authority over believers (Muslims) {Qur'an 4:141}. For God - Glory be to Him - has elevated Muslims to the highest rank (over all men) and foreordained to them the might, by virtue of the Qurtanic text in which God the Almighty said: 'Might and strength be to Allah, the Prophet (Muhammad) and the believers (Muslims) {Qur'an 63:8}.

Thus, the authority of non-Muslim over a Muslim is incompatible with these two verses, since the Muslim has to submit to and obey whoever is in charge over him. The Muslim therefore becomes inferior to him, and this should not be the case with the Muslim.

Dr. Salih Al-Sadlan, professor of Shari'a at the School of Islamic Law, Riyadh, cites the same verses and asserts that it is not permissible for a infidel (in this case is a Christian) to be in charge over Muslims whether in the private or public sector. Such an act:

"Entails the humiliaton of the Muslim and the exaltation of the infidel (Christian). This infidel may exploit his position to humiliate and insult the Muslims who work under his administration. It is advisable to the company owner to fear God Almighty and to authorize only a Muslim over the Muslims. Also, the injunctions issued by the ruler, provides that an infidel should not be in charge when there is a Muslim available to assume the command. Our advice to the company owner is to remove this infidel and to replace him with a Muslim."

In his response Dr. Fahd Al-'Usaymi, professor of Islamic studies at the Teachers' College in Riyadh, remarks that the Muslim owner of the company should seek a Muslim employee who is better than the Christian (manager), or equal to him or even less qualified but has the ability to be trained to obtain the same skill enjoyed by the Christian. It is not permissible for a Christian to be in charge of Muslims by the virtue of the general evidences which denote the superiority of the Muslim over others. Then he quotes (Qur'an 63:8) and also cites verse 22 of Chapter 58:

Thou wilt not find any people who believe in Allah and the Last Day, loving those who resist Allah and His Apostle, even though they were their fathers or their sons, or their brothers, or their kindred.

'Usaymi claims that being under the authority of a Christian may force Muslims to flatter him and humiliate themselves to this infidel on the hope to obtain some of what he has. This is against the confirmed evidences. Then he alludes to the story of Umar Ibn Al-Khattab the second Caliph, who was displeased with one of his governors who appointed a Zimmi as a treasurer, and remarked: "Have the wombs of women become sterile that they gave birth only to this man?" Then 'Usaymi adds:

Muslims should fear God in their Muslim brothers and train them... for honesty and fear of God are, originally, in the Muslim, contrary to the infidel (the Christian) who, originally, is dishonest and does not fear God.

Does this mean that a Christian who owns a business cannot employ a Muslim to work for him? Even worse, does this mean that a Zimmi, regardless of his unequal qualification, cannot be appointed to the right position where he would serve his country the best? This question demands an answer.

FREEDOM OF EXPRESSION

Mawdudi, who is more lenient than most Muslim scholars, presents a revolutionary opinion when he emphasizes that in an Islamic state:

"All non-Muslims will have the freedom of conscience, opinion, expression, and association as the one enjoyed by Muslims themselves, subject to the same limitations as are imposed by law on Muslims."

Mawdudi's views are not accepted by most Islamic schools of law, especially in regard to freedom of expression like criticism of Islam and the government. Even in a country like Pakistan, the homeland of Mawdudi, it is illegal to criticize the government or the head of state. Many political prisoners are confined to jails in Pakistan and most other Islamic countries. Through the course of history except in rare cases, not even Muslims have been given freedom to criticize Islam without being persecuted or sentenced to death. It is far less likely for a Zimmi to get away with criticizing Islam.

In Mawdudi's statement, the term "limitations" is vaguely defined. If it were explicitly defined, you would find, in the final analysis, that it curbs any type of criticism against the Islamic faith and government.

Moreover, how can the Zimmis express the positive aspects of their religion when they are not allowed to use the media or advertise them on radio or TV? Perhaps Mawdudi meant by his proposals to allow such freedom to Zimmis only among themselves. Otherwise, they would be subject to penalty. Yet, Muslims are allowed, according to the Shari'a (law) to propagate their faith among all religious sects without any limitations.

MUSLIMS AND ZIMMIS

Relationships between Muslims and Zimmis are classified in two categories: what is forbidden and what is allowable.

1. The Forbidden

A Muslim is not allowed to:

- Emulate the Zimmis in their dress or behavior.
- Attend Zimmi festivals or support them in any way which may give them any power over Muslims.
- Lease his house or sell his land for the construction of a church, temple, liquor store, or anything that may benefit the Zimmi's faith.
- Work for Zimmis in any job that might promote their faith such as constructing a church.
- Make any endowment to churches or temples.
- Carry any vessel that contains wine, work in wine production, or transport pigs.
- Address Zimmis with any title such as: "my master" or "my lord."

2. The Allowable

A Muslim is allowed to:

- Financially assist the Zimmis, provided the money is not used in violation of Islamic law like buying wine or pork.
- Give the right of pre-emption (priority in buying property) to his Zimmi neighbour. The Hanbilites disapprove of this.
- Eat food prepared by the People of the Book.
- Console the Zimmis in an illness or in the loss of a loved one. It is also permissible for a Muslims to escort a funeral to the cemetery, but he has to walk in front of the coffin, not behind it, and he must depart before the deceased is buried.
- Congratulate the Zimmis for a wedding, birth of a child, return from a long trip, or recovery from illness. However, Muslims are warned not to utter any word

which may suggest approval of the Zimmis' faith, such as: "May Allah exalt you," "May Allah honor you," or "May Allah give your religion victory."

This study shows us that non-Muslims are not regarded as citizens by any Islamic state, even if they are original natives of the land. To say otherwise is to conceal the truth. Justice and equality require that any Christian Pakistani, Melanesian, Turk, or Arab be treated as any other citizen of his own country. He deserves to enjoy the same privileges of citizenship regardless of religious affiliation. To claim that Islam is the true religion and to accuse other religions of infidelity is a social, religious and legal offense against the People of the Book.

Christians believe that their religion is the true religion of God and Islam is not. Does that mean that Great Britain, which is headed by a Queen, the head of the Anglican Church, should treat its Muslim subjects as a second class? Moreover, why do Muslims in the West enjoy all freedoms allotted to all citizens of these lands, while Muslim countries do not allow native Christians the same freedom? Muslims in the West build mosques, schools, and educational centers and have access to the media without any restriction. They publicly advertise their activities and are allowed to distribute their Islamic materials freely, while native Christians of any Islamic country are not allowed to do so. Why are Christians in the West allowed to embrace any religion they wish without persecution while a person who chooses to convert to another religion in any Islamic country, is considered an apostate and must be killed if he persists in his apostasy? These questions and others are left for readers to ponder.

2

The Rights of Non-Muslims in Islam

Islam is a religion of mercy to all people, both Muslims and non-Muslims. The Prophet was described as being a mercy in the Quran due to the message he brought for humanity:

"And we have not sent you but as a mercy to all the worlds." (Quran 21:107)

When a person analyzes the legislations of Islam with an open mind, the Mercy mentioned in this verse will definitely become apparent. One of the aspects constituting an epitome of this Mercy is the way the legislations of Islam deal with people of other faiths. The tolerant attitude of Islam towards non-Muslims, whether they be those residing in their own countries or within the Muslim lands, can be clearly seen through a study of history. This fact is not only purported by Muslims, but many non-Muslim historians also accept it. Patriarch Ghaytho wrote:

'The Arabs, to whom the Lord has given control over the world, treat us as you know; they are not the enemies of Christians. Indeed, they praise our community, and treat our priests and saints with dignity, and offer aid to churches and monasteries.'

Will Durant wrote:

'At the time of the Umayyad caliphate, the people of the covenant, Christians, Zoroastrians, Jews, and Sabians, all enjoyed degree of tolerance that we do not find even today in Christian countries. They were free to practice the rituals of their religion and their churches and temples were preserved. They enjoyed autonomy in that they were subject to the religious laws of the scholars and judges.'

These just relations between Muslims and people of other faiths were not due to mere politics played by Muslim rulers, but rather they were a direct result of the teachings of the religion of Islam, one which preaches that people of other religions be free to practice their own faith, only accepting the guidance offered by Islam by their own choice. God says in the Quran:

"There is no compulsion in religion..." (Quran 2:256)

Not only does Islam demand their freedom to practice religion, but also that they be treated justly as any other fellow human. Warning against any abuse of non-Muslims in an Islamic society, the Prophet stated:

"Beware! Whoever is cruel and hard on a non-Muslim minority, curtails their rights, burdens them with more than they can bear, or takes anything from them against their free will; I (Prophet Muhammad) will complain against the person on the Day of Judgment." (Abu Dawud)

How far is this mannerism than the majority of nations, to this day, which not only suppress the rights of foreign religions, but also foreign peoples and races! In a time when Muslims were being tortured to death in then pagan Mecca, Jews were being persecuted in Christian Europe and various peoples were being subjugated due to their particular race or caste, Islam called to the just treatment of all peoples and religions, due to its merciful tenets which gave humanity the right to their humanness.

NON-MUSLIM RESIDENTS

There is much talk these days about the allowance Islam gives to the existence of other religions in the world. Some of the opinion that Islam orders that Muslims fight the world until everyone becomes Muslim, creating ill feelings without actually knowing what the religion actually says in this regard, much more the existence of non-Muslims within an Islamic country.

In terms of residence within Muslim society, non-Muslims are classified into three types. To understand these types will deepen one's understanding of the relationship between Muslims and peoples of other faith in an Islamic society:

CLASSIFICATION OF NON-MUSLIMS

Permanent Residents

Muslim jurists use the term 'People of the Covenant' (Arabic 'dhimmi' or 'Ahl ul-Dhimma') to refer to non-Muslim residents. It is not a derogatory term, as some have made it seem. In Arabic language the word 'dhimma' means a treaty of protection for non-Muslims living in Muslim territory. A similar term, 'Ahl ul-Dhimma', means 'People of the Covenant,' because they are protected under the covenant extended to them by Prophet Muhammad and the Muslims. Non-Muslims are guaranteed protection in the Muslim society as long as they pay a head tax and abide by the specific legislations mentioned in Islamic Law. This covenant of protection is not limited to a specific duration; rather, stays in effect as long as those with whom the covenant is made abide by its conditions. The good intent behind the term 'dhimmi' can be seen in the letter written by the Caliph Abu Bakr as-Siddiq to the non-Muslims of Najran:

'In the Name of God, the Beneficent, the Merciful. This is the written statement of God's slave Abu Bakr, the successor of Muhammad, the Prophet and Messenger of God. He affirms for you the rights of a protected neighbor, in yourselves, your lands, your religious community, your wealth, retainers, and servants, those of you who are present or abroad, your bishops and monks, and monasteries, and all that you own, be it great or small. You shall not be deprived of any of it, and shall have full control over it...'

Another example is the statement of a famous classical scholar of Islam, Imam Awza'i in his letter to the Abbasid governor Salih b. 'Ali b. Abdullah about the People of the Covenant, "They are not slaves, so beware of changing their status after they have lived in freedom. They are free People of the Covenant."

Acknowledging this fact, Ron Landau wrote:

'In contrast to the Christian Empire, which attempted to impose Christianity on its subjects, the Arabs extended recognition to religious minorities, and accepted their presence. Jews, Christians, and Zoroastrians were known to them as the People of the Covenant; in other words, the nations who enjoyed a protected status.'

Temporary Residents

This category includes two types:

1. The residents of non-Muslims countries who are at peace with Muslims through specific peace agreements, international treaties, or other mechanisms, who temporarily come to Muslim countries for work, education, business, diplomatic missions, and so forth. Muslim jurists refer to them in Arabic as mu'aahadoon, which means, "those with whom there is a pact".
2. The residents of non-Muslims countries with whom Muslims do not have a pact of peace, or who may be at war with Muslims, who temporarily come to Muslim countries for work, education, business, diplomatic missions, and so forth. Muslim jurists refer to them in Arabic as musta'minoon, which means, "seekers of protection".

All classes have general rights common to them, and exclusive rights specific to each group. We will limit our discussion mostly to the most general, common rights to avoid excessive details.

THE GENERAL RIGHTS OF NON-MUSLIMS

The expression "human rights" is relatively new, having come into everyday usage only since World War II, the founding of the United Nations in 1945, and the adoption by the UN General Assembly of the Universal Declaration of Human Rights in 1948. Although its emergence in international law is a relatively recent development, the idea of human rights itself is not new. If one were to study and compare the Universal Declaration of Human Rights to the human rights granted by Islam 1400 years ago, one can clearly see the level of high moral ground achieved by Islam before the Universal Declaration. This moral standard did not come as a result of human intellectual endeavor. The source of Islamic morality is God. The divine standard provides true comprehensiveness and depth in human needs. It provides for everything that benefits the human race and shields it from any harm. Objective study is likely to conclude, 'there is no religion or moral code on earth that has given more generous attention to faithfully affirming these rights than Islam, detailing them, clarifying them, and expressing them.'

The Shariah, which is the legal and moral code of Islam, does not confine itself to giving rights to Muslims only. One of its distinguishing features is that non-Muslim share many of these rights. As a matter of fact, the general principle is that non-Muslims have the same rights and obligations as Muslims. This aspect of religion is unique to Islam, and perhaps has not been attained by any other world religion. If we look at Christianity, for example, Professor Joseph Heath of the University of Toronto, says, 'It should go without saying that you can scour the Bible and not find one single mention of "rights." You can also pick through the following 1500 years of Christian thought without finding any rights. That's because the idea is entirely absent.'

Non-Muslims have many rights in Islam. We will limit our discussion to the most important of them, such as the freedom of belief, right to work, housing, freedom of movement, and education.

RIGHT TO PRESERVATION OF DIGNITY AS HUMAN BEINGS

God has created human beings with certain dignity, Muslims and non-Muslims alike, and has elevated their status above much of His creation. God says in the Quran:

"We have honored the children of Adam; provided them with transport on land and sea; given them for sustenance things good and pure; and conferred on them special favors, above a great part of our creation." (Quran 17:70)

As a token of honor and to elevate his status, God commanded the angels to prostrate out of humility before Adam, the father of humanity. God informs us in the Quran:

"When we said to the angels, 'Prostrate yourselves to Adam,' they prostrated themselves, but not Satan; he refused." (Quran 20:116)

God bestowed many favors on humanity, some of which are obvious, while others are hidden. For instance, He subjected the heavens and earth to human beings to honor them. He says:

"It is God who created the heavens and earth and sends down rain from the sky, and with it brings out fruits therewith to feed you; it is He Who has made the ships subject to you, that they may sail through the sea by His command; and the rivers (also) He has made subject to you. And He gives you of all that you ask for, but if you count the favors of God; never will you be able to count them. Surely, man is given up to injustice and ingratitude." (Quran 14:32-34)

The God-given status of humanity forms the basis of the principle of human dignity in Islam, whether the person is Muslim or non-Muslim. Islam emphasizes the origin of all humanity is one; therefore all human beings have certain rights over one another. God says:

"O mankind! We created you from a single (pair) of a male and female, and made you into nations and tribes, that you may know each other (and not hate one another). Surely, the most honored of you in the sight of God is (he who) is the most righteous of you. And God has full knowledge and is well acquainted (with all things)." (Quran 49:13)

The Messenger of God declared in his farewell sermon, addressing the largest gathering in Arab history till that point:

"People, hear that your Lord is One, and that your father is one. You must know that no Arab has superiority over a non-Arab, no non-Arab has superiority over an Arab, or a red man over a black man, or a black man over a red, except in terms of what each person has of piety. Have I delivered the message?"

An example of the preservation of the human dignity of non-Muslims is the right that their feelings be respected, for example, that they are shown good manners in speech and debate in obedience to the divine command:

"And dispute you not with the People of the Scripture, except in the best way, unless it be with those who do wrong, but say, 'We believe in the revelation which has come down to us and in that which came down to you; our God and your God is One; and it is to Him we submit (in Islam).'" (Quran 21:46)

Non-Muslims have the right not to have their religious beliefs mocked. It may not be an exaggeration to state that no other religion or sect in the world is as fair as Islam to people of other faiths. For example, let us look at a verse from the Quran:

"Say, 'Who gives you sustenance from the heavens and the earth?' Say, 'It is God; and it is certain that either we or you are on the right guidance or in manifest error.'" (Quran 34:24)

The verse ends with what Arabs linguists call a rhetorical question whose answer is common knowledge to the intended audience. The verse blends certainty with doubt: Muslims following guidance and the error of the unbelievers is presented as something doubtful. In doing so, God emphasizes the truth by allowing the reader to draw his own conclusion. God does not state in this verse who is following guidance and who is not. The verse treats the fictitious "opponent" with justice by presenting the argument and allowing the listener to judge. Az-Zamakhshiri, a classical linguist and exegete of the Quran, elaborates this point:

'This is equitable speech: whoever hears it, supporter or opponent, will tell the person to whom the speech is directed that the speaker has treated him justly. It draws the listener to the inevitable conclusion, after the argument has been presented, that there is no doubt about who is following guidance and who is in error. Suggestion of the facts, as if the question were a conundrum, provides a more cogent proof of the truth, the opponent being gently disarmed, without resort to heated quarrelling.'

An example of the style employed by the Quran would be someone saying in a debate, 'God knows who is telling the truth and who is a liar.'

God has also forbidden Muslims from speaking ill of the gods and deities worshipped by non-Muslims so that they do not speak ill of the One, True God. It will be difficult to find a similar example in any scripture of the major world religions. If the polytheists were to hear Muslims speak ill of their gods, it might lead them to speak ill of Allah (the personal and proper Name of God). Also, if Muslims were to speak ill of pagan gods, it might instigate the polytheists to soothe their wounded feelings by hurting the feelings of Muslims. Such a scenario is against human dignity of both sides and would lead to mutual rejection and hatred. God says in the Quran:

"Do not revile those whom they call upon besides God, lest they revile God out of spite in their ignorance. Thus, we have made alluring to each people its own doings. In the end will they return to their Lord and He shall then tell them the truth of what they did." (Quran 6:108)

Another example of how Islam gives regard to human dignity in the following example. A famous story illustrates the degree to which the caliphs of early Islam protected the dignity of non-Muslims. Amr ibn al-As was the governor of Egypt. One of his sons beat up a Coptic Christian with a whip, saying, 'I am the son of a nobleman!" The Copt went to Umar ibn al-Khattab, the Muslim caliph who resided in the city of Medina, and lodged a complaint. These are the details as related by Anas ibn Malik, the personal servant of the Prophet in his lifetime:

"We were sitting with Umar ibn al-Khattab when an Egyptian came in and said, 'Commander of the Faithful, I come to you as a refugee.' So, Umar asked him about his problem and he answered, Amr had a custom of letting his horses run free in Egypt. One day, I came by riding my mare. When I passed by a group of people, they looked at me. Muhammad, the son of Amr got up and came to me, saying, 'I swear by the Lord of the Kaaba, this is my mare!' I responded, 'I swear by the Lord of the Kaaba, the mare is mine!' He came up to me and began beating me with a whip, saying, 'You may take her, because I am the son of a nobleman (meaning I am more generous than you).' The incident got to Amr, who feared that I might come to you, so he put me in jail. I escaped, and here I am before you."

Anas continued:

"I swear by God, the only response Umar made was to tell the Egyptian to take a seat. Then, Umar wrote a letter to Amr, saying, 'When this letter reaches you, come and bring me your son, Muhammad.' Then he told the Egyptian to stay in Medina until he was told Amr has arrived. When Amr received the note, he called his son and asked him, 'Did you commit a crime?' His son stated he has not. Amr asked, 'Then why is Umar writing about you?' They both went to Umar."

Ana narrates the incident further:

"I swear by God, we were sitting with Umar, and Amr arrived wearing the clothes of common people. Umar looked around for the son, and saw him standing behind his father (to appear less conspicuous). Umar asked, 'Where is the Egyptian?' and he responded, 'Here I am!' Umar told him, 'Here is the whip. Take it and beat the son of the nobleman.' So he took it and beat him vigorously, while Umar said over and over, 'Beat the son of the nobleman.' We did not let him stop until we were satisfied he had beaten him enough. Then, Umar said, 'Now you must take it and hit me on my bald head. This all happened to you because of my power over you.' The Egyptian responded, 'I am satisfied and my anger has cooled.' Umar told him, 'If you had beaten me, I would not have stopped you until you had wished to. And you, Amr, since when have you made the people your slaves? They were born free.' Amr began to apologize, telling him, 'I did not know that this is what happened.' So, Umar said turned back to the Egyptian, telling him, 'You may go, and be guided. If anything untoward happens to you, write to me.'"

Such was Umar who said when first chosen as Caliph, 'The weak will be made strong, because I take for them what is their right. And the strong will be made weak because I will take from them what is not rightfully theirs.' History has recorded him as a just ruler because of his equity towards the oppressed, regardless of their social status, and because of his firmness against the oppressor, regardless of their rank.

'The value of this story is that it records how people had a sense of their humanity and dignity under the rule of Islam. Even an unjust blow was disapproved and despised. Many incidents of injustice similar to this story occurred at the time of the Byzantine Empire, but nobody moved to rectify them. However, under the protection of the Islamic state, we see an example of an oppressed person having the conviction of his dignity and access to his rights so strong that he was willing to undertake the hardship and privation of a trip from Egypt to Medina, because of his trust that he would find someone to listen to his compliant.'

RIGHT TO FREEDOM OF BELIEF

Islam does not compel people of other faiths to convert. It has given them complete freedom to retain their own faith and not to be forced to embrace Islam. This freedom is documented in both the Quran and the prophetic teachings known as Sunnah. God addresses the Prophet Muhammad in the Quran:

"If it had been your Lord's will, they would all have believed - all of who are on earth! Will you then compel humankind, against their will, to believe?" (Quran 10:99)

Prophet Muhammad may the mercy and blessings of God be upon him, would give people a choice between entering Islam and retaining their religion. He would ask them to accept Islam only after making an agreement with them, once they had become residents in the Islamic state and felt secure about their personal safety and property. This allowed them to appreciate the security of the covenant with God and His Prophet. It is precisely for this reason that the non-Muslim citizens are referred to as dhimmis. When the Prophet of God sent a commander of an army or a battalion off to war, the Prophet would command him to be conscious of God in his conduct and to treat his Muslim companions well. Then the Prophet of Mercy would instruct him:

"Set out for battle for the sake of God and fight those who disbelieve in Him. Go into battle, but do not go to extremes, behave treacherously, mutilate their dead, or kill children. When you meet your enemies, the unbelievers, offer them three options, and accept any one of them to which they agree and cease the battle:

a. Invite them to join Islam. If they agree, then accept this and cease the battle. Then invite them to move from their lands to the Land of the Immigrants (Medina), and inform them that if they do so, they will have the same privileges and obligations as the other migrants. If they refuse to migrate from their lands, inform them that they will have the same status as the nomadic Muslims: that they will be subject to the Law of God which applies to all Muslims, and that they do not have a share in wealth obtained from conquest, unless they participate in the jihad with the Muslims.
b. If they refuse, then ask them to pay the jizyah, and if they agree, then accept it from them and cease the battle.
c. If they refuse all this, then seek God's help and battle with them."

These directives of the Prophet were in obedience to what God says in the Quran:

"Let there be no compulsion in religion; truth stands clear from error: whoever rejects false gods and believes in God has grasped the most trustworthy hand-hold that never breaks. And God hears and knows all things." (Quran 2:256)

Edwin Calgary, an American scholar, wrote about this verse, 'There is a verse in the Quran that is filled with truth and wisdom, and it is known to all Muslims. Everyone else should know it as well; it is the one that says there is no compulsion in religion.'

This verse was revealed concerning some of the residents of Medina. When none of the children of the pagan women of Medina survived infancy, they would make a vow to make the child a Jew or a Christian if he lived. When Islam came to Medina, they had adult children who were Jewish or Christian. The parents tried to compel them to embrace the new religion, so this verse was revealed to prevent them from doing so. The verse and the history of its revelation reveal that it is not permissible to force anyone to become a Muslim. This is the case even if it is the parent who wants the best for their offspring, and their children become members of another religion. The Quran rejects forcing anyone to join Islam. God says in the Quran:

"Say, 'The truth is from your Lord,' let him who will, believe and let him who will, reject, it. For the wrongdoers we have prepared a Fire whose (smoke and flames are) like the wall and roof of a tent, will hem them in: if they implore relief they will be granted water like molten brass that will scald their faces. How dreadful the drink! How uncomfortable a couch to recline on!" (Quran 18:29)

Not only does Islam give the freedom of religious freedom to non-Muslims, its tolerant law extends to the preservation of their places of worship. God says in the Quran:

"(They are) those who have been evicted from their homes without right - only because they say, 'Our Lord is God.' And was it not that God checks the people, some by means of others, there would have been demolished monasteries, churches, synagogues, and mosques in which the name of God is much mentioned (praised). And God will surely support those who support Him (meaning His cause). Indeed, God is Powerful and Exalted in Might." (Quran 22:40)

The Muslim caliphs used to order their military leaders who went on military campaigns to take steps to guarantee this matter. The first example is the command of Abu Bakr to Usamah bin Zayd:

'I command you to do ten things: kill no woman, no child, nor an elderly person; do not cut down fruit trees, or vandalize homes, or wound a sheep or camel except if you must eat it; do not drown a palm tree, or burn it, do not be treacherous; do not be cowardly; and you will pass by people who have devoted themselves to monastery life; leave them alone to their devotions.'

The second example is the treaty of Umar ibn al-Khattab with the people of Iliya of Jerusalem:

'This is the security given by the slave of God, Umar, the Commander of the Faithful, to the people of Iliya: they are guaranteed the security if their persons, possessions, churches, crucifixes, and everyone within, whether sick or in good health, as well as everyone in their community. Their churches will not be occupied or demolished, nor will anything be taken from them: neither furnishings nor crucifixes or money. They will not be forced away from their religion, or harmed because of it. They will not be occupied by the Jewish settlers in Iliya.'

As a result, since the era of the rightly-guided caliphs, Jews and Christians have held their services in freedom and security.

Muslims protected Christian churches in the lands they occupied from being harmed. In a letter to Simeon, the Archbishop of Rifardashir and leader of all the bishops of Persia, the Nestorian Patriarch Geoff III wrote:

'The Arabs, to whom God has given power over the whole

world, know how wealthy you are, for they live among you. In spite of this, they do not assail the Christian creed. To the contrary, they have sympathy with our religion, and venerate our priests and saints of our Lord, and they graciously donate to our churches and monasteries.'

One of the Muslims caliphs, Abdul-Malik, took the Church of John from the Christians and made it part of a mosque. When Umar bin Abdulaziz succeeded him as the new Caliph, the Christians complained to him about what his predecessor had done to their church. Umar wrote to the governor that the portion of the mosque that was rightfully theirs be returned to them if they were unable to agree with the governor on a monetary settlement that would satisfy them.

The Wailing Wall in Jerusalem is known to historians to be the one of the holiest places of worship in Judaism. Some time ago, it was completely buried under rubble and heaps of debris. When the Ottoman caliph Sultan Sulayman came to know of this, he ordered his governor in Jerusalem to remove all the rubble and debris, clean the area, restore the Wailing Wall, and make it accessible for Jews to visit.

Unbiased Western historians acknowledge these facts. LeBon writes:

'The tolerance of Muhammad towards the Jews and Christians was truly grand; the founders of other religions that appeared before him, Judaism and Christianity in particular, did not prescribe such goodwill. His caliphs followed the same policy, and his tolerance has been acknowledged by skeptics and believers alike when they study the history of the Arabs in depth.'

Robertson wrote:

'The Muslims alone were able to integrate their zeal for their own religion with tolerance for followers of other religions. Even when they bore swords into battle for freedom for their religion to spread, they left those who did not desire it free to adhere to their own religious teachings.'

Sir Thomas Arnold, an English Orientalist, wrote:

'We never heard of a report of any planned attempt to compel non-Muslim minorities to accept Islam, or any organized persecution aimed at uprooting the Christian religion. If any of the caliphs had chosen any of these policies, they would have overwhelmed Christianity with the same ease with which Ferdinand and Isabella exiled Islam from Spain or with which Louis XIV made following Protestantism a punishable crime in France, or with which the Jews were exiled from England for 350 years. A that time Eastern churches were completely isolated from the rest of the Christian world. They had no supporters in the world as they were considered heretical sects of Christianity. Their very existence to this day is the strongest evidence of the policy of Islamic government's tolerance towards them.'

The American author, Lothrop Stoddard wrote, 'The caliph Umar took the utmost care to tend to the sanctity of the Christian holy places, and those who became caliph after him followed his footsteps. They did not harass the many denominations of pilgrims who came annually from every corner of the Christian world to visit Jerusalem.'

The reality is that non-Muslims were treated with more tolerance among the Muslims than anything they experienced with other sects of their own religion. Richard Stebbins spoke of the Christian experience under the rule of the Turks:

'They (the Turks) allowed all of them, Roman Catholics and Greek Orthodox, to preserve their religion and follow their consciences as they chose: they allowed them their churches to perform their sacred rituals in Constantinople and many other places. This is in contrast to what I can testify to from living in Spain for twelve years; not only were we forced to attend their Papist celebrations, but our lives and the lives of our grandchildren were in danger also.'

Thomas Arnold mentions in his 'Invitation to Islam' that there were many people in Italy at that time who longed for Ottoman rule. They wished they could be granted the same freedom and tolerance that the Ottomans gave to their Christian subjects, for they had despaired of achieving it under any Christian government. He also mentions that a great many Jews fled persecution in Spain at the end of the 15th century and took refuge in Ottoman Turkey.

It is worthwhile to reemphasize the following point. The existence of non-Muslims for centuries across the Muslim world, from Moorish Spain and Sub-Saharan Africa to Egypt, Syria, India, and Indonesia are clear evidence of the religious tolerance extended by Islam to people of other faiths. This tolerance even led to the elimination of Muslims, such as in Spain, where the remaining Christians took advantage of Muslim weakness, attacked them, and wiped them out from Spain by either killing them, forcing them to convert, or expulsion. Etienne Denier wrote, 'The Muslims are the opposite of what many people believe. They never used force outside of the Hejaz. The presence of Christians was evidence of this fact. They retained their religion in complete security during the eight centuries that the Muslims ruled their lands. Some of them held high posts in the palace in Cordoba, but when the same Christians obtained power over the country, suddenly their first concern was to exterminate Muslims.'

RIGHT TO FOLLOW THEIR RELIGIOUS LAWS

Islam does not compel non-Muslims citizens living in Muslim lands to be ruled by Islamic Laws. They are exempt from paying the zakah. Under Islamic Law, a Muslim who does not pay the zakah and refuses its obligation becomes an unbeliever. Also, Islamic Law requires military duty from able Muslims, but non-Muslims are exempt from it, even though it is of benefit to Muslims and non-Muslims alike. In return for these two exemptions, non-Muslim citizens pay a nominal tax known as jizya. Sir Thomas Arnold wrote, 'The jizya was so light that it did not constitute a burden on them, especially when we observe that it exempted them from compulsory military service that was an obligation for their fellow citizens, the Muslims.'

Islam also permitted non-Muslims to observe their civil law in matters such as marriage and divorce. Regarding criminal justice, Muslim jurists would pass sentences on non-Muslims in issues considered sinful in their religion such as theft, but exempted them from issues they held to be permissible such as drinking wine and eating pork. This is based clearly of the practice of the Prophet himself when he first came to Medina and established a 'constitution'. He allowed for individual tribes who were not Muslims to refer to their own religious scriptures and their learned men in regards to their own personal affairs. They could though, if they opted, ask the Prophet to judge between them in their matters. God says in the Quran:

"...If they do come to you, either judge between them or decline to interfere..." (Quran 5:42)

Here we see that Prophet allowed each religion to judge in their own matters according to their own scriptures, as long as it did not stand in opposition to articles of the constitution, a pact which took into account the greater benefit of the peaceful co-existence of the society.

Umar ibn Abdulaziz, a Muslim ruler, found it hard to accept how non-Muslims continued to follow their social regulations that went against the Islamic injunctions. He wrote a letter to Hasan al-Basri seeking his legal advice, saying, 'How is it that the Rightly-Guided Caliphs before us left the People of the Covenant as they did, marrying close relatives, and keeping pigs and wine?' Hasan's responded, 'They paid the jizya so that they could be left to practice what they believed, and you may only follow the Islamic Law, not invent something new.'

The People of the Covenant had their own courts to settle their disputes, but if they wished, they could resort to Islamic courts. God commanded His Prophet:

"So if they come to you, (O Muhammad), judge between them or turn away from them. And if you turn away from them never will they harm you at all. And if you judge, judge between them with justice. Indeed, God loves those who act justly." (Quran 5:42)

Adam Metz, a Western historian, writes in the Islamic Civilization in the Fourth Century of the Hegira:

"Since the Islamic Law was specifically for Muslims, the Islamic state allowed the people of other religious affiliations to their own courts. What we know about these courts is that they were church courts and prominent spiritual leaders were the chief justices. They wrote a great number of books on canon law, and their rulings were not confined to matters of personal status. They included such problems as inheritance and much of the litigations between Christians that did not involve the state."

Therefore, it can be seen that Islam did not punish non-Muslims for doing what they viewed as permissible according to their religious law, such as consuming alcohol or eating pork, even though they are forbidden in Islam. The tolerance extended by Islam towards non-Muslims is unmatched by any other religious law, secular government, or political system in existence even today. Gustav LeBon writes:

"The Arabs could have easily been blinded by their first conquests, and committed the injustices that are usually committed by conquerors. They could have mistreated their defeated opponents or forced them to embrace their religion, which they wished to spread all over the world. But the Arabs avoided that. The early caliphs, who had a political genius that was rare in proponents of new religion, realized that religions and systems are not imposed by force. So they treated the people of Syria, Egypt, Spain, and every country they took over with great kindness, as we have seen. They left their laws, regulations, and beliefs intact and only imposed on them the jizya, which was paltry when compared to what they had been paying in taxes previously, in exchange for maintaining their security. The truth is that nations had never known conquerors more tolerant than the Muslims, or a religion more tolerant than Islam."

RIGHT TO JUSTICE

God requires Muslims to be just in all their affairs and to act equitably towards everyone. God says:

"And the sky He has raised; and He has set the Balance (of justice), that you may not exceed the (due) balance. But neither observe the measure strictly, nor fall short thereof." (Quran 55:7-10)

Muslims are divinely ordained to act with justice, even if it means acting against themselves or those close to them, as the Quran states:

"O you who have believed, persistently stand firm in justice, witnesses for Allah, even if it be against yourselves or parents and relatives. Whether one is rich or poor, Allah is more worthy of both. So follow not [personal] inclination, lest you not be just. And if you distort [your testimony] or refuse [to give it], then indeed Allah is Ever-Acquainted with what you do." (Quran 4:135)

God requires that we apply justice at all times:

"Indeed, Allah commands you to render trusts to whom they are due, and when you judge between people, to judge with justice. Excellent is that which Allah instructs you. Indeed, Allah is ever hearing and seeing." (Quran 4:58)

Islamic justice towards non-Muslims is multifaceted. Islam gives them the right to go before their own courts; it also guarantees them equality in seeking justice with Muslims, if they choose to present their case in an Islamic court. God says:

"So, if they come to you, (O Muhammad), judge between them, or turn away from them. And if you turn away from them - never will they harm you at all. And if you judge, judge between them with justice. Indeed, Allah loves those who act justly." (Quran 5:42)

If a Muslim were to steal from a non-Muslim dhimmi, he would be liable to the same punishment as the dhimmi would have been had he stolen from the Muslim. If a Muslim were to rape a dhimmi woman, he would be liable to the same punishment as that for raping a Muslim woman. Similarly, a Muslim is liable to receive a sentence for defamation if he slanders a man or woman protected under the covenant.

Islamic history has some beautiful examples of justice

meted out by Muslims towards non-Muslims. A man named Ta'ima stole a suit of armor from Qataada, his neighbor. Qataada had hidden the armor inside a sack of flour so, when Ta'ima took it, the flour leaked out of the sack through a hole, leaving a trail up to his house. Ta'ima then left the armor in the care of a Jewish man named Zayed, who kept it in his house, in order to conceal his crime. Thus, when the people searched for the stolen armor, they followed the trail of flour to Ta'ima's house but did not find it there. When confronted, he swore to them he had not taken it and knew nothing about it. The people helping the owner also swore that they had seen him breaking into Qataada's house at night, and had subsequently followed the tell-tale trail of flour, which had led them to his house. Nevertheless, after hearing Ta'ima swearing he was innocent, they left him alone and looked for further clues, finally finding a thinner trail of flour leading to the house of Zayed, and so arrested him.

The Jewish man told them that Ta'ima had left the armor with him, and some Jewish people confirmed his statement. The tribe to which Ta'ima belonged sent some of their men to the Messenger of God to present his side of the story, and asked them to defend him. The delegation was told, 'If you do not defend our clansman, Ta'ima, he will lose his reputation and be punished severely, and the Jew will go free.' The Prophet was subsequently inclined to believe them, and was about to punish the Jewish man when God revealed the following verses of the Quran to vindicate the Jew. The verse continues to be recited by Muslims today as a reminder that justice must be served for all:

"Indeed, we have revealed to you, (O Muhammad), the Book in truth so you may judge between the people by that which God has shown you. And do not be an advocate for the deceitful. And seek forgiveness of God. Indeed, God is ever Forgiving and Merciful. And do not argue on behalf of those who deceive themselves. Indeed, God loves not one who is a habitually sinful deceiver. They conceal [their evil intentions and deeds] from the people, but they cannot conceal

[them] from God, and He is with them (in His knowledge) when they spend the night in such as He does not accept of speech. And God ever is encompassing of what they do. Here you are – those who argue on their behalf in [this] worldly life – but who will argue with God for them on the Day of Resurrection, or who will [then] be their representative?" (Quran 4:105-109)

Once, a dispute arouse between Ali bin Ali Talib, when he was the Caliph, and a Jewish man who went to Judge Shuray al-Kindi. Shuray tells the details of what happened:

"Ali found he was missing a suit of mail, so he went back to Kufa and found it in the hands of a Jewish man who was selling it in the market. He said, 'O Jew! That suit of mail is mine! I did not give it away or sell it!'

The Jew responded 'It is mine. It is in my possession.'

Ali said, 'We will have the judge rule on this for us.'

So they came to me and Ali sat next to me and said, 'That suit of mail is mine; I did not give it away or sell it.'

The Jew sat in front of me and said, 'That is my suit of mail. It is in my possession.'

I asked, 'O Commander of the Faithful, do you have any proof?'

'Yes,' Ali said. 'My son Hasan and Qanbar can testify that it is my suit of mail.'

I said, 'Commander of the Faithful, the testimony of a son in his father's favor is not admissible in court.'

Ali exclaimed, 'How Perfect is God! You cannot accept the testimony of a man who has been promised Paradise? I heard the Messenger of God saying that Hasan and Husain are the princes of the youth in Paradise.'

The Jewish man said, 'The Commander of the Faithful takes me before his own judge and the judge rules in my favor against him! I bear witness that no one deserves worship except God and that Muhammad is His Messenger [the Jewish man accepted Islam], and that the suit of armor is yours, Commander of the Faithful. You dropped it at night and I found it.'

Another amazing story of Muslim justice towards non-Muslims pertains to the conquest of the city of Samarkand. Qutayba, the Muslim military general, had not given the residents of Samarkand a choice between accepting Islam, entering into a protective covenant with the Muslims, or to accept fighting at the time. Years after the conquest, the people of Samarkand lodged a complaint with 'Umar bin Abdulaziz, the then current Muslim Caliph. Umar, upon hearing their complaint, ordered the governor of the city to turn it over to the people and vacate it, and then to give the people the three alternatives to choose from. Astounded by this display of instant justice, many of the residents of Samarkand embraced Islam!

We also read in history instances where the general Muslim population was aware of the rights of the non-Muslim minorities and would demand justice for non-Muslims from their rulers. Waleed ibn Yazeed, an Omayyad Caliph, exiled the inhabitants of Cyprus and forced them to settle in Syria. The scholars of Islam did not approve his move at the time and declared it to be oppression after the event. They brought the issue up with his son when he became Caliph so that the people could be resettled in their native land once again. He agreed to the proposal, and is thus known to be one of the fairest rulers of the Umayyad dynasty. Another similar historical instance is when the governor of Lebanon, Salih ibn Ali, expelled an entire village of non-Muslims because some of them refused to pay the land tax. The governor was a close advisor of the Caliph, yet Imam Awza'i, a renowned Muslim scholar of Syria, came to their defense and wrote to letter of protest. Part of the letter reads:

'How can you collectively punish people for the misdeeds of a few, going so far as to expel them from their homes? God states:

"No bearer of burdens will bear the burden of another." (Quran 53:38)

It is the most compelling evidence to consider and follow.

And the most deserving command of the Prophet to preserve and follow is:

"If anyone oppresses a dhimmi or burdens him with something he can not bear, I will argue against him on the Day of Judgment"

They are not slaves whom one is able to take from one place and move to another as one pleases. They are the free People of the Covenant.'

Secular writers and historians have been compelled to acknowledge the justice of Islam towards non-Muslims in their midst. The British historian, H.G.Wells, wrote the following:

'They established great traditions of just tolerance. They inspire people with a spirit of generosity and tolerance, and are humanitarian and practical. They created a humane community in which it was rare to see cruelty and social injustice, unlike any community that came before it.'

Discussing the Christian sects at the beginning centuries of Islamic rule, Sir Thomas Arnold writes:

'Islamic principles of tolerance forbade these actions [mentioned previously], that always involved some oppression. Muslims were the opposite of others, and it appears that they spared no effort in treating all of their Christian subjects with justice and equity. An example was the conquest of Egypt, when the Jacobites took advantage of the removal of the Byzantine authorities to dispossess the Orthodox Christians of their churches. The Muslims returned them to their rightful owners when the Orthodox Christians presented them with proof of ownership.'

Amari, a Sicilian Orientalist, observed:

'At the time of the Muslim Arab rule, the conquered inhabitants of the island of (Sicily) were comfortable and content compared to their Italian counterparts, who were collapsing under the yoke of the Langiornians and Franks.'

Nadhmi Luqa commented:

'No law can eradicate injustice and prejudice better than one that states:

"...and do not let the hatred of a people prevent you from being just." (Quran 5:8)

'Only when a person holds himself to these standards, settling for no other, and devotes himself to a religion with these lofty principles and rectitude accepting no other... only then can he claim to have honored himself.'

3

Security of Life, Property, and Honor

Islamic Law protects basic human rights like the preservation of life, property, and honor for Muslims and non-Muslims alike. Whether the non-Muslims are residents or visitors, they are guaranteed these rights. These rights cannot be taken away except in a justified case permitted by law. For instance, a non-Muslim may not be killed unless he is guilty of killing. God says:

"Say, 'Come, I will recite what your Lord has prohibited to you. (He commands) that you not associate anything with Him, and to parents, good treatment, and do not kill your children out of poverty; we will provide for you and them. And do not approach immoralities - what is apparent of them and what is concealed. And do not kill the soul which God has forbidden [to be killed] except by [legal] right. This has He instructed you that you may use reason.'" (Quran 6:151)

The Prophet of Islam declared that the life of non-Muslims residents or visitor has sanctity when he said:

"Whoever kills a person, with whom we have a treaty, will not come close enough to Paradise to smell its scent, and its scent can be found as far as forty years of travel [away]." (Saheeh Al-Bukhari)

Islam does not allow assaulting a non-Muslim, violating his honor or property, or hurting him. If someone steals from a dhimmi, he must be punished. If anyone borrows from a dhimmi, the property must be returned. The Prophet of Islam said:

"You must know that it is not lawful for you to take the property of the People of the Covenant unless it is (in payment) for something."

He also said:

"Indeed God, Mighty and Majestic, has not allowed you to ener the homes of the People of the Book except by their permission, nor has He allowed you to hit their women, nor eat their fruit if they give you what is obligatory upon them [from the jizyah]." (Abu Dawood)

There is an interesting story from the era of Ahmad ibn Tulun of Egypt. One day a Christian monk came to Tulun's palace to complain about his governor. Upon noticing him, a guard inquired about the problem. On finding out that the governor had taken 300 dinars from the monk, the guard offered to pay the monk on the condition that he does not complain, and the monk accepted his offer.

The incident reached Tulun who ordered the monk, guard, and the governor to come to his court. Tulun said to the governor, 'Are not all your needs met with a sufficient income? Do you have needs that justify taking from others?'

The governor conceded to the force of his argument, yet still Tulun kept on questioning him, eventually removing him from his post. Tulun then asked the monk how much the governor had taken from him, and the monk told him it was 300 dinars. Tulun said, 'It is too bad you did not say 3000, as he needs a larger punishment, but I can only base it on your statement,' and took the money from the governor and returned it to the monk.

Non-Muslims have the right that their honor be protected. This right is extended not only to non-Muslim residents, but also to visitors. They all have the right to be secure and protected. God says:

"And if any one of the polytheists seeks your protection, then grant him protection so that he may hear the words of

God (the Quran). Then deliver him to his place of safety. That is because they are a people who do not know." (Quran 9:6)

The right to asylum makes it a duty on every Muslim to respect and uphold the asylum granted by another Muslim according to the Prophet's statement:

"The obligation imposed by the covenant is communal, and the nearest Muslim must try hard to fulfill it. Anyone who violates the protection granted by a Muslim will be under the curse of God, the angels, and all people, and on Judgment Day no intercession will be accepted on his behalf."

One of the female companions, Umm Hani, said to the Prophet:

"Messenger of God, my brother Ali claims that he is at war with a man whom I have granted asylum, a man with the name of Ibn Hubayra."

The Prophet answered her:

"Anyone you have given asylum to is under the protection of all of us, O Umm Hani."

The right to asylum and protection requires a Muslim to give asylum and grant security to a non-Muslim who seeks it and warns of severe punishment for anyone who violates it. Asylum guarantees protection from aggression, or attack for anyone who has been given security, a right that is not explicitly granted in any other religion.

GOOD TREATMENT

The Quran instructs Muslims to treat non-Muslims courteously in a spirit of kindness and generosity, given they are not hostile towards Muslims. God says:

"God does not forbid you from those who do not fight you because of religion and do not expel you from your homes – from dealing kindly and justly with them. Indeed, God loves those who act justly. God only forbids you from those who fight you because of religion and expel you from your homes and aid in your expulsion – (forbids) that you make allies of them. And whoever makes allies of them, then it is those who are the wrongdoers." (Quran 60:8-9)

Al-Qarafi, a classical Muslim scholar, describes the depth of the meaning of "dealing kindly" referred to in the above verse. He explains the term:

'...gentleness towards the weak, providing clothing to cover them, and soft speech. This must be done with affection and mercy, not by intimidation or degradation. Furthermore, tolerating the fact that they may be bothersome neighbors whom you could force to move, but you do not out of kindness towards them, not out of fear or financial reasons. Also, praying they receive guidance and [thus] join the ranks of the blessed with external reward, advising them in all wordily and spiritual matters, protecting their reputation if they are exposed to slander, and defending their property, families, rights, and concerns. Assisting them against oppression and getting them their rights.'

Divine commandments to treat non-Muslims in this manner were taken seriously by Muslims. They were not just verses to be recited, but Divine Will to be acted upon. The Prophet may the mercy and blessings of God be upon him, himself was the first person to put the divine commands into practice, followed by his caliphs and the general population of believers. The life-story of the Prophet of Islam gives many instances of his kind, tolerant co-existence with non-Muslims. Some of his neighbors were non-Muslims and the Prophet would be generous towards them and exchange gifts. The Prophet of Islam would visit them when they fell sick and do business with them. There was a Jewish family he regularly gave charity to and the Muslims after his death maintained his charity towards them.

When a Christian delegation from Ethiopian churches came to Medina, the Prophet opened up his mosque for them to stay in, hosted them generously, and personally served them meals. He said:

"They were generous to our companions, so I wish to be generous to them in person..."

...referring to the event when they provided asylum to a number of his companions after they fled persecution in

Arabia and took asylum in Abyssinia. In another instance, a Jewish man named Zayd bin Sana came to the Prophet of Islam to reclaim a debt. He grabbed the Prophet by his robe and cloak, pulled the Prophet close to his face, and said, 'Muhammad, are you not going to give me my due? You and your clan Banu Muttalib never pay debts on time!' Umar, one of the companions of the Prophet, got agitated and said, 'Enemy of God, am I really hearing what you just said to God's Prophet. I swear by the One who sent him with truth, if I were not afraid that he would blame me, I would have taken my sword and cut your head off!' The Prophet looked calmly at Umar and censured him gently:

"Umar that is not what we needed to hear from you. You should have counseled me to pay my debts in time and asked him to seek repayment in a respectful manner. Now take him, repay him his debt from my money and give him an extra twenty measures of date."

The Jewish man was so pleasantly surprised by the Prophet's behavior that he immediately declared his acceptance of Islam!

The companions of Prophet Muhammad followed his example in how they treated non-Muslims. Umar set-up a permanent stipend for the Jewish family the Prophet used to take care of in his lifetime. He found justification for allotting funds for the People of the Scripture in the following verse of the Quran:

"Alms are only for the poor and for the needy and for those employed to collect (the funds) and for bringing hearts together, and for freeing captives (or slaves) and for those in debt and for the cause of God, and for the (stranded) traveler – an obligation (imposed) by God. And God is Knowing and Wise." (Quran 9:60)

Abdullah ibn 'Amr, a famous companion of the Prophet Muhammad would regularly give charity to his neighbors. He would send his servant to take portions of meat on religious occasions to his Jewish neighbor. The surprised servant asked about Abdullah's concern for his Jewish neighbor. Abdullah told him the saying of Prophet Muhammad:

"The angel Gabriel was so adamant in reminding me to be charitable with my neighbor that I thought he might make him my heir."

Turning to the pages of history, we find a marvelous example of how a Muslim ruler expected his governors to treat the Jewish populace. The Sultan of Morocco, Muhammad ibn Abdullah, issued an edict on February 5th, 1864 CE:

'To our civil servants and agents who perform their duties as authorized representatives in our territories, we issue the following edict:

'They must deal with the Jewish residents of our territories according to the absolute standard of justice established by God. The Jews must be dealt with by the law on an equal basis with others so that none suffers the least injustice, oppression, or abuse. Nobody from their own community or outside shall be permitted to commit any offense against them or their property. Their artisans and craftsmen may not be scripted into service against their will, and must be paid full wages for serving the state. Any oppression will cause the oppressor to be in darkness on Judgment Day and we will not approve of any such wrongdoing. Everyone is equal in the sight of our law, and we will punish anyone who wrongs or commits aggression against the Jews with divine aid. This order which we have stated here is the same law that has always been known, established, and stated. We have issued this edict simply to affirm and warn anyone who may wish to wrong them, so the Jews may have a greater sense of security and those intending harm may be deterred by greater sense of fear.'

Renault is one of the unbiased Western historians who has acknowledged the kind and fair treatment of Muslims towards the non-Muslim minorities. He comments:

'The Muslims in the cities of Islamic Spain treated the non-Muslims in the best possible way. In return, the non-Muslims showed respect to the sensibilities of the Muslims and would circumcise their own children and refrain from eating pork.'

SOCIAL SECURITY

Modern welfare states provide social benefits to their poor citizens, but Islam preceded all nations in establishing social security services. Islamic law set up financial provisions for needy Muslims through zakah (obligatory charity) and sadaqa (voluntary charity). Zakah was made obligatory on wealthy Muslims to take care of the poor, whereas sadaqa was left on individual discretion to help the needy. Social security provided by Islam includes non-Muslims as well. Islamic Law requires the state to provide for its citizens with disabilities – Muslim or non-Muslim - that prevent them from employment. They are provided for by the public treasury and the ruler is negligent if he does not do so. Many instances of Muslims providing social security to the non-Muslim citizens are recorded in history. Umar ibn al-Khattab the second caliph of Islam, once passed by a old, blind man begging in front of a house. Umar asked him which religious community he belonged to. The man said he was Jewish. Umar then asked him, 'What has brought you to this?' The old man said, 'Do not ask me; ask ...poverty, and old age.' Umar took the man to his own home, helped him from his personal money, and then ordered the head of the treasury, 'You must look after this man and others like him. We have not treated him fairly. He should not have spent the best years of his life among us to find misery in his old age.' Umar also relieved him andothers in his situation of paying the jizya.

Another example is found in Khalid ibn al-Walid's letter to the people of the Iraqi city of Hira. It contains the terms of truce he offered them:

'If God gives us victory, the people of the covenant will be protected. They have rights promised to them by God. It is the strictest covenant God has made incumbent on any of His prophets. They are also held by the duties that it places upon them and must not violate it. If they are conquered, they will live comfortably with everything due to them. I am commanded to exempt from jizya the elderly who cannot work, the disabled, or the poor who receive charity from their own community. The treasury will provide for them and their dependants as long as they live in Muslim lands or in the communities of Muslim emigrants. If they move outside of Muslim lands, neither they nor their dependants shall be entitled to any benefits.'

In another instance, Umar ibn al-Khattab, the Muslim Caliph, was visiting Damascus. He passed by a group of Christian lepers. He ordered that they be given charity and regular stipends for food.

Umar ibn Abdul-Aziz, another Muslim Caliph, wrote to his agent in Basra, Iraq, 'Search for the people of the covenant in your area who may have grown old, and are unable to earn, and provide them with regular stipends from the treasury to take care of their needs.'

Some of the early Muslims used to distribute part of their post-Ramadan charity (zakat ul-fitr) to Christian monks, based on their understanding of the verse of Quran:

"God does not forbid you from those who do not fight you because of religion and do not expel you from your homes - from dealing kindly and justly with them. Indeed, God loves those who act justly. God only forbids you from those who fight you because of religion and expel you from your homes and aid in your expulsion - (forbids) that you make allies of them. And whoever makes allies of them, and then it is those who are the wrongdoers."(Quran 60:8-9)

Finally, there are other rights that we have not discussed here, because of the assumption that they are elementary and taken for granted, such as the right to work, housing, transportation, education, and so forth. However, before concluding, I would like to make the following observation. Our discussion has clarified how non-Muslims living in Muslim countries enjoy rights that they might not be granted in non-Muslim countries. Some readers may respond with the objection that these rights might have existed in history, but the experience of non-Muslims living in Muslim countries today is different. The author's personal observation is that non-Muslims still enjoy many of these same rights today, perhaps even more. Allah Almighty has commanded us to be truthful, in the verse:

"O you who believe! Stand out firmly for justice, as witnesses to Allah; even though it be against yourselves, or your parents, or your kin, be he rich or poor, God is a Better Protector to both (than you). So follow not the lusts (of your hearts), lest you avoid justice; and if you distort your witness or refuse to give it, verily, Allah is Ever Well-Acquainted with what you do."(Quran 4:135)

Further, when we compare the conditions of non-Muslims living in Muslim countries to the status of Muslim minorities living in non-Muslim countries, whether now or in history, we see a profound difference. What happened to Muslims during the Crusades, under the Spanish Inquisition, in Communist China, or the Soviet Union? What is happening to them today in the Balkans, Russia, Palestine, and India? It would be worthwhile to reflect in order to give an answer based on fairness and declaration of truth and justice. Allah is the best of Judges, and He states:

"O you who believe! Stand out firmly for God as just witnesses; and let not the enmity hatred of others make you avoid justice. Be just: that is nearer to piety; and fear God. Verily, God is Well-Acquainted with what you do."(Quran 5:8)

Protection from Foreign Aggression

Non-Muslim citizens have a similar right to be protected from external enemies just as a Muslim fellow citizen does. The payment of jizya ensures protection against outside aggression, defense against enemies, and ransom to be paid on their behalf if they are taken captive by an enemy.

Writing a few centuries ago, Ibn Hazm, a classical scholar of Islam, said:

'If we are attacked by an enemy nation who is targeting the People of the Covenant living among us, it is out duty to come fully armed and ready to die in battle for them, to protect those people who are protected by the covenant of God and His Messenger. Doing any less and surrendering them will be blameworthy neglect of a sacred promise.'

History has recorded many examples of Muslims fulfilling their sacred promise towards the dhimmis. The companion of Prophet Muhammad, Abu Ubayda al-Jarrah, was the leader of the army that conquered Syria. He made agreement with its people to pay the *jizya*.

Realizing the faithful loyalty of the Muslims, the Syrian people of the covenant resisted Muslim enemies and aided the Muslims against them. The residents of each town would send some of their people to spy against the Byzantines, who conveyed the news of the gathering of Byzantine army to Abu Ubayda's commanders. Finally, when the Muslims feared they would not be able to guarantee their protectect, Abu Ubayda wrote to his commanders to return all the money they had collected as jizya with the following message for the Syrians:

'We are returning your money to you because news has reached us of the awaiting armies. The condition of our agreement is that we protect you, and we are unable to do so, therefore, we are returning what we have taken from you. If God grants us victory, we will stand by out agreement.'

When his commanders returned the money and conveyed his message, the Syrian response was:

'May God bring you back safely to us. May He grant you victory. If the Byzantines had been in your place, they would not have returned anything, they would have taken everything we own and left us with nothing.'

The Muslims were victorious in the battle. When people of other towns saw how their allies were defeated, they sought to negotiate a truce with the Muslims. Abu Ubayda entered into a truce with all of them with all the rights he had extended in the first treaties. They also requested that the Byzantines hiding among them be given safe passage back home, with their families and possessions, without any harm, which Abu Ubayda agreed to.

Then the Syrians sent the jizya and opened their cities to welcome Muslims. On the way back home, Abu Ubayda was met by the representatives of townspeople and villagers requesting him to extend the treaty to them as well, to which he happily complied.

Another example of Muslims' defending the non-Muslim citizens can be seen in the actions of Ibn Taimiyya. He went to the Tartar leader after they had sacked Syria for release of their captives. The Tartar leader agreed to release the Muslim prisoners, but Ibn Taimiyya protested:

'We will only be satisfied if all the Jewish and Christian prisoners are released as well. They are people of the covenant. We do not abandon a prisoner whether from our own people or from those under a covenant.'

He persisted until the Tartars released all of them.

Furthermore, Muslim jurists have stated that protecting non-Muslims from external aggression is a duty just as their protection from internal harassment. Al-Mawardi stated:

'The payment of the jizya entitles the people of the covenant to two rights. First, they be left undisturbed. Second, that they be guarded and protected. In this way, they can be secure in society and protected from outside threats.'

Islam considers abandoning the protection of its non-Muslim citizens a form of wrongdoing and oppression that is forbidden. God says:

"...And whoever commits injustice among you - We will make him taste a great punishment." (Quran 25:19)

Therefore, harming or oppressing people of the covenant is considered a serious sin. Upholding treaties with them is an obligation on the Muslim Caliph and his representatives. The Prophet promised to argue on the Day of Judgment on behalf of the dhimmi against someone who harms him:

"Beware! Whoever is cruel and hard on a non-Muslim minority, curtails their rights, burdens them with more than they can bear, or takes anything from them against their free will; I (Prophet Muhammad) will complain against the person on the Day of Judgment." (Abu Dawood)

All evidence in Islamic Law points towards protecting the people of the covenant.

Al-Qarafi, another classical Muslim scholar, wrote:

'The covenant is a contract that has conditions that are compulsory for us, for they are under our protection as neighbors, and the covenant of God and His Messenger, and the religion of Islam. If someone harms them with inappropriate speech, defamation, any type of harassment, or is an accomplice to such actions, then he has made light of the covenant of God, His Messenger, and Islam.'

Umar, the second Caliph of Islam, would inquire from the visitors coming to meet him from other provinces about the situation of the people of the covenant and would say, 'We may know that the treaty is still being upheld.' On his deathbed, Umar is reported to have said, 'Command whoever becomes Caliph after me to treat well the people of the covenant, to uphold the treaty, to fight whoever wants to harm them, and not to overwhelm them with burden.'

The writings of Muslim scholars and the actions of many Muslim rulers demonstrate the Islamic commitment from the earliest times to this right of non-Muslims.

The Forgiveness of Muhammad Shown to Non-Muslims

The Prophet Muhammad may God praise him, was described as a "Mercy for all the Worlds", as God said in the Quran:

"We have sent you as a mercy for all the worlds." (Quran 21:107)

The recipients of this quality were not limited to just the Muslim nation, but it also extended to non-Muslims, some of who spent all their effort trying to harm the Prophet and his mission. This mercy and forgiveness is clearly demonstrated in the fact that the Prophet, may the mercy and blessings of God be upon him, never took revenge on anyone for personal reasons and always forgave even his staunch enemies. Aisha said that the Prophet never took revenge on his own behalf on anyone. She also said that he never returned evil for evil, but he would forgive and pardon. This will, God willing, become clear after a deep analysis of the following accounts of his life.

In the earlier portion of his mission, the Prophet traveled to the city of Taif, a city located in the mountains nearby to Mecca, in order to invite them to accept Islam. The leaders of Taif, however, were rude and discourteous in their treatment of the Prophet. Not being content with their insolent attitude towards him, they even stirred up some gangs of the town to harass him. This riff-raff followed the Prophet shouting at and abusing him, and throwing stones at him, until he was compelled to take refuge in an orchard. Thus the Prophet had to endure even more obstacles in Taif than he had had to face in Mecca. These ruffians, stationed either side of the path, threw stones at him until his feet were injured and smeared with blood. These oppressions so grievously dejected the Prophet and plunged him into in such a state of depression that a prayer, citing his helplessness and pitiable condition and seeking the aid of God, spontaneously came from his lips:

"O God, to You I complain of my weakness, lack of resources and humiliation before these people. You are the Most Merciful, the Lord of the weak and my Master. To whom will You consign me? To one estranged, bearing ill will, or an enemy given power over me? If You do not assign me any worth, I care not, for Your favor is abundant upon me. I seek refuge in the light of Your countenance by which all darkness is dispelled and every affair of this world and the next is set right, lest Thy anger should descend upon me or Your displeasure light upon me. I need only Your pleasure and satisfaction for only You enable me to do good and evade the evil. There is no power and no might but You."

The Lord then sent the angel of mountains, seeking the permission of the Prophet to join together the two hills and crush the city of Taif, between which it was located. Out of his great tolerance and mercy, the Messenger of God replied,

"No! For, I hope that God will bring forth from their loins people who will worship God alone, associating nothing with Him." (Saheeh Muslim)

His mercy and compassion was so great that on more than one occasion, God, Himself, reprimanded him for it. One of the greatest opponents of Islam and a personal enemy was Abdullah bin Ubayy, the leader of the hypocrites of Medina. Outwardly proclaiming Islam, he surreptitiously inflicted great harm to the Muslims and the mission of the Prophet. Knowing his state of affairs, the Prophet Muhammad still offered the funeral prayer for him and prayed to God for his forgiveness. The Quran mentions this incident in these words:

"And never (O Muhammad) pray for one of them who dies, nor stand by his grave. Lo! They disbelieve in God and His Messenger, and they died while they were evil doers." (Quran 9:84)

Abdullah bin Ubayy worked all his life against Muhammad and Islam and left no stone unturned so as to bring him into disrepute and try to defeat his mission. He withdrew his three hundered supporters in the battle of Uhud and thus almost broke the backbone of the Muslims at one stroke. He engaged in intrigues and acts of hostility against the Prophet of Islam and the Muslims. It was he who tried to bring shame to the Prophet by inciting his allies to falsely accuse the Prophet's wife, Aisha, of adultery in order to discredit him and his message.

The mercy of the Prophet even extended to those who brutally killed and then mutilated the body of his uncle Hamzah, one of the most beloved of people to the Prophet. Hamzah was one of the earliest to accept Islam and, through his power and position in the Quraishite hierarchy, diverted much harm from the Muslims. An Abyssinian slave of the wife of Abu Sufyan, Hind, sought out and killed Hamzah in the battle of Uhud. The night before the victory of Mecca, Abu Sufyan accepted Islam, fearing the vengeance of the Prophet, may the mercy and blessings of God be upon him. The latter forgave him and sought no retribution for his years of enmity.

After Hind had killed Hamzah she mutilated his body by cutting his chest and tearing his liver and heart into pieces. When she quietly came to the Prophet and accepted Islam, he recognized her but did not say anything. She was so impressed by his magnanimity and stature that she said, "O Messenger of God, no tent was more deserted in my eyes than yours; but today no tent is more lovely in my eyes than yours."

Ikrama, son of Abu Jahl, was a great enemy of the Prophet and Islam. He ran away after the victory of Mecca and went to Yemen. After his wife embraced Islam, she brought him to the Prophet Muhammad under her protection. He was so pleased to see him that he greeted him with the words:

"O emigrant rider, welcome."

Safwan bin Umaya, one of the chiefs of Mecca, was also a great enemy of Muhammad and Islam. He promised a reward to Umair ibn Wahab if he managed to kill Muhammad. When Mecca was conquered, Safwan ran away to Jeddah in the hope of finding a berth that would take him to Yemen by sea. Umair ibn Wahab came to Muhammad and said, "O Messenger of God! Safwan ibn Umayya, a chief of his tribe, has run away from fear of what you might do to him and threatens to cast himself into the sea." The Prophet sent him a guarantee of protection and, when he returned, he requested Muhammad to give him two months to come to a decision.. He was given four months, after which he became a Muslim by his own will.

Habir ibn al-Aswad was another vicious enemy of Muhammad and Islam. He inflicted a serious injury to Zainab, daughter of the Noble Prophet when she decided to migrate to Medina. She was pregnant when she started her migration, and the polytheists of Mecca tried to stop her from leaving. This particular man, Habbar bin al-Aswad, physically assaulted her and intentionally caused her to fall down from her camel. Her fall had caused her to miscarry her baby, and she herself, was badly hurt. He had committed many other crimes against Muslims as well. He wanted flee to Persia but, when he decided to come to Muhammad instead, the Prophet magnanimously forgave him.

The tribe of Quraish the were archenemies of Islam and, for a period of thirteen years while he was still in Mecca, they would rebuke the Prophet, taunt and mock him, beat him and abuse him, both physically and mentally.They placed the afterbirth of a camel on his back while he prayed, and they boycotted him and his tribe until the social sanctions became unbearable. They plotted and attempted to kill him on more than one occasion, and when the Prophet escaped to Medina, they rallied the majority of the Arab tribes and waged many wars against him. Yet, when he entered Mecca victorious with an army of 10,000, he did not take revenge on anyone. The Prophet said to the Quraish:

"O people of Quraish! What do you think I will do to you?

Hoping for a good response, they said: "You will do good. You are a noble brother, son of a noble brother."

The Prophet then said:

"Then I say to you what Joseph said to his brothers: 'There is no blame upon you.' Go! For you all free!"

Rarely in the annals of history can we read such an instance of forgiveness? Even his deadliest enemy Abu Sufyan, who led so many battles against Islam, was forgiven, as was any person who stayed in his house and did not come to fight him.

The Prophet, may the mercy and blessings of God be upon him, was all for forgiveness and no amount of crime or aggression against him was too great to be forgiven by him. He was the complete example of forgiveness and kindness, as mentioned in the following verse of the Quran:

"Keep to forgiveness (O Muhammad), and enjoin kindness, and turn away from the ignorant." (Quran 7:199)

He always repelled evil with the good of forgiveness and kind behavior for, in his view, an antidote was better than poison. He believed and practiced the precept that love could foil hatred, and aggression could be won over by forgiveness. He overcame the ignorance of the people with the knowledge of Islam, and the folly and evil of the people with his kind and forgiving treatment. With his forgiveness, he freed people from the bondage of sin and crime, and also made them great friends of Islam. He was an epitome of the verse of the Quran:

"Good and evil are not alike. Repel evil with what is better. Then he, between whom and you there was hatred, will become as though he was a bosom friend." (Quran 41:34)

NO COMPULSION IN RELIGION

The dealings of the Prophet may the mercy and blessings of God be upon him, with other religions can best be described in the verse of the Quran:

"To you be your religion, to me be mine."

The Arabian Peninsula during the time of the Prophet was a region in which various faiths were present. There were Christians, Jews, Zoroastrians, polytheists, and others not affiliated with any religion. When one looks into the life of the Prophet, one may draw on many examples to portray the high level of tolerance shown to people of other faiths.

In order to understand and judge this tolerance, one must look into the period in which Islam was a formal state, with the specific laws laid down by the Prophet in accordance with the tenets of religion. Even though one can observe many examples of tolerance shown by the Prophet in the thirteen years of his stay in Mecca, one may incorrectly think that it was only due to seeking to raise the profile of the Muslims and the social status of Islam and in general.

The Saheefah

The best example of the tolerance shown by the Prophet to other religions may be the constitution itself, called the 'Saheefah' by early historians. When the Prophet migrated to Medina, his role as a mere religious leader ended; he was now the political leader of a state, governed by the precepts of Islam, which demanded that clear laws of governance be laid out to ensure harmony and stability in a society which once had been distraught by decades of war, one which must ensure the peaceful coexistence of Muslims, Jews, Christians and polytheists. Due to this, the Prophet laid down a 'constitution' which detailed the responsibilities of all parties which resided in Medina, their obligations towards each other, and certain restrictions which were placed on each. All parties were to obey what was mentioned therein, and any breach of its articles was regarded as an act of treachery.

ONE NATION

The first article of the constitution was that all the inhabitants of Medina, the Muslims as well as those who had entered the pact from the Jews, Christian, and idolaters, were "one nation to the exclusion of all others." All were considered members and citizens of Medina society regardless of religion, race, or ancestry. People of other faiths were protected from harm as much as the Muslims, as is stated in another article, "To the Jews who follow us belong help and equity. He shall not be harmed nor his enemies be aided." Previously, each tribe had their alliances and enemies within and without Medina. The Prophet gathered these different tribes under one system of governance which upheld pacts of alliances previously in existence between those individual tribes. All tribes had to act as a whole with disregard to individual alliances. Any attack on other religion or tribe was considered an attack on the state and upon the Muslims as well.

The lives of the practitioners of other religions in the Muslim society were also given protective status. The Prophet said:

"Whoever kills a person who has a truce with the Muslims will never smell the fragrance of Paradise." (Saheeh Muslim)

Since the upper hand was with the Muslims, the Prophet strictly warned against any maltreatment of people of other faiths. He said:

"Beware! Whoever is cruel and hard on a non-Muslim minority, or curtails their rights, or burdens them with more than they can bear, or takes anything from them against their free will; I (Prophet Muhammad) will complain against the person on the Day of Judgment." (Abu Dawud)

To each their own Religion

In another article, it states, "the Jews have their religion and the Muslims have theirs." In this, it is clear that anything other than tolerance would not be tolerated, and that, although all were members of a society, each had their separate religion which could not be violated. Each was allowed to practice their beliefs freely without any hindrances, and no acts of provocation would be tolerated.

There are many other articles of this constitution which may be discussed, but emphasis will be placed on an article which states, "If any dispute or controversy likely to cause trouble should arise, it must be referred to God and His Messenger." This clause maintained that all inhabitants of the state must recognize a higher level of authority, and in those matters which involved various tribes and religions, justice could not be meted out by individual leaders; rather it must be adjudicated by the leader of the state himself or his designated representatives. It was allowed, however, for individual tribes who were not Muslims, to refer to their own religious scriptures and their learned men in regards to their own personal affairs. They could though, if they opted, ask the Prophet to judge between them in their matters. God says in the Quran:

"…If they do come to you, either judge between them or decline to interfere..." (Quran 5:42)

Here we see that Prophet allowed each religion to judge in their own matters according to their own scriptures, as long as it did not stand in opposition to articles of the constitution, a pact which took into account the greater benefit of the peaceful co-existence of the society.

RELIGIOUS AUTONOMY AND POLITICS

There are many other examples during the lifetime of the Prophet, may the mercy and blessings of God be upon him, in addition to the Saheefah that practically portray the tolerance Islam shows for other religions.

FREEDOM OF RELIGIOUS ASSEMBLY AND RELIGIOUS AUTONOMY

Given consent by the constitution, the Jews had the complete freedom to practice their religion. The Jews in Medina at the time of the Prophet had their own school of learning, named Bait-ul-Midras, where they would recite the Torah, worship and educate themselves.

The Prophet emphasized in many letters to his emissaries that religious institutions should not be harmed. Here in a letter addressed to his emissary to the religious leaders of Saint Catherine in Mount Sinai who has sought the protection of the Muslims:

"This is a message from Muhammad ibn Abdullah, as a covenant to those who adopt Christianity, near and far, we are with them. Verily I, the servants, the helpers, and my followers defend them, because Christians are my citizens; and by God! I hold out against anything that displeases them. No compulsion is to be on them. Neither are their judges to be removed from their jobs nor their monks from their monasteries. No one is to destroy a house of their religion, to damage it, or to carry anything from it to the Muslims' houses. Should anyone take any of these, he would spoil God's covenant and disobey His Prophet. Verily, they are my allies and have my secure charter against all that they hate. No one is to force them to travel or to oblige them to fight. The Muslims are to fight for them. If a female Christian is married to a Muslim, it is not to take place without her approval. She is not to be prevented from visiting her church to pray. Their churches are declared to be protected. They are neither to be prevented from repairing them nor the sacredness of their covenants. No one of the nation (Muslims) is to disobey the covenant till the Last Day (end of the world)."

As one can see, this Charter consisted of several clauses covering all important aspects of human rights, including such topics as the protection of minorities living under Islamic rule, freedom of worship and movement, freedom to appoint their own judges and to own and maintain their property, exemption from military service, and the right to protection in war.

On another occasion, the Prophet received a delegation of sixty Christians from the region of Najran, then a part of Yemen, at his mosque. When the time for their prayer came, they faced the direction of east and prayed. The Prophet ordered that they be left in their state and not harmed.

POLITICS

There are also examples in the life of the Prophet in which he cooperated between with people of other faiths in the political arena as well. He selected a non-Muslim, Amr-ibn Umaiyah-ad-Damri, as an ambassador to be sent to Negus, the King of Ethiopia.

These are only some of the examples of the Prophet's tolerance of other faiths. Islam recognizes that there are a plurality of religions on this earth, and gives the right to individuals to choose the path which they believe to be true. Religion is not to be, and was never, forced upon an individual against their own will, and these examples from the life of the Prophet, may the mercy and blessings of God be upon him, are an epitome of the verse of the Quran which promotes religious tolerance and sets the guideline for the Muslims' interaction with people of other faiths. God says:

"...There is no compulsion in religion..." (Quran 2:256)

SOCIAL SECURITY

The laws of social security in Islam do not exist in codified form. But they consist of the injunctions of the Quran, hadith, precedents of the 'Righteous Caliphate' and the views of the jurists deduced from the original sources through qiyas and ijtihad. In order to examine these laws of social security with reference to non-Muslim subjects of an Islamic State, one should have recourse to these sources.

Before coming to the subject proper an appreciation of the contemporary concept of social security and its evolution is necessary. The term 'social security' denotes the programmes established by law to provide for the economic security and social welfare of the individual and his family.

Nowadays these programmes have assumed the shape of old-age pension, unemployment benefit, sickness benefit, death grant, disablement allowance, family allowance, etc. Some European authors try to trace the evolution of these laws to some practices of the late medieval period. But the truth is that Europe first got acquainted with the laws of social security at the end of the last century only. Before 1883, the functions that now come under social security law, were discharged by private arrangements made chiefly by co-operative movements among workers.

The practices considered to be the primitive forms of this concept have no relation to it. One of the instances referred to is the practice at some places in England where local magistracy was empowered in 1531 to licence the aged, sick and crippled persons to beg in their neighbourhood.

Another statute referred to is that of 1536 which provided for organization of relief of those unable to work through voluntary funds. The attitude of the central government towards these local initiatives was nothing more than that of supervision and advice.

The first instance of social security laws in Europe can be seen in the scheme of compulsory State insurance which was introduced by Bismark in Germany in 1883. Germany was followed by Austria and some other countries. By the beginning of this century most of the European countries initiated promulgation of laws in this direction. In America, except the Workmans Compensation Act passed in 1908, no significant legislation was enacted until 1935 when the Social Security Act was passed by the Congress.

Contrary to the European tradition, in Islam, right from the beginning, fulfillment of the basic needs of the subjects was conceived to be the concern of the State. Zakat is the first institution of social security in Islam. Payment of 2l1/2 percent of his/her savings of the zakat fund is one of the fundamental duties of a Muslim. The State is responsible to collect zakat and make arrangements for its distribution. Non-payment of it is tantamount to waging war against the State. The Caliph Abu Bakr subjugated by force all those who refused to pay it.

Non-Muslims are also included in one of the categories of the recipients of zakat. While prescribing laws for the distribution of zakat, the Quran includes them among those 'whose hearts are to be conciliated'.

Some jurists are of the view that this clause is inoperative after the time of the Prophet. Their views are based on a precedent of 'Umar ibn al-Khattab who got it cancelled by Abu Bakr towards some recipients of this category. Some prominent scholars of the past and present are of the view that this injunction is operative even today. It must be noted here that this share of the people belonging to this category is not on account of their inability to meet their material needs but for 'reconciliation' of their hearts. There are also some reports which suggest that the needy among the non-Muslims were also helped from the zakat funds during the early days of Islam.

Majority of scholars hold it to be unlawful. Their opinion is based on the precept of the Prophet who directed Mu'adh to take zakat from rich Muslims for distributing it among poor Muslims.

Some present day scholars also hold the view that poor and destitute among non-Muslims can be helped out of the zakat funds. It is reported that 'Umar interpreted the word masakin in the verse "Alms are for the poor and the needy (masakin) and those employed to administer the funds...." as non-Muslims. Besides zakat, the Quran provides for collection of sadaqat. Although sadaqah is not an obligatory duty like zakat, the Quran has given great Importance for it. Emphasizing the payment of sadaqah, the Quran goes to the extent of declaring, "You will never attain piety until you spend of what you love."

The difference between zakat and sadaqah is that while the former is to be paid at a fixed rate, no such rate has been prescribed for the latter, In the words of al-Sayyid Qutub, "The rich are obliced to contribute as much as is sufficient to meet the necessities of the needy.... There is no restriction or condition except that it should be sufficient for their needs". The guidance of the Quran to the believers as to what they should give in the way of Allah is 'the superfluity.' So far as meeting the needs of non-Muslims from the funds of sadaqah is concerned, most of the scholars' view is positive. Elaborating the position of the Hanafis, al-Hidayah states, "Our doctors base their opinion regarding this point on the precept of the Prophet (S) who has ordained that alms should be bestowed upon persons of every religion indiscriminately. And they also argue that had not there been the Prophet's directions to Mu'adh, bestowing of zakat on dhimmis would have been deemed legal". Collection and distribution of sadaqah along with zakat are among the fundamental duties of the government.

If the funds raised out of zakat and sadaqah are insufficient to meet the needs of the poor, the State can

Impose other taxes to realize funds for this purpose. While prescribing the rules of zakat and sadaqah, the Quran emphasizes that the needs of those who are economically hard-pressed and unwilling to ask for help out of self-respect should be given priority. Thus it is clear that these funds are to be spent primarily to relieve people from immediate hardships without creating a class of social parasites. Besides Quranic institutions of zakat and sadaqah, there are several Prophetic traditions which hold the State responsible for the fulfillment of the basic needs of all its subjects. The Prophet (S) is reported to have said: "I am the guardian of a person who has no guardian". Another hadith declares: "The State is the guardian of a person who has no guardian".

The guardianship, mentioned in the above traditions, is of a general nature which necessarily implies the fulfillment of basic needs. In another tradition the Prophet (S) is reported to have told: "The son of Adam has basic rights for three things a house to live in, a piece of cloth to cover his body, a loaf of bread and water". In the above traditions there is no reference to a particular community. By referring to 'the son of Adam' any ambiguity in defining the scope of these traditions has been removed. Thus it is obvious that the Islamic State is bound to provide for the basic necessities of its people irrespective of their religion. Examination of the extent of applying these injunctions of the Quran and Sunnah during the period of Righteous Caliphate, will further clarify the scope of their implementation. Keeping in view the topic of discussion, the injunctions and precedents related to non-Muslims only are cited here. The earliest instance of fulfillment of basic necessities of non-Muslims during this period can be seen in one of the treaties concluded by the Muslim general Khalid ibn al-Walid during the days of Abu Bakr. The treaty reads:

"And I have granted the right that if an old person becomes incapable of working or is suffering from ill health or is a destitute after being rich, so much so that his co-religionists start giving him alms, then his jizyah will be remitted; he and his family will receive the allowance for maintenance from public treasury as long as he lives in the Islamic State". Explaining the legal importance of the dhimmi treaties, of which the above extract forms a part, Majid Khadduri says: "The dhimmi treaties, it will be recalled, were in the form of constitutional guarantees from the moment dhimmi communities ceased to be separate entities. Finally Muslim authorities tended to regard their contractual understandings as religious obligations which should be strictly observed".

Other instances of observance of social security laws can be found in the following practices of the Righteous Caliphs. Before going through the practices, it must be made clear that the nature of these practices was not that of compassion shown by some kings or rulers of the past towards some of their needy subjects. The exercise of the kings was in the nature of royal bounty rather than the realization of the rights of their subjects.

The Righteous Caliphs on the other hand considered these

functions as discharging their duties and fulfilling the rights of their subjects. The legal significance of these can be gathered from the following words of an eminent jurist al-Hasan al-Basri. While answering the questions of a ruler regarding some precedents of the Pious Caliphs, he stated: "You have only to follow what your predecessors did".

Other Muslim jurists have also referred to these as the basis of their argument while giving their opinions. The Kitab al-kharaj of Imam Abu Yusuf is replete with such references.

The Caliph 'Umar, on seeing an old Jew begging, brought him to his house. He gave him some cash and ordered the treasury officer that such people who could not earn their living should be granted stipends from the public treasury. Once, seeing some non-Muslim lepers on his way back from a journey, he issued orders that they should be provided maintenance from the State funds.

In a letter addressed to Adi ibn Artah, 'Umar ibn 'Abd al-'Aziz wrote: "Be kind towards dhimmis. If you find some of them old or helpless, give maintenance to them".

The above-mentioned instances bear clear evidence as to how Islamic Shari'ah assures thee basic material needs of the non-Muslim subjects of an Islamic State. The legal guarantees of the material requirements of the citizens, with which the West became acquainted only in the beginning of this century, were given by Islamic Shari'ah fourteen hundred years ago. This attitude towards religious minorities is of great importance in view of the fact that such minorities are deprived of even basic human rights in the so-called welfare states of the twentieth century.

4

Tolerance and the Qur'an

With Islam coming to the West through immigration and conversion, it is to be expected that attitudes in the "public square" are going to be affected. The social reality of religious pluralism, where Islam and other religions cannot live in isolation any more, forces us to take seriously the implications of such a plurality of religious views and examine the effects on religious freedom and tolerance. Can Muslims and other religious people live together in peace and harmony?

What makes some Muslims behave as they did in the streets of a French city? What leads some Muslims to blow up the World Trade Center towers in an American city, killing thousands of civilians? Is this behavior and expression of true Islam or a perversion of it? What does Islam teach on religious tolerance? These are questions that cannot be answered quickly or easily and yet the answers are there if one looks diligently.

THE IMPORTANCE OF UNDERSTANDING THE ISLAM OF THE QUR'AN

As Jacques Ellul says: "It is impossible to judge the Islamic world in a general way: a hundred different cultures have been absorbed by Islam. It is impossible to study all the doctrines, all the traditions, and all their applications together. Such a study can only be undertaken if one limits oneself to the study of specific questions, disentangling what is true from what is false."

It is important to clarify that the Islam I have in view in this writing is the Qur'anic Islam – the Islam that is faithful to its source, the Islam which cannot exist without the Qur'an as it is – not innovative forms of Islam, or the Islam of people who do not understand and do not follow their religion as prescribed for them in the Qur'an. I will not analyze the differences between numerous branches of Islam with their specific teachings and beliefs. I choose to focus on the teaching of the Qur'an since this is the common denominator for all the different branches of Islam. It is the one source which all Muslims accept, whilst other sources of authority are interpreted and believed (or denied) in unpredictable ways. My concern, therefore, deals exclusively with the unavoidable Islam, that form of Islam which will exist as long as the Qur'an exists.

DEFINING TOLERANCE

Since we need to understand what the Qur'an teaches about religious tolerance we must define what tolerance is, and then we must see if there is such a thing taught in the Qur'an. Some Muslims may object to this approach, saying that the Qur'an ought to define the meaning of tolerance. The goal here, however, is to compare the concept of tolerance as generally understood in the democratic West with "Qur'anic tolerance."

Tolerance is different from toleration. Jay Newman wrote:

> ... [W]e are reminded that there are two different nouns corresponding to the verb 'tolerate' – 'tolerance' and 'toleration.' The latter seems to have a broader application; it refers to any instance of tolerating. But 'tolerance' is more closely related to the adjective 'tolerant.' Toleration is merely instantiated in each instance of toleration; the term is entirely behavioural. Tolerance is expressed as well as instantiated in tolerant actions. A person can be tolerant on one occasion and intolerant on another. But most of us believe that some men are generally tolerant while others are not. 'Tolerance,' then, unlike 'toleration,' is often seen as a character trait, a disposition, and usually as that kind of disposition that we call a 'virtue.'

To describe a person, a religion, or a doctrine as both tolerant and intolerant says nothing about the disposition or character of such an entity with regard to tolerance. It is not possible to characterize any person or religion as both tolerant and intolerant if tolerance is understood as a normative and defining virtue. One person or religion can be intolerant, although at times may show toleration; another can be tolerant but, inconsistently with the tolerant character, may show lack of toleration in specific or isolated occasions. This distinction between "tolerance" as a normative virtue (something we ought to exemplify consistently) and "toleration" merely as an instantiation of tolerance (occasioned by expediency), is important to bear in mind as we investigate Muslim scripture and history where there may be examples of toleration.

TOLERANCE AND THE VIEW OF TRUTH

What does it mean to tolerate another's beliefs? To "tolerate" another's beliefs does not mean that one accepts them as true; but in being tolerant one respect another's right to free will to choose what to believe. As Newman clarifies, "Tolerating a religious belief, then, does not involve a half-hearted acceptance or endurance of the belief in itself, but rather it involves acceptance or endurance of someone's holding that belief that is of a certain case of believing."

Relativists modify this meaning of tolerance to make it more of a propositional attitude, which involves respecting another's religious beliefs as being of equal value to all other truth claims, even one's own convictions. If this line of thought, however, is followed to its logical conclusion, a person could end up holding as equally true both propositions, even if they are obviously contradictory.

Metaphysical relativism considers metaphysical constructs as valuable in that they give significance to our lives; but it is not necessary for them to correspond with something objective outside of our minds. They are basically our own constructs. The motivation for such a conclusion may be epistemological (doubting the possibility to know things as they are in themselves, following the Kantian postulation of the categories of the mind that give shape to reality as experienced by us) or moral (in seeking to accommodate everybody's view).

When metaphysical relativism is considered as a foundation for tolerance, we end up with no tolerance at all because it deprives the belief of any significance which makes it worth holding. On the other hand, this view also ends up being dogmatism itself, as Newman writes: "Tolerance, after all, does not demand that one believe that every other person's metaphysical views are as true or as reasonable or as profound as his own. Indeed ... tolerance is possible only because we are capable of putting up with things that we do not like ... or agree with." This condition implies: (1) having a certain belief and (2) being introduced to another person who holds beliefs with which you disagree. If we didn't have to put up with those who hold beliefs contrary to ours, there would be no need for tolerance. If all believed the same thing, namely, that all religious beliefs are not to be taken seriously, but rather are to be considered merely as different keys in a piano (which may be different but not true or false), than what is there to tolerate?

In conclusion, we can say that tolerance means exemplifying an attitude of respect or endurance toward another's views, even those one may consider false, and tolerance as such can rightly be a virtue in one who believes in absolute truth. Muslims and Christians (and others who believe in the nature of truth as absolute and objective), have a real opportunity to be tolerant in this sense of the word, while relativists don't.

MUSLIM BACKGROUND BELIEFS

To understand the Muslim view of tolerance we need to understand some basic concepts of the Muslim worldview and sources of authority. The answer to many questions about Islam and its nature is connected with understanding "the very structure of Islam as a religious and political complex." Although the so called Christian Byzantine Empire and the Western Holy Roman Empire, with the close association of the Christian Church and the State throughout the Middle Ages might suggest a similarity with the Islamic religious-political structure, it is a wrong assumption to consider them identical. Islam is radically different in that in its very identity is a political-religious structure. Fazlur Rahman, a well respected Muslim scholar writes: "Islam insisted on the assumption of political power since it regarded itself as the repository of the Will of God which had to be worked on earth through a political order ... To deny this fact would be both to violate history and to deny justice to Islam itself."

The concept of God as "Allah" is of a being that is totally other, wholly transcendent to the point of implying that Allah is unknowable in himself but known in his will and requirements revealed in the Qur'an (Sura 42:11; 112:1-4). In the words of a Muslim scholar: "You may not have complete transcendence and self-revelation at the same time." This view of God is accompanied by a view of humans as the "slaves" of God (Sura 19:93). One major concept in Islam is captured in the very meaning of the word "Islam" itself: namely "submission," which carries the sense of laying down arms before the victor and is taken to exemplify the total submission of every aspect of life, as an individual and society to Allah (The God).

The Qur'an teaches about itself that it is God's direct and verbal word, that it is eternal and came down from what is preserved in heaven (Sura 85:22) as the "Mother of the Book" (Sura 3:7; 13:39; 43:4). Although the Qur'an considers the Old and New Testaments as God's word (Sura 3:93; 4:163; 5:46 etc.), it considers its own authority as greater than theirs (Sura 5:48). Even the Arabic language of the Qur'an is considered an integral part of Allah's word (Sura 20:113; 12:2), therefore, Muslims consider the Islamic culture as of heavenly origin.

So, Islam is a political, cultural and religious system. Religion, as based primarily on the Qur'an, is a part of the system, which informs all the other aspects of the Islamic system. Religious doctrine, however, is viewed in Islam as a preamble to Islamic law, the Shariah (divine law), which is a comprehensive code governing every aspect of life, because Islam is a religion primarily oriented toward law rather than theology.

Another important Muslim concept is the "Umma," or "the community of submission." Although Muhammad, the prophet of Islam, had been reciting the earliest Suras of the Qur'an starting in A.D. 610 for about 13 years, it is A.D. 622 that marks the beginning of the Muslim era, because this marks the emergence of the "Umma," the establishment of the Muslim political- religious structure. Dr. W. Bonar Sidjabat writes: "... the Islam of the Qur'an is theocratic and the Muslim state was a theocracy from its first ascent to power."

Prior to A.D. 622, Muhammad had not attracted many with his monotheistic message. The people of Mecca, the city of Muhammad's birth and his first decade of religious activity (which started when he was 40 years old), were not responding positively to Muhammad's message. They eventually made life so miserable for Muhammad and his few followers that they decided to flee to Medina, another city three hundred miles to the north, where some people had invited Muhammad to mediate differences between various tribal groups. William J. Saal writes:

That well-known event, the Hijra [emigration to Medina], gave Muhammed opportunity to gain control of Medina and eventually extend that control to the entire Arabian Peninsula and beyond.

This event is the pivotal event of Islamic history and has become the starting point of the Muslim calendar. Muslims believe that God's ultimate objective was the creation of a new universal social order. The Hijra marks the beginning of this new world order, today identified with the Nation or Community of Islam, the Ummah.

There are many issues that require further development at this point in tracing the history of Islam; the looting of Meccan caravans and subsequent battles with Meccan protectors of the caravans (Sura 2:216-218) in A.D. 624; the conquering of Mecca in A.D. 630; massacres of Jews; and military campaigns against the Christians in the north of Arabia under the leadership of Muhammad. He died in A.D. 632 "... but not without ordering about a month before his death another expedition to the North." We should turn to our main question now and will pursue history only in relation to defining the Qur'anic view of religious tolerance.

THE QUR'AN AND ITS IMPORTANCE

The Qur'an is the absolute authority of Islam (socio-political-economic-cultural-religious system). Fazlur Rahman writes: "This 'Other' [Allah] through some channel 'dictated' the Qur'an with an absolute authority." The high esteem with which Muslims regard the Qur'an seems best captured by a Muslim scholar, Yusuf K. Ibish, who says: "It is not a book in the ordinary sense, nor is it comparable to the Bible, either the Old or New Testaments. ... If you want to compare it with anything in Christianity, you must compare it with Christ Himself ... Christ was the expression of the Divine among men, the revelation of the Divine Will. That is what the Qur'an is."

With regard to the importance of the Qur'an in forming a concept of tolerance in Islam, Sidjabat correctly observes:

[A]lthough the Muslim opinion about any problem does not always find its answer literally in the Qur'an, but also in and supported by the Sunnah (custom) and Hadith (tradition), the Ijma (consensus) and Qias (analogy), the value of the Qur'an as the primary source of any Islamic religious problem is decisive. ... Its significance for the concept of religious tolerance is obvious, if we realize that the Qur'an can be considered as the command of God ... Following the contents of the Qur'an means practically being obedient to the will of Allah no matter how tolerant or intolerant this might be for others.

Sidjabat even goes so far as to suggest that Muhammad's "political tolerance or intolerance should not be primarily attributed to Mohammad himself but rather to Allah from Whom - as Mohammad believed - came the Qur'an."

Through the sequences of [Muhammad's] career-yearning, vision, utterance, pertinacity, controversy, endurance, rejection, emigration, militancy and triumph - the accumulation of the Qur'an moves in parallel relation, fusing meaning with mission, and truth with setting. It is as events unfold that the whole grows into entirety ... [But] In many circles, the non-chronological form of the Qur'an as it stands, however we account for it, becomes in this way a virtue in disguise or, rather, a proper parable of the necessary transcendence of mere point and circumstance which the believer should attain. God had not allowed the Qur'an to be arranged in sequence, in order to preclude notions of the time factor and of calendar time itself, seen as embarrassments to its celestial status.

The Qur'an was not written down systematically during the time of Muhammad but was primarily memorized by Muhammad's followers. It was not until after his death, and due to the fear that those who knew the Qur'an by heart were dying in the conquering battles Muslims were fighting, that Umar got the idea to ask Muhammad's successor (caliph) Abu Bakr (632-634) to "order that the Qur'an be collected." Although that compilation of the Qur'an doesn't exist and there was another compilation made during the third successor, Uthman (644-656), the order of the chapters (Sura) was decided at the time of the first official copy as the order of length rather than chronology. All the other competing variants of Qur'an, "whether written in fragmentary manuscripts or whole copies, [were ordered to] be burned."

The Qur'an itself does not help in determining the order of the chapters and sometimes, even verses from one chapter come from different periods. Cragg observes: "... the Surahs, especially the longer ones, are composite within themselves as well as irregular in time, so that the continuous reader oscillates bewilderingly across the years and has, indeed, a better chance of being in historical step if he starts at Surah 114 and reads back to Surah 2, than if he lets the paging guide him."

On the one hand, Muslims believe that since the Qur'an is eternal there is no need for a chronological order but, on the other hand, as Fazlur Rahman says: "the 'occasions of revelation' were recorded [in the Hadith] as a necessary aid for fixing the correct meaning of the Word of God." Some construction of the chronological order therefore has been undertaken by scholars, which should be supplemented with the "historical traditions containing reports about how those among whom the Qur'an first appeared understood its injunctions and statements."

The reason chronology is very important for our search

for a definition of Qur'anic tolerance is related to the doctrine of abrogation taught therein. Sura 2:106 says: "Whatever communications we abrogate or cause to be forgotten, we bring one better than it or like it." Zamakshari, a famous Muslim scholar, commenting on this verse, wrote: "To abrogate a verse means the God removes (azala) it by putting another in its place. To cause a verse to be abrogated means that God gives the command that it be abrogated. ... Every verse is made to vanish whenever the well-being (maslaha) (of the community) requires that it be eliminated ... We bring a verse which is better for the servants (of God), that is, a verse through which one gains a greater benefit, or one which is equal to it in this respect."

In the earlier Meccan period, Muhammad may well have taught that he was to "declare openly ... and turn aside from the polytheists" (Sura 15:94) or to "call to the way of your Lord with wisdom and goodly exhortation, and have disputations with them in the best manner" (Sura 16:125). But when Muhammad went to Medina "it was ... time for a different watchword: '... kill the idolaters wherever you find them; take them prisoner, lay siege to them, and wait for them in every ambush' (9:5); 'fight in the way of God' (2:244)." Have the later verses of Medina abrogated the earlier ones in this case to serve better the interests of the Muslim Community? Many commentators think that this is the case, although they disagree about the extent of the abrogation and the specific suras it applies to.

Following some chronological arrangement for the Suras (according to Nöldeke's listing) that is generally accepted by Muslim scholars, we will now look at some pertinent verses from the Qur'an.

QUR'ANIC TEACHING ON RELATING TO RELIGIOUS OTHERS

Although the majority of Surahs (90 out of 114) were recited during the first 13 years of persecution in Mecca, it is interesting to notice that none of them contains commands to fight and kill. It is after the Hijra, the establishing of the first Muslim community in Medina, that the teaching on attacking religious others unfolded. Rev. Richard Bailey, in his study "Jihad," traces the progression of the attitude toward religious others in four stages: (1) No retaliation (in Mecca), (2) Defensive fighting permitted (in Medina), (3) Defensive fighting commanded (in Medina), and (4) Offensive war commanded (after conquering Mecca).

THE INTERPRETATION OF QUR'AN IS A FOSSILIZED TEACHING BEYOND CHANGE

The Qur'anic teaching on how to relate to religious others is normatively exemplified in the life of Muhammad and the first community. Muslims cannot be free to interpret Qur'an differently from Muhammad's interpretation throughout his life and as shown in the way his earliest followers imitated him. The Qur'an says: "And it behoves not a believing man and a believing woman that they should have any choice in their matter when Allah and His Apostle have decided a matter; and whoever disobeys Allah and His Apostle, he surely strays off a manifest straying" (Sura 33:36). Yvone Yazbeck Hadad writes: "Islam is one as revealed in the Qur'an, and the ideal and perfect Islamic community is that of Medina where the Umma lived under divine guidance through the mediation of the Angel Gabriel and the Prophet Muhammad."

As said earlier, the flight to Medina in A.D. 622 is the watershed event that marks the emerging of the Muslim community (umma), which would remain the model for the future as a God-ordained model for society. Bat Ye'or, traces several significant events in the life of Muhammad and the first Muslim Community:

In 624 Muhammad, joined by more followers, called upon the Qaynuqa, one of the Jewish tribes of Medina, to recognize his prophetic mission. When they refused, he besieged and overcame them. ... their lives were spared, but they were expelled from the city, their lands and a part of their possessions being confiscated by the Muslims. The following year the Jewish Nadir tribe suffered a similar fate: Muhammad burned down their palm groves and divided all their fields and houses among the community of the Believers.

... In 627 ... guided by the angel Gabriel, Muhammad ...

turned his host against the Jewish tribe of the Qurayza. ... Because the Jews refused conversion, Muhammad attacked and overwhelmed them ... six to nine hundred of them ... were led forth in batches and decapitated. ... The Prophet then divided the women, children, houses, and chattels among the Muslims.

... In 628, taking advantage of a treaty of nonbelligerency (Hudaybiya) with the Meccans, he attacked the oasis of Khaybar. ... The assailants came to the oasis at night and in the morning attacked the peasants as they were coming out in the fields, carrying spades and baskets. After a siege lasting a month and a half, the inhabitants surrendered under the terms of a treaty known as the dhimma. According to this agreement Muhammad allowed the Jews to continue cultivating their oasis, on condition that they ceded to him half of their produce; he also reserved the right to break the agreement and expel them whenever he wished.

Based on the dhimma of Khaybar, the relationship between Muslims and conquered peoples everywhere and for all time was held as an example for the future status of peoples under Muslim rule, the status of the dhimmi. When the early successor of Muhammad, Umar Al-Khattab, expelled the Jews and Christians from the Hijaz (Mecca and Medina) in A.D. 640, he referred to what Muhammad had said at the siege of Khaybar: "The land belongs to Allah and his Messenger." Based also on the Prophet's advice: "Two religions shall not remain together in the peninsula of the Arabs," even to this day there are no non-Muslims that can set foot in Mecca.

It is because of such examples left by Muhammad for all of his followers in all times and places, that one is baffled to learn of Muslim scholars like Pickthall who go "to the extent of asserting that Muhammad's attitude to Jews and the Christians remained tolerant till he died."Against such a background, it defies understanding to read some evaluations of history by Hassan Al-Turabi who, as of 1983, was Attorney General of the Sudan. He wrote: "The historical record of Muslims' treatment of Christians and Jews is quite good especially compared with the history of relations between different religions and religious denominations in the West." After reading the Qur'an, it is surprising to encounter declarations such as Ahmad A. Galwash made: "There is not even a single verse in the Holy Qur'an which directly or indirectly insinuates the alternative of death or Islam for the unbelievers." Another Muslim claims that: "Mohammad did not merely preach toleration; he embodied it into law. In all conquered nations he offered liberty of worship. A nominal tribute was the only compensation they were required to pay for the observance and enjoyment of their faith." (Emphasis mine.)

What, then, are the implications of having to pay "compensation" for the "favor" of observing one's religion? This clearly denies the "fundamental and inalienable human right – the freedom to reach, hold, freely exercise, or change our beliefs independent of governmental control."

It is important to clarify that people who lived under Muslim rule didn't have rights that flow from the mere fact of being a human being, but only as prescribed by a "concessionary charter" (the dhimma) which could be changed at the decision of the Muslim ruler. As Ellul notes: "... In the case of the 'concessionary charter,' ... one enjoys rights only to the extent that they are recognized in the charter and only for as long as it remains valid. As a person, by the mere fact of one's 'existence,' one has no claim to any rights. And this, indeed, is the dhimmi's condition."

This view of human rights is diametrically opposed to the rights that a liberal democracy envisions for its citizens. Nicholas Wolterstorff gives a definition of what democracy involves: "Equal protection under law for all people, equal freedom in law for all citizens, neutrality on the part of the state with respect to the diversity of religious and other comprehensive perspectives present in society, and equal voice for all citizens within the fair voting schemes." Weigel says: "Democracy is a way of public life, a way of being a political community," which will work if it includes people "who have made their own the values, the moral truths that teach us to be civil, tolerant, respectful – in a word, democratic." I am fully aware that democracy is a fairly recent phenomenon even in the West but the point here is to see if Islam, with the Qur'an as its defining factor, can ever be compatible with democracy and the religious tolerance democracy epitomizes.

In light of the Muslim concept of the Umma, the status of religious others in Qur'anic Islam is not negotiable. Ellul says that the status of the dhimmi:

> ... was not the product of historical accident but was that which ought to be from the religious point of view and according to the Muslim conception of the world. In other words, it was the expression of the absolute, unchanging, theologically grounded Muslim conception of the relationship between Islam and non-Islam. ... One must know as exactly as possible what the Muslims did with these unconverted conquered peoples, because that is what they will do in the future.

Given the Muslim view of God as rule-giver but not relational, tolerance as a concept is understood to be the undeserved and capricious generosity of a ruler toward the ruled. Epistemologically, given the authority of the Qur'an and Muhammad's example, tolerance is defined according to the regulations of the Shariah law (divine law of the Muslim theocracy) and the normatively interpretative example of Muhammad and the first Muslim Community. Theologically, Muslims view everything in light of the destiny of Islam to rule the world and, therefore, they are committed to what they believe is God's will, involving jihad (holy war). Moreover, there is the utilitarian dimension of Muslim intolerance, which includes reasoning that the greater good (for the umma) justifies hard measures. The same worldview and understanding of Islam as superior (not only as a religion but also as a form of government with which it is inseparably linked) persists today among Muslims generally. As Watt writes: "... the thinking of the fundamentalist Islamic intellectuals and of the great masses of ordinary Muslims is still dominated by the standard traditional Islamic world-view and the corresponding self-image of Islam."

THE WILL TO DENY THE OBVIOUS

Nevertheless, even among those who should know better, there is a tendency to behave like the proverbial ostrich, denying the obvious implications of the Qur'anic teaching. Daniel Pipes, who surveyed about 25 experts in religion (professors in Harvard, Georgetown, Duke University, Baylor, Rutgers, University of Wisconsin etc.), found only four of them who considered the term "jihad" to have any military component whatsoever and this, he says "is quite as if historians of medieval Europe were to deny that the word "crusade" ever had martial overtones ... [but rather the term "crusade" actually meant] 'crusade on hunger' or 'crusade against drugs.'" It is also disturbing that, even in post 9/11 America, as Pipes testifies, "one who dares to dissent and utter the truth on the matter of jihad falls under enormous censure ... We have thus reached a point where merely to state a known fact about Islam earns one the status of a hostile bigot."

The will to believe that Islam is a religion of tolerance may cause some to be convinced that it is; but in reality it doesn't make Islam a religion of tolerance. After being confronted with the facts of Islamic teaching, some still continue to say: "Please tell me this is not Islam." Even when one correctly observes that "Islam cannot but be ruling – and ruling on its own terms, and deciding what minorities it will allow and how," exemplifying the ostrich mentality, the same person still hopes against hope that Muslims will choose "Meccan priority (choose to make normative the Meccan attitude of toleration), in terms of the twenty-first century, [which] must emphasize an Islam that ... tolerates diversity ..." This is just another way of saying, "please tell me this is not Islam."

We live during the worst time for the West to confront Islam because of the loss of clarity on the nature of truth. The relativistic view of truth explained earlier in relation to tolerance is prevalent in the affluent, sleepy (even if restless) western society. The openness of the West toward third world religions is not because the West has become more tolerant (relativism just stupefies the mind giving the illusion of tolerance), but because it is confused about its own identity; it has educated itself to be ignorant and dismissive of its own heritage; it is embarrassed by colonialism and blows out of proportion the mistakes of the past throwing out the baby with the bath water.

It is as if the West is living the tale of the ugly duckling in reverse. Westerners, for a time, thought the West was beautiful but lured by the "nonconformists" and looking at the exotic "others" they now feel like as if the West is the ugly duckling. There is a need for people like Dinesh D'Souza, who emigrated from the East to the West and can't be fooled by the hype of criticism against the West, to convincingly declare how beautiful America and the West, still are.

The West built a legacy of religious tolerance because it believed that objective truth existed; because truth mattered and because people should be free to pursue it. As was made clear earlier, in order to have tolerance at all, a view of truth as objective and an attitude of respect for humans (who are endowed by the Creator with dignity and rights that involve the exercise of their free will), is essential. This view of tolerance is part of the glorious legacy the West has bestowed upon the world. Therefore, it is tragic that one can be considered a bigot today in the West because one believes that another view can be wrong. America and the world have an opportunity to overcome this untenable relativistic stance as we face the ugliness of ideologies which result in events such as September 11th 2001.

CONTEMPLATING CHANGE: THE IMPOSSIBLE

At the end of his book Foundations of Religious Tolerance, Newman wants to strike an optimistic note: "... we ... still have a moral obligation to believe that further civilization - further civilizing - is possible. If the prospects for religious tolerance are not bright, then it is our business as human beings to make them bright." Another hopeful voice was Watt, suggesting that: "... a programme for the correction of the faulty self-image of Islam may seem utopian and unlikely to be realized. [but] ... That at least is the outcome for which the believer in God, Muslim or non-Muslim, should be praying."

After all, ideas and concepts are known to change. ... But precisely what seems to me interesting and striking about Islam, one of its peculiarities is the fixity of its concepts. ... Wherever the social organization is based upon a system, it tends to reproduce itself far more exactly. Islam, even more than Christianity, is a religion that claims to give a definite form to the social order, to human relations, and claims to embrace each moment in the life of every person. Thus, it tends toward an inflexibility that most other forms of society have not had. Moreover, it is known that the whole of Islamic doctrine (including its religious thought) took on a juridical form. ... Of course, there can be an evolution (in practical matters, in jurisprudence, etc.), but when there is a text, which is regarded in some way as an "authoritative" source, one has only to go back to that text and recent innovations will collapse. And this is exactly what has happened in Islam. ...

One should be aware that when one is dealing with some Islamic term or institution of the past, as long as the basic text - in this case, the Koran - remains unchanged, one can always return to the original principles and ideas whatever apparent transformations or developments have taken place, especially because Islam has achieved something that has always been very unusual: an integration of the religious, the political, the moral, the social, the juridical, and the intellectual, thus constituting a rigorous whole of which each element forms an integral part.

These words express exactly the thrust of my argument: there is an Islam that is unavoidable, namely the Qur'anic Islam, which can be rediscovered time and again. Just as Kenneth Woodward says: "Israeli commandos do not cite the Hebrew prophet Joshua as they go into battle but Muslim insurgents can readily invoke the example of their Prophet Muhammad who was a military commander himself. And while the Crusaders may have fought with the cross and their shields, they did not - could not - cite words from Jesus to justify their slaughters." It is the Qur'an that binds Islam to intolerance and since Islam without the Qur'an is not Islam, there cannot ever exist true Islam that is tolerant. Again we may wish to believe that Islam can become tolerant but we will have to live with the consequences, which are inevitable given the hard evidence.

CONTEMPLATING CHANGE: THE POSSIBLE

It is true that the Qur'an ultimately does not teach tolerance but rather intolerance toward other religions in the society it seeks to dominate that there is nothing we can do about it; we cannot change the Qur'an. This doesn't preclude on the other hand sympathizing with Muslims and seeking to understand where they come from so we may responsibly address the issues of concern. They are fellow human beings, much more similar to us than different. Not every Muslim believes what the unavoidable Islam may suggest, and Muslims can and have changed or converted to another worldview.

Given the content of the Qur'an and the unquestioned place it has in Muslim religion and system, one fails to see how the Qur'anic Islam – the unavoidable Islam can possibly change but a change in its adherents is a different matter. Therefore, we should not get tired of upholding the truth, exposing falsehood, showing the consequences of certain views, seeking to win all people to the truth, and being prepared to stand our ground when the evil hour comes, as people who have hope.

5

Islam's Global War against Christianity

From Nigeria to Indonesia, Christians are under siege in virtually every single country in the Muslim world, the victims of countless acts of discrimination, depredation, brutality, and murder that are so widespread and systematic that it can rightfully be called the new Holocaust. This time, however, the perpetrators of this Holocaust aren't wearing swastikas, but kufi skull caps and hijabs.

Some of the oldest Christian communities in the world are subject to relentless attack and teeter on the brink of extinction at the hands of the "Religion of Peace": Palestinian Christians in Gaza and the West Bank; Assyrian, Syriac and Chaldean Christians in Iraq; Coptic Christians in Egypt; Evangelical and Orthodox Christians in Eastern Ethiopia and Eritrea; Armenian Orthodox Christians in Turkey; and Maronite Christians in Lebanon.

Several of these communities date back to the beginning decades of Christianity and all have weathered wave after wave of Islamic persecution for centuries and more, but in the very near future some will simply cease to exist. In our lifetime, the only trace of their past existence will be in footnotes in history books (and probably only Western history books at that).

Meanwhile, we in the West hear much from radical Islam's apologists how the US is engaged in a war against Islam citing of our military actions in Afghanistan and Iraq. We are lectured on the inviolability of the Muslim ummah and justifications of defensive jihad.

But an extensive search this past weekend of the websites of the Council on American-Islamic Relations, the Islamic Society of North America, the Islamic Circle of North America, the Muslim American Society, the Muslim Student Association, the Fiqh Council of North America, and the Muslim Public Affairs Committee - the most visible institutional representatives of Islam in America - found not a single mention or reference of the religious persecution of Christians by their Islamic co-religionists, thereby making them tacit co-conspirators in the Final Solution to the Christian problem in the Muslim world.

The global war on Christianity by Islam is so massive in size and scope that it is virtually impossible to describe without trivializing it. Inspired by Muslim Brotherhood ideology and fueled by billions of Wahhabi petrodollars, the religious cleansing of Christians from the Muslim world is continuing at a break-neck pace, as the following recent examples demonstrate.

IRAQ

In the current issue of the American Spectator, Doug Bandow observes that centuries of dhimmitude have left Christians in the war-torn country without any means of self-defense. Washington policymakers have refused to lend assistance for fear of showing partiality, despite the murder of hundreds of Iraqi Christians, the kidnapping and torture of Christian clerics, the repeated bombings of Christian churches, the torching of Christian businesses, and the flight of close to half of the entire Iraqi Christian population since April 2003. Those who remain have been subject to the imposition of shari'a by the Shi'ite Mahdi Army and Sunni militias (al-Qaeda doesn't bother with such niceties, preferring to murder them immediately instead), including the recent published threat in Mosul of killing one member of every Christian family in that city for Christian women not wearing the hijab and continuing to attend school. (Be sure to remember that the next time an Islamist apologist claims that the hijab is a symbol of women's liberation.)

EGYPT

Journalist Magdi Khalil chronicles in a new report ("Another Black Friday for the Coptic Christians of Egypt") the campaign of violence directed against Christian Copts almost weekly immediately following Friday afternoon Muslim prayers. Inspired by Islamist imams preaching religious hatred in mosques all over the country and protected by government officials willing to look the other way, rampaging mobs of Muslims set upon Christians churches, businesses and individuals, from Alexandria to cities all the way up the Nile. Coptic holy days are also favorite times for Muslim violence, which the Egyptian media likes to describe as "sectarian strife" - as if it were actually a two-sided affair.

GAZA

Ethel Fenig recently noted here at American Thinker ("More Gaza Multiculturalism") the systematic destruction of churches and desecration of Christian religious objects by Jihadia Salafiya following the HAMAS takeover of the Gaza Strip from their Fatah rivals and the imposition of Islamic rule. The head of Jihadia Salafiya told reporter Aaron Klein that any suspected Christian missionary activity in the area will be "dealt with harshly". (*Ynet News*)

SAUDI ARABIA

According to the Arab News, a Sri Lankan Christian man barely escaped with his life in late May when he was found working in the city of Mecca, Islam's holiest city, which is officially barred to non-Muslims. In December, an Indian man had been sentenced to death for accidentally entering the city, but was spared after the Indian embassy made an urgent appeal to the Saudi Supreme Court.

PAKISTAN

In Islamabad, Younis Masih was sentenced last month to

death under the country's frequently invoked blasphemy laws, which were also used against six Christian women suspended from a nursing school after they were accused of desecrating a Quran. And as protests against Salman Rushdie's knighthood raged, a Muslim mob armed with guns, axes and sticks attacked Christians worshipping in a Salvation Army church in Bismillahlpur Kanthan. (*Associated Press; United Press International; Mission News Network*)

BANGLADESH

Almost a dozen Christian converts in the Nilphamari district were beaten last week by Muslim villagers wielding bricks and clubs, and threatened with death if they did not leave town immediately. Local hospitals subsequently refused them treatment. Christians in the area have also been prevented from using the only potable water well in the area after a pronouncement by religious authorities at the mosque in Durbachari. This came after 42 former Muslims were baptized as Christians in the local river on June 12. (*Compass News Direct*)

MALAYSIA

Government authorities demolished a church building on June 4th in Orang Asli settlement in Gua Musang in Ulu Kelantan, despite prior government approval of the project. The church was built on donated property after the entire village had converted to Christianity just a few months ago. Also in late May, the Malaysian high court ruled that Muslims who convert to Christianity must appeal to the religious shari'a courts to officially be deregistered as Muslims and reregistered as a Christians. (*Journal Chretien; Associated Press*)

INDONESIA

Agence France Presse reported last month on an attack by the Islamic Anti-Apostate Movement, who stormed a church service in a Protestant church in the West Java town of Soreang. The AFP report notes that more than 30 churches have been forced to close in West Java and dozens more throughout the country in recent years due to Muslim violence, churches which were among the few spared during the outbreak of hostilities during 1997-1998, where hundreds of Christian churches were burned to the ground and never rebuilt.

TURKEY

The Christian community is still reeling from the torture nd ritual slaughter of three Protestants at a Christian publishing house in Malatya in April by an armed Islamist gang, which was preceded by the murder last year of Catholic priest Andrea Santoro in Trabzon and the assassination of Armenian journalist Hrant Dink in Istanbul in January. An additional six men allegedly associated with the same Muslim gang were arrested on May 30th for plotting an attack on a Christian pastor in Diyarbakir. (*Lebanon Daily Star; ADKNI*)

CYPRUS

The Cyprus Mail reports that during a meeting last month in Rome the Archbishop of the Cypriot Greek Orthodox Church pleaded with the Vatican Secretary of State for the Pope's assistance to pressure Turkish authorities in restoring and repairing Christian sites and churches in areas occupied since the invasion of the island nation by Turkey in July 1974 and the ethnic cleansing of 160,000 Greek Christian Cypriots.

LEBANON

More than 60,000 Christians have left the country since last summer's war between Hezbollah and Israel, fearing the rise of both Sunni and Shi'ite extremism and terrorist activity. The Sunday Telegraph recently revealed the results of a poll finding that at least half of Lebanon's Maronite community was considering leaving the country. More than 100,000 have already submitted visa applications at foreign embassies.

ALGERIA

In what is considered one of the more "moderate" Muslim regimes, Al-Quds Al-Arabi announced that the Algerian government has just issued regulations requiring advance permission for non-Muslim public events, following a 2006 law aimed at limiting Christian evangelism in the Kabylia region and the Sahara. (*MEMRI*)

MOROCCO

In the country that The Economist magazine in 2005 anointed "the best Arab democracy", all Moroccans are considered Muslims at birth and face three years in prison if they attempt to convert. They are also prohibited from entering any of the few churches permitted to operate for the foreign inhabitants of the country. Moroccan Christians must operate covertly for fear of imprisonment by the government and attacks by Islamists. They cannot bury their dead in Christian cemeteries, and they must be married by Islamic authorities or face charges of adultery. Late last year, a 64 year-old German tourist, Sadek Noshi Yassa, was sentenced to six months in jail and fined for missionary activity. (*Journal Chretien*)

NIGERIA

Police in Gombe arrested sixteen suspects after a Muslim mob stoned, stripped, beat, and finally stabbed to death a Christian teacher, Christiana Oluwatoyin Oluwasesin, after she caught a student cheating on an exam in March. Her body was then burned beyond recognition by the mob who falsely accused her of desecrating a Quran. The suspects were released last month without any charges being filed, prompting Christian leaders to accuse government authorities of a cover-up and raising concerns about additional attacks. (*Christian Today*)

ERITREA

Just a few weeks ago, the Islamic government installed a new Orthodox Patriarch after they removed the previous Patriarch and placed him under house arrest for no stated reason. Compass News Direct reported in February the death of Magos Solomon Semere, a Christian who had been imprisoned in a military jail for four and a half years for illegal Christian worship, the third Christian to die in government custody since October. Authorities have also cracked down on unapproved churches, jailing at least two thousand Protestants and members of the Medhane Alem Orthodox renewal movement since the beginning of the year and publicly burning confiscated Bibles. (*Christian Post; Compass News Direct; Journal Chretien*)

It is not an exaggeration to say that I could extend this brief list ad infinitum with additional Islamic countries and news items from just the past few weeks' worth of incidents of violence, discrimination, intimidation and murder targeting Christians in the Muslim world. In many instances, the government and religious authorities in these Muslim countries work hand-in-hand in their campaign of religious persecution.

A scene in the Academy Award-winning movie Schindler's List gives us some insight into what is happening all across the Muslim world with respect to Christianity. As the SS Commandant Amon Göth and his Nazi Stormtroopers prepare to liquidate the Jewish ghetto in Krakow, Poland, Göth (played in the movie by Ralph Fiennes) gives his men a peptalk:

For six centuries there has been a Jewish Krakow. Think about that. By this evening, those six centuries are a rumor. They never happened. Today is history.

This scene is being repeated in the Friday sermons in mosques and on Islamic satellite TV all over the world, only this time it is the Christians in addition to the Jews who are targets. Great efforts are being made to make the two-thousand year history of Christianity in North Africa, the Middle East and Southeast Asia a blasphemous rumor. Soon students in Turkey will be taught that the Hagia Sophia, the greatest architectural structure in the Muslim world, wasn't built by the Christian Emperor Justinian in the Sixth Century, but by the Sultan Mehmed II a thousand years later after the Ottomans seized the Byzantine capital. That Christians lived at all in the Muslim world, let alone that much of the territory occupied by Muslims used to be Christian lands before the Islamic Wars of

Conquest, will be nothing but a rumor by the end of this century punishable according to the precepts of shari'a.

President Bush announced last week that he will be sending a special envoy to the 57-member Organization of Islamic Countries. Hopefully, the systematic persecution of Christians and other religious minorities will be the first and primary item in the new envoy's portfolio, with the 2007 annual report of the US Commission on International Religious Freedom and the State Department's Annual Report on International Religious Freedom, which name virtually every single country in the OIC for its human rights abuses and religious cleansing, as evidence for our country's concern.

The fact remains that not a single Christian or Jew lives in peace in the Muslim world, and if it is truly our nation's foreign policy to spread democracy around the world, this issue is the perfect topic for us to press. Back at home, raising Islam's global war on Christianity should be the immediate response to the seemingly endless media grievance machine of radical Islam's Western apologists. Until they begin to address the new Holocaust perpetrated in the name of Islam, their complaints and denials are nothing but bald hypocrisy.

TREATMENT OF CHRISTIANS GENERALLY

Overall, whether a Christian is a convert or born into the faith, he or she is ostracized by the Muslim majority. Over and over converts told stories of losing their jobs when their Muslim employers learned they had become Christians; then others would not employ them because they are Christians.

Those who are Christian from birth-who are born into Christian families-often, can only find jobs that Muslims would not want to do, such as being sanitary workers. Others work for Muslims as their domestic servants, farm workers, or factory employees. Clearly Christians exist at all levels of society in Pakistan, but most are at the lower rungs of the ladder.

In Peshawar, in the North-West Frontier Province next to Afghanistan, a man who had been the General Secretary of his labor union lost his job after his conversion to Christianity, and he has been unable to obtain other employment. He currently is trying to find translation work; only another Christian will employ him. He has a wife and a young son. They live in a part of his father's house currently, although his father previously had forced him out of the home, leaving the three no place to live.

At the time of this report, he had not paid his father rent or been able to pay his electricity for some months and had been without electricity for that period of time. This is a man with a special technical skill who went from 5,000 rupees per month (approximately $100.00 USD) to zero, only because he believes in and follows the teachings of Jesus Christ.

Also in Peshawar, a former Mullah of a Madrassa, bent over from age, earns money as a cobbler, provided anyone will bring him work. On a particular day another Christian brought him an old canvas duffel bag, ripped to shreds. He will get 100 rupees to repair it, about $2.00 USD. He cannot find regular employment because he is a Christian.

In Lahore, in the Punjab province, a Christian convert no longer is employed as a teacher-or as anything else. He is unable to find work. He was a professional, and now he finds himself and his family destitute. At one time a daughter brought in support for the family. Then it was learned that she was a Christian, too, however. She has fled the country to save her life. He hopes she is safe, but he cannot be certain.

One may be tempted to call the foregoing "circumstantial persecution." Overlooked, ostracized, despised-this is sad, some may say, but such are the circumstances of being or becoming a Christian in Pakistan.

Much more than circumstances, however, is the actual persecution that is occurring in Pakistan on a routine basis. It is the result of discriminatory laws being implemented, interpreted and applied by the government, police and judiciary to persecute the Christians. Likewise it is the result of protective laws the police refuse to implement or active misconduct on their part, knowing that the government and the judiciary will do nothing to them.

This report provides an objective and factual account of this persecution in Pakistan as it is happening.

The cases cited and details described, therefore, serve to reveal only a portion of the truth. Many more such cases have occurred in Pakistan; many more are ongoing; and many more unfortunately will arise. These matters need attention now; delay only inflames the cause of Islam. As one is reading this, more and more of its victims await their unjust fate.

PERSECUTION UNDER THE CONSTITUTION

One may ask how such misconduct can occur under the law. Is there no equality of citizenry, no freedom of religion, no freedom of speech, and one may ask. It is a matter of how the Constitution is written and applied-or not applied.

It is a Constitution whose Preamble provides for the principles of "democracy, freedom, equality, tolerance and social justice" to be observed, but it is further stated that these principles are those as are "enunciated by Islam."

With the enactment of the 1973 Constitution, Islam officially was made the "State religion of Pakistan," by Article 2. Since that time, further Constitutional amendments and legislation have made it clear that Islamic laws shall govern all the people of Pakistan and that these laws shall give distinct advantage to Muslims and distinct disadvantages to non-Muslims.

In 1985, Article 2A of the Constitution, called the "Objectives Resolution," was added. This Resolution made it clear that Christians and other minorities would not be free to practice their religions.

The original Constitution had stated that provisions would be made "for the minorities freely to profess and practice their religions and develop their cultures." The Objectives Resolution restated this provision but without the word "freely." What had been occurring already in Pakistan now became written law. There was to be no freedom of religion for any non-Muslim.

PERSECUTION BY ISLAMIC RELIGIOUS ORDINANCES

The most egregious laws in Pakistan's Penal Code are being used to persecute Christians and other non-Muslims at every turn. These are the blasphemy laws, which have made certain speech or conduct criminal and punishable by prison or death. Even further these provisions are being used to fuel the fire of fundamentalist Muslims, and with each victory, whether in or out of the courtroom, these fundamentalists become more fierce.

PERSECUTION BY DESTRUCTION OF PROPERTY

Churches and other property of Christians are targets for Muslim fanatics. What little the Christians do have is taken from them.

St. Peter's Church

On 22 October 1999, St. Peter's Catholic Church, located in Lahore Township, was set on fire. It was the second incident of communal attack on a Christian church in one month.

Fifteen hundred Christian families live in Lahore Township, where seven churches of different denominations exist. Adjacent to St. Peter's is a high school for males and females, and George Yaqoob, his wife and family live on the church premises. On the day of the fire, his wife saw smoke coming from a room used in the church to store all the items used for worship. When she ran out to tell the nuns at the school, some of the students heard her, saw a man running toward the school with a container of gas, and caught him.

By then, however, all the church's possessions had been lost: twenty Bibles, sixty hymn books, other religious books, a large wooden cross, and items used for the altar, musical equipment and wooden furniture.

Three days before the fire, George Yaqoob had gone to close up the church and found the picture of a cross that hung on the altar smashed on the floor.

The man who was caught, a Muslim, was questioned and admitted to burning the church and wanting to burn the Christian school. His reason: Because America had urged Pakistan to call back its troops from Kargil while thousands of Muslims were being killed in Kashmir, and because America is a Christian nation, he had burned the church. He wanted to show Americans that Muslims are not afraid. He was charged with arson and also with blasphemy under 295 and 295A; however, the maximum punishment he can receive for the greater of the two blasphemy charges is ten years, not life. He could receive as little as a fine. At this moment, however, the culprit is walking free, still on bail.

The Village of Qila Didar Singh

Qila Didar Singh, a village in the Punjab province, contains a Christian development. Although Muslims have lived in peace for some years also in the village, during the last few years, a Muslim resident, Khalid Mehmood, together with several other Muslims, have tried to seize the land where the Christians live. Having been unsuccessful previously, on 5 June 1994, they destroyed a boundary wall on the church premises. Although charges of breaking into private property were filed against the men, none were ever held on the charges.

The Muslims, however, seeking revenge for the charges having been brought, attacked the Christian compound with firearms on 17 June, injuring seven of the Christians. They also desecrated Bibles, a cross and the Church. The mob stayed in the compound some five hours, but policemen never came. Only three hours after this, did any appear; and then the police refused to allow the Christian residents to file charges. Only when a team from a legal aid office went to the villages and cases were registered against the mob members.

The matter took a new twist in 1998-99. The Muslims involved registered cases against the Christian complainants, and the situation between the Muslims and Christians has become very critical. The Muslims want the church leader killed and have offered a large amount of money for the murder. The attorney assisting the Christians also has been threatened with his life.

The Christian Colony in Sahiwal

In 1996, more than eighty Christian families settled on barren land near a Christian graveyard in Sahiwal. These people built concrete houses on the land and applied to the proper authority-the Deputy Commissioner-to obtain proprietary rights to the land. Most of the women in the Christian colony worked as domestic servants in the posh areas of Sahiwal City.

Even while the applications were pending, on 28 November 1997, the local government bulldozed their houses. Although the working people were not home at the time, their children were. The houses were completely razed, furniture and other objects destroyed. Although the local government's Disposal Committee had not objected on paper to the settlement, having issued "Non-Objection Certificates" to the families on 3 May 1997, it did not want the Christians to occupy the land. Thus occurred the bulldozing.

The Settlement of Shantinagar

On 5 February 1997, a huge mob of Muslims attacked Christian settlements in Khanewal City and in nearby Shantinagar, completely destroying the houses and all the furnishings in them, along with any bicycles or other vehicles parked outside, by using petrol bombs to burn out everything.

To this very day, none of the some 350 cases filed against the perpetrators have been prosecuted. Also to this very day, the investigative report prepared by a government-appointed tribunal never has been released to the public. The problems began when the house of a Christian named Raji Baba was raided by the police in Shantinagar; they suspected Raji Baba of selling alcohol and of gambling. During the raid, one-or more-of the police officers threw a Bible to the floor.

Raji Baba told people in the village about the Bible incident, which upset many of the Christians. Later a group of Christians went to the police station to register a case against the four police officers who raided the house and threw down the Bible, but the police administration refused to allow a case to be registered. Raji Baba, however, was arrested by the police on suspicion of selling alcohol and of gambling.

The Christian group, unwilling to accept the police administration's failure to register a case, went again to the police station and demonstrated outside and also in Khanewal City. This got into the newspapers, which brought more impassioned pleas that something is done about the four police officers. Finally it was agreed that they would be suspended.

However, they were not. Again, the Christians became upset, and again demanded that a case be registered against the officers. Also they demanded that Raji Baba be released from jail. By this time, he had been held some two weeks, and there was no evidence that he was guilty of either matter with which he stood accused. Finally Baba was released, and a case was registered against the four police officers, with Raji Baba as the complainant. This angered the officers, who were Muslim, and they then registered a case against Baba himself and three others. The charge: burning pages from the Quran. The officers had taken pages from a Quran, burned the edges of them, and then written the names of each of the four alleged blasphemers on the pages. The pages then were left in a mosque, and when Muslims came to pray at the next call to prayer, the pages were found. Immediately the imam of the mosque was called in and shown the pages, and just as quickly an announcement was made over the mosque loudspeakers-used for the calls to prayer-for all Muslims to come out into the streets to punish the Christians for defiling the Quran.

The huge mob that gathered headed to Khanewal City, burning the Christians' houses and everything in and outside of them. All together about 35 homes and 13 Christian churches were destroyed, along with hundreds of Bibles, hymn books and other religious books and items used for worship. The Christians in Shantinagar heard about the mob and went to authorities there, asking for protection. The authorities refused to try and stop the mob, so when the mob got to Shantinagar, there was no one to stop them. They cut all communication lines, so that no one in the village could call out, and they proceeded to fire bomb the entire village. In addition to houses, they burned out the Catholic Church and the Salvation Army Church there, again also destroying Bibles and other religious books and items used for worship.

The mob had gathered early in the morning, and by late

afternoon, the burning and looting still was going on. Only after everything was destroyed and looted did the authorities come, but the mob was so large and the situation was so out of control that the army had to be called in. Not one person in the mob was arrested.

Not until a legal assistance office got involved did any of the some 350 cases get registered by the police against the Muslim offenders. Again, to this very day, none has been prosecuted by the government.

According to the HRCP's Report, referenced hereinabove, the residents of Shantinagar, as of early 1999, still were struggling with the government over its failure to provide rehabilitation in and restoration of Shantinagar. Burned and lost identity cards, which every Pakistani citizen must have, had not been replaced. The Agricultural Development Bank had not written off loans as promised and had detained people who were in arrears. The utility company, which had promised to cancel all electric bills for February and March, 1997, had not done so. Rather, it had cut off electricity for nonpayment of bills in those months. Also according to the Report, only a few of the houses had been rebuilt.

Some Shantinagar Christians were beneficiaries of donations from people in other countries who had heard of their predicament; these were the more fortunate ones, if indeed fortunate even can describe these Christian people. Those who did not receive such donations still were suffering greatly, continuing to live in the middle of destruction.

Many more situations illustrate the plight of persecuted Christians in Pakistan. A few brief summaries follow:

Muzaffargarh District

Nine hundred Christian families in some nine villages in Muzaffargarh, not far from Khanewal, cannot obtain proprietary rights to property on which they have lived since 1976. During the past few years a group of influential local Muslims have been active in land seizing, and many Christian families already have evicted from their land and left shelterless. Other Christian families have been threatened that if they did not give up their land, they would be treated like their Christian brothers in Shantinagar and Khanewal.

Narowal District

Six hundred Christian families settled in an area of Narowal District on lands given to them on lease in 1947, when India and Pakistan were partitioned. They have continued to pay the government for the lands, but proprietary rights have not been given to them as promised. One Christian man was killed in a Christian-Muslim riot over this land, but no case was registered against the accused killer.

Sheikhupura

Here lived a man named Ismaeel Bhatti, a Christian. He had received 12-1/2 acres of land from his father in a particular village. A group of Muslims from this same village wanted the land and so falsely accused him and his son of abducting a woman and getting her married to some person. He was fined 75,000 rupees (approximately $1,500.00 USD) by the village council called to hear this matter, and told that if he did not pay this, his land would be taken. Bhatti and his family were driven off the land by this Muslim group.

The reality is a society rife with hatred and active, actual persecution of Christians and other minorities, with permission to carry this out given by the law itself to the Muslim civilian, police and judiciary.

In a December 1999 interview with I. A. Rehman, Director of HRCP and himself a Muslim, Mr. Rehman acknowledged to the authors problems with the Constitution and its resultant discrimination against minorities. While agreeing that the Constitution states equality as a principle, he said, "We have problems. There are things such as Article 2 and Article 2A-even the name of the state of Pakistan-we [HRCP] took a position some years ago to abolish Articles 2 and 2A." This, however, has never happened.

He further noted that HRCP "knows" that the Constitutional provisions "providing protection for religious minorities is inadequate." The Commission, he says, just wants

Pakistan to be "nonsectarian, if [people] don't like calling it secular." He added that the Commission already is "under attack" for opposing Islamisation of Pakistan.

When questioned about particular issues, such as one's religion being added to National Identification Cards, Mr. Rehman emphasized that the Commission had noted this problem and had concluded that "religious discrimination on the basis of recording goes much deeper than just having such a registration law. We have not been able to get far enough away from these laws that we can raise these issues successfully."

When asked whether in the Commission's report, HRCP tread lightly on Christian issues so as not to offend the Muslim majority, Mr. Rehman said there was no intent to do so-that "we've stated clearly Christians are discriminated against."

Mr. Rehman continued by saying that the judges are not interpreting the law; rather they are using their own subjective social values. The judicial system, he believes, "is acting outside the law." Further there is "no system of redress for the general people."

When asked about the inability to build churches, he replied, "So? It is, of course, discrimination." He advised that the Commission is looking into this issue and into the problem of the taking of Christians' lands.

PERSECUTION IN THE JUDICIARY

The discrimination against and persecution of the Christians in Pakistan does not occur only among the village people; it also occurs at all other levels of the citizenry, even among the judiciary.

The Shariat Courts

Article 175 of the Constitution of 1973 established a Supreme Court for the entire country, a High Court for each of the four provinces, and "such other courts as may be established by law."

In 1979, for the first time a religious court was established by Constitutional amendment. Called the Federal Shariat Court, it is at the same level as the High Courts. However, its judges all must be Muslim; in fact up to three may be ulema, who are Muslim scholars trained in Islam and Islamic law. It has the power to determine whether any law is repugnant to the injunctions of Islam and then strike down that law if it is found to be so. This Court also has the power to hear appeals of convictions under the Hudood Ordinance.

At the same time, a Shariat Bench in the Supreme Court of Pakistan also was established to hear appeals from the Federal Shariat Court. Again, only Muslim judges can sit on the Shariat Bench, and it has the last word on all such appeals.

One final point: Only Muslim lawyers are allowed to appear before either

As discussed above, as Islamisation has progressed, so, too, has the discrimination against Christians and other non-Muslims in the courtroom. Whether it be refusing to appoint and seat Christian judges or refusing to allow Christian judges to hear certain types of cases or disallowing Christian lawyers to represent citizens in the courtroom, the situation is worsening, not improving, for Christians and other non-Muslims in Pakistan.

Recommendations

As a result of having seen the current situation in Pakistan, detailed hereinabove, the writers of this report make the following recommendations:

1. All Christians in jail awaiting trial under any section of the blasphemy law-295, 295A, 295B, or 295C-must be released immediately and remain free until proven guilty beyond a reasonable doubt. The accuser must be required to state-and do so under oath-exactly what the words or actions of blasphemy were before a case can be registered and a person arrested.
2. Whether in the accusatory stage or at trial, the evidence offered and admitted and the conduct of the proceedings

otherwise must be that which would be comply with internationally recognized procedures. Evidence obtained under duress shall be inadmissible, and so shall hearsay and other questionable forms of proof. Perjury must be prosecuted.

3. All property of Christians that has been confiscated shall be returned, whether it is individual, church or mission. Compensation must be made to these Christian individuals, churches or missions for all such property destroyed that cannot be returned. At the very least they must be made whole again.
4. Likewise a compensation plan must be instituted immediately to pay Christian victims for the injustices committed against them and their families by individuals as well as by the Islamic mobs. These are the victims of prejudice and of persecution through religious violence: the widow and ten fatherless children of Manzoor Masih; 9-year-old Nagina Masih, her mother, and her sisters and brothers, who cannot go to school and do not have food to eat because their father is falsely imprisoned; Ayub Masih, who is dying in jail, and his family; Emmanuel Bhatti, who will never eat on his own or dress himself; and so many others.
5. Many of these families must be relocated to other areas, even other countries, where they can get a fresh start. They must be given opportunities and the funds to do this.
6. Just as in cases such as Emmanuel Bhatti's, the corrupt police and others who have acted illegally must be brought to justice; they must be prosecuted for their actions and made to pay for their crimes.
7. The abductors of minors must be brought to justice and the minors returned to their parents. The law regarding kidnapping must be implemented and applied in these situations, as this is a most egregious matter whereby minor children can be removed from their parents without parental notification, opportunity for hearing or input from the child.
8. So, too, the Muslim fundamentalists be brought to justice for abduction, rape and forced conversion to Islam of Christian girls? They must be prosecuted for these crimes.

In order to do this, the laws regarding evidence must be changed to remove the unequal weight given to a male's testimony over that of a female and especially to remove the unequal weight given a Muslim's testimony over that of a Christian. The evidence law requiring multiple witnesses to a rape also must be struck.

A PLEA AND A PLEDGE

The writers hereof issue a plea-a plea for the recommendations above to be implemented.

We also issue an urgent plea to all the international organizations of which Pakistan is a member to boldly and intensely look into and investigate the matters reported herein and the innumerable other human rights violations that are occurring daily in that country.

We ask them to verify these for themselves and to hold the Pakistan government accountable for these atrocities, demanding that such cease immediately and that measures be implemented forthwith to prevent any further such harm to the Christians in Pakistan and to protect their interests in the future.

We call on the following specifically: The United Nations, together with the United Nations Conference on Trade and Development and the United Nations High Commissioner for Refugees; the International Labor Organization; the World Trade Organization; the World Bank; the World Health Organization; the Organization of American States; and the Commonwealth of Nations.

We ask them to enforce the terms of the human rights treaties and conventions to which Pakistan is a signatory or party:

1. The United Nations
   a. The International Convention on the Elimination of All Forms of Racial Discrimination;
   b. The Convention on the Elimination of All Forms of Discrimination Against Women;
   c. The Convention on the Rights of the Child; and
2. The International Labour Organisation
   a. The Convention Concerning Discrimination in Respect of Employment and Occupation.

Each of the foregoing documents clearly affirms "The Universal Declaration of Human Rights" as its basis. This Declaration proclaims:

"Everyone is entitled to all the rights and freedoms set forth in this Declaration, without distinction of any kind, such as race, colour, sex, language, religion, political or other opinion, national or social origin, property, birth or other status."

We call generally on all other associations in which Pakistan shares membership and all countries with which Pakistan has treaties to step forward and use all available resources and means to stop this persecution and demand equal rights for all citizens of Pakistan. Pakistan must be brought to account for these killings, these tortures, and the other inhumane and discriminatory treatment imposed on those unable to defend themselves because their rights have been abolished.

The writers also issue a plea to business organizations that operate within Pakistan to take a very long and close look at the atrocities revealed in this report, to use this as a springboard to investigate for themselves the unjust and evil practices ongoing in the country and to determine whether or not they will continue to do business with those who promote such denial of human rights.

We issue this plea specifically to McDonald's; the Pepsi-Cola Company; American Express Bank Ltd.; Bank of America, NT & SA; Chase Manhattan Bank, NA; Citibank, NA, all of America; Standard Chartered Bank, of the United Kingdom; ANZ Grindlays Bank Ltd., of Australia; and Deutsche Bank AG, of Germany.

Further the authors make a plea to the trading partners of Pakistan also to take these matters very seriously and to apply every pressure possible to change the existing system. We issue this plea specifically to the European Union, the United States and Japan and generally to all other countries trading with Pakistan that value and promote human rights and fundamental freedoms for all.

A very special appeal goes out to all Christian bodies-international, national, state, regional and local-to telephone, write and lobby their representatives on behalf of the Pakistani Christians to bring pressure to bear on the Pakistani government for release of all the Christians currently charged with violations of the blasphemy law-Sections 295A, B or C- and otherwise imprisoned on false charges arising from personal vendettas. We also implore these Christian bodies to pray daily for the Christians, for their continued strength, and for the release of those in prisons.

The writers also implore each and every concerned Christian to pledge to continue to fight individually, through every peaceful means, for justice on behalf of the Pakistani Christians, for an end to the atrocities that these fellow Christians are suffering, and for specific guarantees that these will not be repeated over and over again.

We beseech all Christians to pledge to pray daily for their suffering brothers and sisters in Pakistan and for the many other tormented Christians elsewhere in the world and to pray always for the culprits-who continue to walk in darkness, under the veil of fear-that they would come to have knowledge of the one and only living Saviour-the One for whom their victims would rather die than deny.

THE JIZYAH TAX: EQUALITY AND DIGNITY UNDER ISLAMIC LAW

It is an oft-repeated assertion of Muslims that other faith-communities have always been treated with respect and dignity by in a genuine Islamic State. Indeed, as one peruses Islamic literature, this claim is noticeable for the frequency of its presence. For example, the Muslim author Suzanne Haneef state about Islam's attitude to other religious communities:

...Islam does not permit discrimination in the treatment of other human beings on the basis of religion or any other criteria... it emphasises neighborliness and respect for the ties of relationship with non-Muslims ...within this human family, Jews and Christians, who share many beliefs and values with Muslims, constitute what Islam terms Ahl al-Kitab, that is,

People of the Scripture, and hence Muslim have a special relationship to them as fellow "Scriptuaries".

Similarly, the German convert Ahmed von Denffer, examining the position of Christians in Islam, states that 'It is thus clear that, seen from the legal perspective, Christians are entitled to have their own prescriptions.' From what he terms 'the Societal Perspective', he tackles the problem of Surah Maidah 5:51 which warn against taking Jews and Christians as 'friends':

On the other hand, Christians being ahl al-kitab may not be harassed or molested for being non-Muslims. It is true that the Qur'an warns against taking Jews and Christians as friends, but that does not mean they should be molested or harmed because of their being non-Muslims.

So far, all very positive, but both Haneef and von Denffer are Muslims residing in the West, thus interacting with Christians, and addressing a Western audience. Thus, their approach will be conditioned by that reality. A somewhat different attitude is exhibited by a Muslim writer based in Saudi Arabia, a state governed largely by Islamic law, and which forbids all expressions of religious liberty:

In a country ruled by Muslim authorities, a non-Muslim is guaranteed his freedom of faith.... Muslims are forbidden from obliging a non-Muslim to embrace Islam, but he should pay the tribute to Muslims readily and submissively, surrender to Islamic laws, and should not practice his polytheistic rituals openly.

To examine the aspects of Islam's attitude to non-Muslims, especially the Jizyah tax, to consider whether Haneef's claim in particular is valid on Islamic law, since that practically regulates everyday relations. Since Muslims in the West, as much as in the Muslim world uphold the divine character of the Shari'ah, based as it is primarily on the Qur'an and the Sunnah, and uphold the Islamic State with Islamic Law as the ideal society, it is important to see what this would mean in practice for non-Muslims, if the Caliphate was ever restored and applied to the West.

THE VALUE OF HUMAN LIFE

In the West, at least in constitution terms, however inadequately outworked in practice in some places, the equality of human beings is a fundamental assumption – 'all men are equal before the law'. For this reason, Justice is often depicted in statues as blindfolded; the class, religion or race of anyone is irrelevant – the law, at least in terms of its goal, applies equally to everyone, and safeguards everyone equally.

In Islamic law, however, this is simply not the case. The life of a Muslim is considered superior to that of a non-Muslim, so much so that whilst a non-Muslim killing a Muslim would be executed, the reverse would not occur. This is despite the fact that murder is normally considered a capital offence in Islam, with regular executions in most Muslim states. This inequity is also demonstrable in the blood rate paid to non-Muslims where murder or injury has occurred, which is half that of a Muslim. Effectively, this ruling means that a Muslim need not fear the usual retribution for murder if he kills a non-Muslim. The law deliberately and consciously does not protect non-Muslims as it does Muslims. The position of Islamic law is not that human life is sacred, but that Muslim life is so.

THE VALUE OF EVIDENCE

What we have just stated about Justice becomes very pertinent when considering evidence in a court. Haneef's assertions can be immediately questioned by pointing to the fact that in Islam, the court testimony of a non-Muslim is considered inferior to that of a Muslim, a practice given official sanction in countries like Pakistan. This means in practice that if a Muslim offends in some way against a Christian, whether by stealing from the latter, inflicting injury or even committing rape, the Christian must gain at least another Christian witness even to match the testimony of the Muslim, and even then in practice the assumption is that the latter is a more credible witness. This rule also carries the insulting presumption that non-Muslims are intrinsically dishonest and unreliable witnesses per se.

Obviously, this considerably disadvantages non-Muslims, and becomes of practical import when we consider the frequent charges of blasphemy used by Muslims against Christians in places like Pakistan, which usually have an ulterior motive (often personal or land disputes). Legal conditions such as these give unscrupulous Muslims the idea that it is 'open season' on minorities. A similar ruling endangers the inheritance rights of Christian wives of Muslims. Again, this gives opportunity to dishonest Muslim relatives of a widow.

THE VALUE OF HUMAN DIGNITY

What we have just examined becomes very important when we consider the issue of human dignity. It almost naturally follows that if the life of a non-Muslim is considered inferior to that of a Muslim, the dignity of the former will be held in the same lack of esteem. Rape in most Muslim countries usually results in execution for the offender where the victim is a Muslim. Where the victim is a non-Muslim, and the perpetrator is a Muslim, this is not the case. Thus, the honour of a Christian woman is not considered equal to that of a Muslim woman. This ruling is quite chilling.

A particularly objectionable ruling concerns the Christian wife of a Muslim man. Their difference in religion precludes their common burial place. Moreover, if she be pregnant at time of death, the foetus, being considered Muslim, cannot be buried in a Christian cemetery, and thus the woman may not be buried there either, and so must be buried in a 'neutral' place. Even in death, Christians are sometimes denied dignity.

THE VALUE OF HUMAN PROPERTY

The right to the defence of personal property is usually considered a fundamental liberty, and its violation by theft is punishable in all societies, again, irrespective of the religious identity of the thief or his victim. This is not the case in all circumstance in Islamic law. The situation is somewhat ambiguous at times, especially if items haram to Muslims are concerned.

Another ruling, however, suggests that if a Muslim stole an item from a Christian, such as a gold crucifix, and then stated that he did so in order to destroy this 'infidel' object, he may escape prosecution. Hence, there is nothing clear-cut in Islamic law which protects the property of Christian subjects, as would be the case in most Western systems which protects all property per se, whatever people's race or faith.

RELIGIOUS LIBERTY

Most Western constitutions today guarantee complete religious liberty, in opinion, practice and propagation. A person is perfectly free to hold or change his opinions, or even hold no religious opinions whatsoever. Under Islamic law, however, this is not the case. Whilst a person may be free to be a Muslim, Jew, Christian or Zoroastrian, he may not hold other religious opinions, as the ban on paganism illustrates.

Moreover, whilst a non-Muslim may change his religion to Islam or one other 'Scriptuary' faith, a Muslim who converts from Islam faces execution. It follows from this that Christians are forbidden to proselytise Muslims, though no such reciprocal ban exists on Muslims. This also affects marriages, since if a Muslim apostatises, the marriage is dissolved, and there is at least one recent example of this in Egypt, where a liberal Muslim was declared apostate by a court, and his marriage dissolved, necessitating the couple's removal to the West, illustrating that the ruling is not merely theoretical.

Most blatantly, whilst the post-war era, especially since the 1970s, have seen an energetic upsurge of mosque construction in the West, there has been no corresponding development in Christian religious buildings in the Muslim world, since Islamic law permits only the repair of existing buildings, forbidding the construction of new ones. The same ruling forbids any Christian presence whatsoever in the Arabian peninsula, so we can see the anomaly that whereas the Saudis recently constructed a giant mosque in Rome, there is no possibility of reciprocity for the Roman Catholics (or anyone else) to build even the smallest chapel in Saudi Arabia.

The issue is not simply one of reciprocity; national Christians in the Muslim world are denied this right as well, whereas Muslims may freely construct mosques.

THE JIZYAH TAX

The American Revolution was fought on the principle 'no taxation without representation', the idea being that constitutional equality was a precondition for the sovereign exercise of levying taxes. The only basis for different levels of taxation is socio-economic distinction, but even here the tax is identical in character, is levied without regard for one's communal origins. The principle of distinction in progressive taxation is ability to pay. The tax imposed does not punish a businessman for his success. Refusal to pay will result in fines or imprisonment, but never execution. Furthermore, the tax he pays grants him entitlement to the full protection of the state, and thus full and equal citizenship. The goal of the tax is the same with everyone - the enabling of the state to provide for the security and well being of all its citizens.

This is not the case with the Jizyah, which is a tax that the Dhimmi uniquely had to pay. It has its origins in Surah Tauba 9:29, where it is explicitly revealed as a sign of the subjugation of conquered non-Muslims. Hence, the tax is clearly a tribute, and a sign of subjection, in no way equivalent to the alms tax Zakat. Yusuf Ali's comment on the Jizyah clarifies this:

The 1281 Jizya: The root meaning is compensation. The derived meaning, which became the technical meaning, was a poll-tax levied from those who did not accept Islam, but were willing to live under the protection of Islam, and were thus tacitly willing to submit to its ideals being enforced in the Muslim State. There was no amount permanently fixed for it. It was in acknowledgment that those whose religion was tolerated would in their turn not interfere with the preaching and progress of Islam. Imam Shafi'i suggests one dinar per year, which would be the Arabian gold dinar of the Muslim States. The tax varied in amount, and there were exemptions for the poor, for females and children (according to Abu Hanifa), for slaves, and for monks and hermits. Being a tax on able-bodied males of military age, it was in a sense a commutation for military service. But see the next note. (9.29)

1282 'An Yadin (literally, from the hand) has been variously interpreted. The hand being the symbol of power and authority. I accept the interpretation "in token of willing submission." The Jizya was thus partly symbolic and partly a commutation for military service, but as the amount was insignificant and the exemptions numerous, its symbolic character predominated. See the last note. (9.29)

Abul 'Ala Mawdudi, Qur'anic exegete and founder of the Islamist Pakistani group Jama'at-i-Islami was quite unapologetic about Jizyah:

...the Muslims should feel proud of such a humane law as that of Jizya. For it is obvious that a maximum freedom that can be allowed to those who do not adopt the way of Allah but choose to tread the ways of error is that they should be tolerated to lead the life they like.

He interprets the Qur'anic imperative to Jihad as having the aim of subjugating non-Muslims, to force them to pay the Jizyah as the defining symbol of their subjection:

... Jews and the Christians ...should be forced to pay Jizya in order to put an end to their independence and supremacy so that they should not remain rulers and sovereigns in the land. These powers should be wrested from them by the followers of the true Faith, who should assume the sovereignty and lead others towards the Right Way.

The consequence of this is that in an Islamic State - specifically the Khilafah - non-Muslims should be denied Government posts, since the state exists for the Muslims, who alone are true citizens, whilst the non-Muslims are merely conquered residents, and the Jizyah signifies this:

That is why the Islamic state offers them protection, if they agree to live as Zimmis by paying Jizya, but it can not allow that they should remain supreme rulers in any place and establish wrong ways and establish them on others. As this state of things inevitably produces chaos and disorder, it is the duty of the true Muslims to exert their utmost to bring an end to their wicked rule and bring them under a righteous order.

Differences of taxation demonstrate distinctions in citizenship. As a symbol of subjection, it signifies that the state is not really the common property of all its permanent residents, but only the Muslims. The non-Muslims are conquered outsiders. It demonstrates their inferior condition. It also punishes them for their disbelief in Islam. Islamic law makes it very clear that the Jizyah is punitive in character. Further, it is too levied with humiliation. Hence, it is in no way comparable to Western tax systems. Even progressive taxation is not a 'punishment' for economic success, nor is any tax specifically humiliating in character.

This illustrates that essentially, in an Islamic State, the non-Muslims are in a worse situation than prisoners out on parole, since they are still being punished - they are not considered 'good, law-abiding citizens' however exemplary their conduct, but rather criminals given day-leave. Their crime is their faith. Moreover, their crime is capital in nature - they deserve death. This demonstrates the unique character of the Jizyah tax - unlike Western taxes, payment does not grant equality and liberty to the payee, but rather merely permission for another tax period to live; failure to pay it results in death. Again, it is rather analogous to a convict on parole regularly visiting the police station or parole officer to register. This is different from the case of someone in the West who refuses to pay his tax for whatever reason; he is punished, though it must be stated not by execution, for breaking the law. The reverse is true with the Jizyah - the tax itself is punishment, and the payee lives in the permanent condition of being punished for his faith until he converts. Essentially, non-Muslims live under a permanent death-threat.

Only by the wildest stretch of the imagination could the situation of non-Muslims under Islamic law be seen as one conferring equal citizenship, whatever Muslim apologists claim. Similarly, only a leap of fantasy could ever believe that such a situation is one that non-Muslims would welcome. The honour, dignity, equality and even the lives of non-Muslims are by no means guaranteed under Islamic law. The Jizyah tax in particular demonstrates the constitutional inferiority and humiliation such a legal arrangement confers. For non-Muslims, it is rather like permanently walking under the sword of Damocles, ready to fall at any moment. If Muslims wish Christians and others to regard an Islamic political order as something attractive, their scholars had best engage in a some heavy work of ijtihad to revise those elements of Islamic jurisprudence and legislation which are particularly offensive to non-Muslims.

6

Exclusion of the Jews and Christians from the Arabian Peninsular

Undoubtedly, one barrier to improved Christian-Muslim relations is the prohibition on the existence of free and public Christian worship, especially with respect to religious buildings, in the Arabian Peninsula. The Saudi Government claims it enforces this ban in loyalty to several ahadith which demand the exclusion of the ahl-ul-Kitab - 'People of the Book' (or any other religious confession) - from the Jazirat al-Arabi (Arabian Peninsula). Islamic historians claim that Muhammad uttered this prohibition near the end of his life, and that it was enforced during the reign of the second Caliph, 'Umar. Both from the standpoint of Christian-Muslim relations and from that of historical criticism, it is therefore an interesting and essential obligation to examine this policy and its historical origins.

To do so, it is essential to study earlier examples of Muhammad's interaction with the ahl-ul-Kitab, and his political and religious policies with respect to them, especially if this reveals a tension with his later policy. This is problematic for Muslims, who, believing Muhammad to be the Great Exemplar, hold him to be both divinely-inspired and thus infallible. To a lesser extent this remains true, at least for Sunnis, with regard to Abu Bakr, the first Caliph, since he was one of the Khulafah Rashidun, the Rightly-Guided caliphs and as

Muhammad's immediate successor, his religious policy sheds great light on the historicity or otherwise of the event. Further, if there is objective historical evidence of a Christian presence remaining after the supposed 'religious cleansing', this raises further questions about the historical veracity of Islamic origins in other aspects.

MUHAMMAD AND THE JEWS

According to the traditional Muslim depiction of Islamic history, the principal interaction of Muhammad with Jews occurred after the Hijra to Medina (Yathrib). The city of Yathrib, two hundred miles north of Mecca was at that time experiencing civil conflict between two rival tribes, the Aws and the Khazraj. According to the hadith literature, a major clash, the 'Battle of Bu'ath' in 617, was the occasion for the invitation to Muhammad. In 622 seventy-five Medinans invited Muhammad and his followers to come to Medina, probably as a peacemaker and political leader. There were several Jewish tribes and individuals, albeit divided, in Yathrib who enjoyed influence, with the Banu Nadir and Banu Qurayza supporting the Aws, and the Banu Qaynuqa supporting the Khazraj. According to the Hadith, the first man to witness the arrival of Muhammad in Medina on 12 Rabi (24 September) 622and to announce the news was a Jew. In this regard, it is noteworthy what purportedly happened at the meeting with Muhammad.

...Allah had set them on the road to Islam, for there were Jews with them in their own country - people who had scriptures, and were endowed with knowledge, while they themselves were polytheists and idolaters The Jews had the upper hand of them in their country. Whenever there was a dispute among them, the Jews said to them: 'Now a prophet will be sent, his time is almost come. We shall follow him and with his help we shall obliterate you as the 'Ad and Iram were obliterated.' When the Messenger of God spoke to them and called them to Allah, they said to one another: 'People! Understand! By Allah, this is surely the prophet with whom the Jews threatened us. We must not let them get ahead of us with him.' ...they believed him and accepted the Muslim dogmas... They told him: 'We renounce our people. No other is so divided by hatred and rivalry. It may be that with your help Allah will bring them together... if Allah unites them in this faith, there will be no man more powerful than you.'

According to Watt, the Jewish tribes had previously dominated the political, economic and intellectual life of Medina. Although the Sira may suggest that the references in the Qur'an to the Torah prophesying the coming of Muhammad may reflect these ideas, it is far more likely that the reverse is true, and the Sira simply attempts a polemical historical reconstruction to justify Muslim holy texts on the beliefs of Jews and Christians which are obviously lacking in factual basis.

After his accession to power, Muhammad purportedly issued the 'Declaration of Medina' addressing the issue of communal relations, effectively forming a tribal confederacy. The basis of relationships was between individual tribes and the Muslims, rather than the Jews en masse. The Muslims were allied with each individual Jewish tribe, although the terms were the same for all. Thus, when conflict arose between the Muslims and individual tribes such as the Banu Nadir, there was no collective punishment of the Jews as a whole. Watt suggests that at this stage Muhammad would have settled for a 'broad church' of Abrahamic monotheists that would not have obliged the conversion of the Jews. He even suggests that this, rather than the Najran visit, may have been the origin of Surah 3 Al-i-Imran Ayah 64. However, his rejection by the Jews set the scene for conflict.

THE BANU QAYNUQA

Relations between the Muslims and the Jewish tribe of Banu Qaynuqa had already deteriorated after some of the tribe had become Muslims, leading to hostility from their former co-religionists. The tribe's principal employment was as craftsmen, particularly as goldsmiths. It was this that was to lead to the first major confrontation between Muslims and Jews in 624 A.D. On one occasion a Muslim woman visited their bazaar, in the course of which she sat down by a goldsmith's stall. Some Jewish youths teased her by attempting to lift her veil, and the goldsmith, probably as a tasteless joke, somehow fastened her skirts to the floor, with the result that her lower body was exposed upon her rising. Rodinson comments that the bystanders hooted with joy while the victim swore vengeance on all and sundry. The honour of everyone connected with the woman, however remotely, was at stake. A Muslim... sprang forward and killed the goldsmith. The Jews fell on the Muslim and killed him. The quarrel was on.

In an oriental context, this would be perceived as an outrage against both personal and tribal honour warranting bloodshed. The Banu Qaynuqa, realising this, withdrew to their strongholds, but were attacked by the Muslims. Rodinson asserts that Muhammad wanted to kill them all, but demurred because of an ally of the Jews, the influential Medinan ibn Ubayy. Rather, the Muhammad imposed upon them was exile, but they were permitted to take with them their families and possessions, with the exceptions of their arms and goldsmith tools. In the contemporary context, this gesture was generous. According to the traditional accounts, the Banu Qaynuqa could field 700 men, 400 armoured, and they possessed allies among the other tribes, even the Muslims. They were thus potentially a serious security risk to the emerging regime. Hence, according to the traditional scenario, it was security considerations and oriental traditions of 'honour', rather than sectarianism, which caused the expulsion.

Having noted this, it should be stated that traditional Muslim accounts are somewhat varied as to the cause of the conflict. According to a Muslim biography of Muhammad ibn Maslamah, the cause of the conflict was a rash, reckless military challenge to the prophet:

After the resounding victory of the Muslims over the Quraysh at the Battle of Badr, one of the three main Jewish groups in Madinah, the Banu Qaynuqa was especially furious and issued a petulant challenge to the Prophet. They said:

"O Muhammad! You really think that we are like your people (the Quraysh)? Don't be deceived. You confronted a people who have no knowledge of war and you took the chance to rout them. If you were to fight against us you would indeed know that we arc men."

They thus spurned their agreement with the Prophet and issued an open challenge to fight. The Qaynuqa however were goldsmiths who dominated the market in Madinah. They were depending on their allies, the Khazraj, to help them in their declared war. The Khazraj refused. The Prophet placed the Banu Qaynuqa's quarters under a siege which lasted for fifteen nights. The fainthearted Qaynuqa finally decided to surrender and ask the Prophet for a free passage out of Madinah.

The Prophet allowed them to leave and the tribe - men, women and children - left unharmed. They had to leave behind them their arms and their goldsmith's equipment. They settled down at Adhraat in Syria.

Mawdudi's account combines both depictions, presenting the picture as being partly a matter of Jewish arrogance, and partly a result of the impugned honour of the Muslim woman:

The first Jewish tribe that, after the Battle of Badr, openly and collectively broke their covenant was the Bani Qainuqa. They lived in a locality inside the city of Madinah. As they practised the crafts of the goldsmith, blacksmith and vessel maker, the people of Madinah had to visit their shops fairly frequently. They were proud of their bravery and valour.

Being blacksmiths by profession even their children were well armed and they could instantly muster 700 fighting men from among themselves. They were also arrogantly aware that they enjoyed relations of confederacy with the Khazraj and Abdullah bin Ubbay, the chief of the, Khazraj, was their chief supporter. At the victory of Badr, they became so provoked that they began to trouble and harass the Muslims and their women in particular, who visited their shops. By and by things came to such a pass that one day a Muslim woman was stripped naked publicly in their bazaar.

This led to a brawl in which a Muslim and a Jew were killed. Thereupon the Holy Prophet (upon whom be Allah's peace) himself visited their locality, got them together and counselled them on decent conduct. But the reply that they gave was; "O Muhammad, you perhaps think we are like the Quraish; they did not know fighting; therefore, you overpowered them. But when you come in contact with us, you will see how men fight." This was in clear words a declaration of war. Consequently, the Holy Prophet (upon whom be Allan's peace) laid siege to their quarters towards the end of Shawwal (and according to some others, of Dhi Qa'dah) A.H. 2. The siege had hardly lasted for a fortnight when they surrendered and all their fighting men were tied and taken prisoners. Now Abdullah bin Ubayy came up in support of them and insisted that they should be pardoned. The Holy Prophet conceded his request and decided that the Bani Qainuqa would be exiled from Madinah leaving their properties, armour and tools of trade behind. (Ibn Sa'd, Ibn Hisham, Tarikh Tabari).

A surprising challenge to the historicity of the event is the lack of any clear reference in either the Qur'an or the Hadith to the event. The former only has an ambiguous statement in Surah Al-Hashr 59:15, usually applied to the Qaynuqah in relation to the expulsion of the Banu Nadir 'Like those who lately preceded them they have tasted the evil result of their conduct and (in the Hereafter there is) for them a grievous Penalty'

Yusuf Ali comments on the verse:

The immediate reference was probably to the Jewish goldsmith tribe of the Qainuqa, who were also settled in a fortified township near Madinah. They were also punished and banished for their treachery, about a month after the battle of Badr, in which the Makkan Pagans had suffered a signal defeat, in Shawwal, A.H. 2. The Nadhir evidently did not take that lesson to heart...

Yet there is nothing explicit in either this text or elsewhere in the Qur'an about the incident. Whilst there are several ahadith mentioning the Banu Qunaiqa, only one refers to their expulsion, and that is in the context of mentioning the general exile of the Jews from Medina. There is no specific historical outline in the hadith corpus of the alleged event and why it occurred. As Mawdudi's quotes show, we have to rely on later Sira material, through which lens Muslim (and other) commentators interpret this verse.

Even then, as we examine the supposed basis of the expulsion, there are grounds for suspicion that there were originally two distinct accounts involved - one involving Jewish recklessness, the other indicating a matter of honour, which Muslims like Mawdudi have redacted and merged, to reconcile their inconsistencies. For one thing, we have no objective evidence as to the actual military strength or otherwise of the Qunayqa, and have to rely on later Muslim accounts. We cannot say for sure if the Qunayqa indeed provoked an incident one way or another, or whether indeed the actual event occurred at all. Moreover, even in the actual accounts as they stand, we do not encounter any supposed divine revelation arising demanding the exile of this section of the ahl-ul-Kitab because of their 'idolatrous' practices, as indicated in the hadith where Muhammad indicated his intention to exile the People of the Book for turning the graves of the prophets into places of worship.

THE CONSEQUENCE OF BADR

At the Battle of Badr in 624, the Meccans were beaten by the Muslims, but remained determined to avenge their defeat. Leadership of the Quraish had fallen to a young man called Abu Sufyan, who had the services of a brilliant Medinan poet-propagandist called Ka'b ibn al-Ashraf, of Pagan paternity but whose mother who came from the Jewish tribe of Banu Nadir, with whom he identified. He composed poetic verses against Muhammad, and poetry of this kind was linked to occult power - i.e. curses. Given the fact that everyone believed in the supernatural power of curses, Muhammad was not inclined to ignore this attack. It should be understood that as a Medinan, and a member of a confederate tribe, Ka'b ibn al-Ashraf was guilty of treason.

Abu Sufyan organised a raid on Medina during which he burned a few young palms as an act of economic sabotage, killed two Medinan field-workers and conversed with two Jews who debriefed him of the situation in the city. This in itself would have called into question the loyalty of the Jews. Ka'b ibn al-Ashraf returned to Medina under the protection of his tribe. Muhammad had him assassinated, the killers placing the head of Ka'b at the feet of Muhammad. The Jews were disturbed, and entered into a new treaty with Muhammad. Similarly, Abu Rafi, a leading Jew of the Banu Nadir, was assassinated on the orders by Muhammad for conspiring against the Prophet after the expulsion of the tribe from Medina.

THE BANU NADIR

The exile of the Banu Nadir in 625 was a consequence of the treachery of a pagan tribe and the Arab obligation of blood-money, the details of which are not pertinent to our theme. Muhammad approached the council of the Jewish tribe Banu an-Nadir to request financial assistance. At first, they were reluctant, but eventually they agreed, and requested that he and his Companions wait while they prepared a meal in his honour. However, Muhammad purportedly received a divine revelation that the Banu Nadir were about to kill him by dropping a millstone from the roof on his head. Commentators such as Rodinson and Watt agree that this scenario was quite possible. Ka'b ibn al-Ashraf was a member of the tribe, and honour demanded that his blood be avenged, and Muhammad's death might also provide an opportunity for the renewal of Jewish influence in Medina. Further, they may have suspected that his request for financial assistance was a precedent for protracted requests of the same nature.

Muhammad reacted to the attempted assassination by sending Muhammad ibn Maslama, a Muslim member of a tribe allied to the Nadir, with an ultimatum: 'Leave my city and live with me no longer after the treason which you have plotted against me'. They were given ten days to leave upon pain of death. They would still be regarded as proprietors of the palm trees, and would receive part of their produce. The tribal chief, Huyayy bin Akhtab, was reluctant to comply, and then made a catastrophic misjudgement by listening to ibn Ubayy, who, seeing a chance to topple Muhammad, promised the Banu Nadir his assistance, that of the Qurayzah and his nomad allies the Ghatafan if they resisted. On this basis, the Nadir retired to their fortresses and resisted the siege for a fortnight. Mawdudi refers to this event:

The day they [the Bani an-Nadir] plotted against the life of the Holy Prophet, and the secret was disclosed, the Holy Prophet ordered them to leave Madinah within ten days and warned that anyone who remained behind after that would be put to death. Abdullah bin Ubayy, the chief of the hypocrites of Madinah, encouraged them to defy the order and refuse to leave Madinah. He even promised to help them with 2,000 men, and assured them that the Bani Ghatafan from Najd also would come to their aid. Accordingly, the Bani an-Nadir sent word that they would not leave no matter what the Holy Prophet might do.

As soon as the time limit of ten days comes to an end, the Holy Prophet laid siege to their quarters, but none of their supporters had the courage to come to their rescue. At last, they surrendered on condition that every three of them would be allowed to load a camel with whatever they could carry and go away leaving the rest of their possessions behind. Thus, the whole suburbs of the city which were inhabited by the Bani an-Nadir, and their gardens and their fortresses and other properties fell to the Muslims, and the people of this treacherous tribe became scattered in Khaiber, Wad il Qura and Syria.

However, the promises of ibn Ubayy proved empty; no-one in the proposed alliance came to the aid of the Banu Nadir. Muhammad then engaged in economic warfare by cutting down the palm trees, a move completely contrary to the Arab code. When the Banu Nadir protested, and some Muslims were uncertain, a divine revelation came in support of Muhammad's action. The sight of the livelihood of the Banu Nadir being destroyed broke their spirits and they surrendered. However, as a result of their obstinacy, Muhammad was not prepared to offer them the same terms as before. They were allowed to take with them whatever their camels could carry; their property, the doors of their houses, and their wood (many dismantled their houses) but they forfeited the palm trees and their armour. Some migrated to Khaybar, where they had property, others to Syria. Yusuf Ali comments on the event as follows:

> They had played a double game. Originally they were sworn allies of the Madinah Muslims under the holy Prophet, but they secretly intrigued with the Makkah Pagans under Abu Sufyan and the Madinah Hypocrites. They even tried treacherously to take the life of the Prophet while he was on a visit to them, breaking both the laws of hospitality and their own sworn alliance. They thought the Pagan Quraish of Makkah and the Hypocrites of Madinah would help them, but they did not help them.
>
> On the contrary the eleven days siege showed them their own helplessness. Their supplies were cut off; the exigencies of the siege necessitated the destruction of their outlying palm trees; and the unexpected turn in their fortunes disheartened them. Their hearts were stack with terror and they capitulated. But they lay waste their homes before they left: Their lives were spared, and they were allowed ten days in which to remove themselves, their families, and such goods as they could carry. In order to leave no habitations for the Muslims they demolished their own houses and lay waste their property, to complete the destruction which the operations of war had already caused at the hands of the besieging force of the Muslims. The punishment of the Banu Nadhir was because in breaking their plighted word with the Messenger and in actively resisting Allah's Message and supporting the enemies of that Message, they rebelled against him. For such treason and rebellion the punishment is severe, and yet in this case it was seasoned with Mercy.

However, the Qur'anic evidence is limited. Surah Al-Hashr 59:1ff is traditionally presented as the text referring to this incident. Yusuf Ali comments on the passage as follows:

> This refers to the Jewish tribe of the Banu Nadhir whose intrigues and treachery nearly undid the Muslim cause during the perilous days of the battle of Uhud in Shawwal, A.H. 3.

Four months after, in Rabi, 1. A.H. 4, steps were taken against them. They were asked to leave the strategic position which they occupied, about three miles south of Madinah, endangering the very existence of the Ummat in Madinah. At first they demurred, relying on their fortresses and on their secret alliance with the Pagans of Makkah and the Hypocrites of Madinah. But when the Muslim army was gathered to punish them and actually besieged them for some days, their allies stirred not a finger in their aid, and they were wise enough to leave. Most of them joined their brethren in Syria, which they were permitted to do, after being disarmed. Some of them joined their brethren in Khaibar...

Their lives were spared, and they were allowed ten days in which to remove themselves, their families, and such goods as they could carry. In order to leave no habitations for the Muslims they demolished their own houses and lay waste their property, to complete the destruction which the operations of war had already caused at the hands of the besieging force of the Muslims. (59.2)...

The punishment of the Banu Nadhir was because in breaking their plighted word with the Messenger and in actively resisting Allah's Message and supporting the enemies of that Message, they rebelled against him. For such treason and rebellion the punishment is severe, and yet in this case it was seasoned with Mercy. (59.4)...

"The people of the townships": the townships were the Jewish settlements round Madinah, of the Banu Nadhir, and possibly of other tribes...

The reference cannot be to the Wadi-ul-Qura (Valley of Towns), now Madain Salih, which was subjugated after Khaibar and Fadak in A.H. 7, unless this verse is later than the rest of the Sura. (59.7)

How the Jews managed to destroy their own homes when they had surrendered to the Muslims, and thus were effectively militarily occupied is difficult to imagine. What is even more surprising, indeed, crucially enigmatic, is that the

Qur'anic text makes no explicit reference to the assassination attempt on the Prophet, merely mentioning that the People of the Book had 'opposed', or more accurately, 'broke away' from Muhammad and thus Allah. The nature of this 'resistance' or 'breach' is very ambiguous. It would be natural to interpret this as referring to a breach of the Constitution of Medina, but the problem is, once again, there is no definite, clear evidence in the Qur'anic text itself, or anywhere else for that matter. The Hadith corpus, while referring to their expulsion, mentions nothing about assassination, or about any breach of agreement. In Abu Dawood, an anonymous narration presents the conflict as a battle instigated by the Quraish. Another text in the same collection contradicts the view that Muhammad let the Jews take all their property with them.

Of course, it should be remembered that Muslims themselves do not regard Abu Dawood's collection as sound, reliable narrations. Other than various texts referring to the cutting-down of the palm-trees, the only reference in a sound collection like Bukhari is to the identification of Surat Al-Hashr with Surat An-Nadir. Even then, we should remember that Bukhari lived about two centuries after the supposed event, and it may be the case, as evidenced from the equation of Surat Al-Hashr and Surat An-Nadir, that the story was 'enlarged' in scope and detail to explain the passage. Moreover, Yusuf Ali's comment on 'the people of the townships' suggest even the Qur'anic passage is composite. It may well be the case that the Nadir (or some of them) was exiled, though why exactly we do not know. The story may have provided a pattern for the saga of the general exile of the People of the Book from Arabia.

THE EXPULSION OF THE BANU QURAYZA

The Battle of the Ditch/Trench in 627, when 10,000 Meccans and their allies unsuccessfully besieged Medina, was a decisive event in Muhammad's career, preparing the way for the conquest of Mecca. It also consolidated his power in Medina. Where it becomes relevant to our theme concerns his action against the last remaining major Jewish tribe in Medina, the Banu Qurayza, and the purported involvement of Jews in the assault on Medina by the Quraish. Mawdudi claims that the Jews of the exiled Banu Nadir played a role in the assault upon Medina:

It had been instigated by the leaders of the Bani an-Nadir, who had settled in Khaiber after their banishment from Madinah. They went round to the Quraish and Ghatafan and Hudhail and many other tribes and induced them to gather all their forces together and attack Madinah jointly. Thus, in Shawwal, A.H. 5, an unprecedentedly large army of the Arab tribes marched against the small city of Madinah. From the north came Jews of Bani an-Nadir and Bani Qainuqa who after their banishment from Madinah, had settled in Khaiber and Wad il Qura.

However, this appears to contradict his picture of inter-Jewish relatons. In his introduction to S. Al-Hashr, he notes that the Jewish tribes were not on good relations with each other: '... the third tribe, Bani Qainuqa, was not on friendly terms with the other two tribes, it stayed inside the city as usual, but had to seek protection of the Khazraj tribe. As a counter measure to this Ban an-Nadir and Bani Quraizah took protection of the Aus tribe so that they could live in peace in the suburbs of Yathrib.' This being so, the picture Mawdudi presents of a united Jewish attack upon Muhammad in alliance with the Quraish must be questioned.

It should be also noted that some Qurayza Jews assisted in constructing the defensive ditch along with the Muslims. Eventually the battle concluded with the withdrawal of the Quraish. However, during the siege, the Meccans had allegedly negotiated a plan with the Banu Qurayza whereby the defenders would be assaulted from the rear, massacring their women and children. Mawdudi writes:

They sent Huyayy bin Akhtab, the Jewish leader of the Bani an-Nadir, to the Bani Quraizah so as to induce them to break the treaty and join the war. In the beginning, they refused to oblige and said that they had a treaty with Muhammad (upon whom be Allah's peace) who had faithfully abided by it and given them no cause for complaint. But when Ibn Akhtab said to them, "Look, I have summoned the united force of entire Arabia against him: this is a perfect opportunity to get rid of him. If you lose it, you will never have another opportunity," the anti Islamic Jewish mind prevailed over every moral consideration and the Bani Quraizah was persuaded to break the treaty.

Watt gives credence to the purported role of the Banu Nadir from Khaybar in this. Apparently the Banu Qurayza discussed the matter, and according to Muslim tradition, some actually joined the siege. They may have been obliged by treaty to assist Muhammad in conflict or at least stay neutral - judging from the terms of the Declaration of Medina, this would seem quite likely. Clearly, by engaging in such intrigue they were guilty of an act of treachery, not to say war, against Muhammad. This was the final straw for Muhammad, whose mind was now set on conquering Mecca, and the last thing he would be willing to tolerate was a fifth column undermining his strategy. On the very day the siege ended he turned his troops on the Qurayzah. According to Islamic tradition, this was not a mere human strategic decision on the part of Muhammad; rather, it had been commanded by God through the agency of Gabriel:

...When the Prophet (peace be upon him) returned from (the battle of) al-Khandaq (i.e. trench) and laid down his arms and took a bath.

Gabriel came to him while he (i.e. Gabriel) was shaking the dust off his head, and said, "You have laid down your arms? By Allah, I have not laid them down. Go out to them (to attack them)."

The Prophet (peace be upon him) said, "Where?"

Gabriel pointed towards Banu Qurayzah...

The following tradition states why the Banu Qurayzah was to be assaulted - they had fought against Muhammad:

Banu An-Nadir and Banu Qurayzah fought (with the Prophet (peace be upon him) violating their peace treaty), so the Prophet (peace be upon him) exiled Banu An-Nadir and allowed Banu Qurayzah to remain in their homes (in Medina) taking nothing from them till they fought the Prophet (peace be upon him)...

Yusuf Ali comments on S. 33:26 in relation to the Battle of the Ditch:

The reference is to the Jewish tribe of the Banu Quraiza. They counted among the citizens of Madinah and were bound by solemn engagements to help in the defence of the City. But on the occasion of the Confederate siege by the Quraish and their allies they intrigued with the enemies and treacherously aided them. Immediately after the siege was raised and the Confederates had fled in hot haste, the Prophet turned his attention to these treacherous "friends" who had betrayed his City in the hour of danger. The Banu Quraiza ... were filled with terror and dismay when Madinah was free from the Quraish danger. They shut themselves up in their castles about three or four miles to the east (or north east) of Madinah, and sustained a siege of 25 days, after which they surrendered, stipulating that they would abide by the decision of their fate at the hands of Sad ibn Muaz, chief of the Aus tribe, with which they had been in alliance.

Although the Jews protested their innocence of treachery, Muhammad, in obedience to the angelic instruction, attacked them by getting his poets to supernaturally abuse them. After twenty-five days the Jews were disheartened. Some families escaped by converting to Islam. The tribe then asked to be set free on the same basis as the Qaynuqah, but Muhammad demanded unconditional surrender. Muhammad then allowed one of the Aws, Sa'd, an old friend of the Jews to pronounce judgement, which was to execute all the men and share-out all the women and children.

At this point, we return to Arafat's critique of the Banu Qurayza story, and note his objections to its veracity, which are relevant to the Najran epic:

Now for the story. The reasons for rejecting the story are the following:

As already stated above, the reference to the story in the Qur'an is extremely brief, and there is no indication whatever of the killing of a large number. In a battle context the reference is to those who were actually fighting. The Qur'an is the only authority which the historian would accept without hesitation or doubt. It is a contemporary text, and, for the most cogent reasons, what we have is the authentic version.

The rule in Islam is to punish only those who were responsible for the sedition.

To kill such a large number is diametrically opposed to the Islamic sense of justice and to the basic principles laid down in the Qur'an - particularly the verse. "No soul shall bear another's burden." It is obvious in the story that the leaders were numbered and were well known. They were named.

It is also against the Qur'anic rule regarding prisoners of war, which is: either they are to be granted their freedom or else they are to be allowed to be ransomed.

It is unlikely that the Banu Qurayza should be slaughtered when the other Jewish groups who surrendered before Banu Qurayza and after them were treated leniently and allowed to go. Indeed Abu 'Ubayd b. Sallam relates in his Kitab al-amwal that when Khaybar felt [sic] to the Muslims there were among the residents a particular family or clan who had distinguished themselves by execesive [sic] unseemly abuse of the Prophet. Yet in that hour the Prophet addressed them in words which are no more than a rebuke: "Sons of Abu al-Huqayq (he said to them) I have known the extent of your hostility to God and to His apostle, yet that does not prevent me from treating you as I treated your brethren." That was after the surrender of Banu Qurayza.

If indeed so many hundreds of people had actually been put to death in the market-place, and trenches were dug for the operation, it is very strange that there should be no trace whatever of all that - no sign or word to point to the place, and no reference to a visible mark.

Had this slaughter actually happened, jurists would have adopted it as a precedent? In fact exactly the opposite has been the case. The attitude of jurists, and their rulings, has been more according to the Qur'anic rule in the verse, "No soul shall bear another's burden."

Indeed, Abu 'Ubayd b. Sallam relates a very significant incident in his book Kifab al-amwal, which, it must be noted, is a book of jurisprudence, of law, not a sira or a biography. He tells us that in the time of the Imam al-Awza'i there was a case of trouble among a group of the People of the Book in the Lebanon when 'Abdullab b. 'Ali was regional governor. He put down the sedition and ordered the community in question to be moved elsewhere. Al-Awza'i in his capacity as the leading jurist immediately objected. His argument was that the incident was not the result of the community's unanimous agreement. "At [sic] far as I know (he argued) it is not a rule of God that God should punish the many for the fault of the few but punish the few for the fault of the many."

Now, had the Imam al-Awza'i accepted the story of the slaughter of Banu Qurayza, he would have treated it as a precedent, and would not have come out with an argument against Authority, represented in 'Abdullah b. 'Ali. Al-Awza'i, it should be remembered, was a younger contemporary of Ibn Ishaq.

In the story of Qurayza a few specific persons were named as having been put to death, some of whom were described as particularly active in their hostility. It is the reasonable conclusion that those were the ones who led the sedition and who were consequently punished - not the whole tribe.

The details given in the story clearly and of necessity imply inside knowledge, i.e. from among the Jews themselves. Such are the details of their consultation when they were besieged, the harangue of Ka'b b. Asad as their leader; and the suggestion that they should kill their women and children and then make a last desperate attack against the Muslims.

Just as the descendants of Qurayza would want to glorify their ancestors, so did the descendants of the Madanese connected with the event. One notices that that part of the story which concerned the judgement of Sa'd b. Mu'adh against Qurayza, was transmitted from one of his direct descendants. According to this part the Prophet said to Mu'adh: "You have pronounced God's judgement upon them [as inspired] through Seven Veils."

Now it is well known that for the purposes of glorifying their ancestors or white washing those who were inimical to Islam at the beginning, many stories were invented by later generations and a vast amount of verse was forged, much of which was transmitted by Ibn Ishaq. The story and the statement concerning Sa'd are one such detail.

Other details are difficult to accept. How could so many hundreds of persons he incarcerated in the house belonging to a woman of Banu al-Najjar?

The history of the Jewish tribes after the establishment of Islam is not really clear at all. The idea that they all departed on the spot seems to be in need of revision, as can be seen on examining the sources.

In other words, the story is a legend, rather than an historical event. It has an historical incident as its basis, but it has magnified the event out of all proportion to what in fact occurred. Of course, in the absence of even Qur'anic evidence for this scenario, we are entitled to ask how Muslim tradition, apart from purported divine revelation, is sure of this picture. What objective evidence is there for its veracity? What proof is there for Mawdudi's assertion about the role of the Banu Nadir in the Quraish attack upon Medina? How does anyone know that the Qurayza and the Quraish were engaged in this supposed conspiracy? It would indeed have displayed a treacherous intention on their part, revealing them to be a genuine security risk, especially if they were willing to massacre innocents. Moreover, it would seem to present a picture of the climax of Jewish/ahl-ul-Kitab treachery right from the beginning of Islam, giving concrete historical expression to the Qur'anic warnings about taking Jews or Christians as 'friends, and other texts implying that the People of the Book are treacherous. Yusuf Ali comments on this verse, displaying how the historical events of Muhammad's life demonstrate why Muslims should be suspicious of the ahl-ul-Kitab: 'That is, look not to them for help and comfort.

They are more likely to combine against you than to help you. And this happened more than once in the lifetime of the Prophet, and in after-ages again and again.' Mawdudi states with regard to this theme:

> The hypocrites, while living among the Muslims, wanted to keep good relations with the Jews and the Christians so that if the conflict ended in the defeat of the Muslims, they might safely take refuge with their enemies. Then there was also the economic factor; at that time the Jews and the Christians were economically the most powerful people in Arabia.... This also led the hypocrites to preserve their old relations with them... In short, they considered it very dangerous to break relations with these people because of the conflict between Islam and *kufr*, for they feared it might ruin them economically and politically.

THE JEWS OF KHAYBAR, FADAK AND ELSEWHERE

The last group of Jews to resist Muhammad was in Khaybar, where, according to Muslim tradition, they plotted with pagan tribes against him, as we have seen. This constituted an act of war, and in 628 he besieged them. Some Jews aided the Muslim 'war effort', attempting to secure their position after the conquest. The terms of surrender were quite merciful for the time. The Hadith tradition [see below] relates that ownership of the land passed to the Muslims, but the Jews were to cultivate it and keep half the produce for themselves. According to Muslim sources, Muhammad returned to the Jews copies of the Torah seized during the siege, as opposed to desecrating them. The rest of the Jewish communities in the area soon fell to Muhammad. The Jews of Fadak submitted, handing over half their wealth to Muhammad. They may have been involved in the Khaybar campaign. The Jews of Wadi'l-Qura offered token resistance, and then capitulated on similar terms. The Jews of Tayma, however, who offered no resistance, merely had to pay the

Jizya tax. The same thing happened to the Jews of Banu Ghaziyah and Banu 'Arid. According to Haykal, the Jews of al Bahrayn were exempted from this tax. The Khaybar conquest is allegedly celebrated in the Qur'an, S. 33:26ff. Yusuf Ali comments with regard to v27:

Sunan of Abu-Dawood Hadith 3000	**Sahih Al-Bukhari Hadith 5.550**
Narrated by Abdullah Ibn Umar	**Narrated by Abdullah**
The Prophet fought with the people of Khaybar, and captured their palm-trees and land, and forced them to remain confined to their fortresses. So they concluded a treaty of peace providing that gold, silver and weapons would go to the Apostle of Allah (peace be upon him), and whatever they took away on their camels would belong to them, on condition that they would not hide and carry away anything. If they did (so), there would be no protection for them and no treaty (with Muslims). They carried away a purse of Huyayy ibn Akhtab who was killed before (the battle of) Khaybar. He took away the ornaments of Banu an-Nadir when they were expelled. The Prophet (peace be upon him) asked Sa'yah: Where is the purse of Huyayy ibn Akhtab. He replied: The contents of this purse were spent on battles and other expenses. (Later on) they found the purse. So he killed Ibn AbulHuqayq, captured their women and children, and intended to deport them. They said: Muhammad, leave us to work on this land; we shall have half (of the produce) as you wish, and you will have half. The Apostle of Allah (peace be upon him) used to make a contribution of eighty wasqs of dates and twenty wasqs of wheat to each of his wives.	The Prophet gave (the land of) Khaibar to the Jews (of Khaibar) on condition that they would work on it and cultivate it and they would have half of its yield.Al-Muwatta Hadith 33.1 Yahya related to me from Malik from Ibn Shihab from Said ibn al-Musayyab that the Messenger of Allah, may Allah bless him and grant him peace, said to the Jews of Khaybar on the day of the conquest of Khaybar, "I confirm you in it as long as Allah, the Mighty, the Majestic, establishes you in it, provided that the fruits are divided between us and you." Said continued, "The Messenger of Allah, may Allah bless him and grant him peace, used to send Abdullah ibn Rawaha, to assess the division of the fruit crop between him and them, and he would say, 'If you wish, you can buy it back, and if you wish, it is mine.' They would take it."

This part of the Sura is considered a prophecy. It may refer to the conquest of Khaibar. Khaibar is a Harrat or volcanic tract, well-watered with many springs issuing from its basaltic rocks. It has a good irrigation system and produces good harvests of grain and dates in its wet valleys, while the outcrop of rocks in the high ground affords sites for numerous fortresses. In the holy Prophet's time there were Jewish colonies settled here, but they were a source of constant trouble especially after Siege of Madinah. It became a nest of all the hostile Jewish elements expelled for their treachery from elsewhere. Its capital, Khaibar, is about 90 miles due north of Madinah. Its inhabitants offered some resistance, and Hadhrat 'Ali, though he had just risen from a bed of illness, performed prodigies of valour. After its surrender, a land settlement was made, which retained the cultivators of the soil on the land, but brought them under control, so that no further focus of active hostility should remain near Madinah. The terms of the settlement will be found in Waqidi.

It can be seen, however, that there is some ambiguity attached to the passage, since Yusuf Ali is uncertain if it actually refers to the Khaybar expedition. Mawdudi, in his Surah introductions, holds that S. 62:1-8 relate to the Khaybar conquest, yet once again, there is an uncertainty about this hypothesis:

The period of the revelation of the first section (vv. 1-8) is A.H. 7, and probably it was sent down on the occasion of the conquest of Khaiber or soon after it. Bukhari, Muslim, Tirmidhi, Nasa'i and Ibn Jarir have related on the authority of Hadrat Abu Hurairah that he and other Companions were sitting in the Holy Prophet's assembly when these verses were revealed. About Abu Hurairah it is confirmed historically that he entered Islam after the truce of Hudaibiyah and before the conquest of Khaiber, and Khaiber was conquered, according to Ibn Hisham, in Muharram, and, according to Ibn Sa'd, in Jamadi al-Awwal, A.H. 7. Thus presumably Allah might have sent down these verses, addressing the Jews, when

Sahih Al-Bukhari Hadith 3.890	**Sunan of Abu-Dawood Hadith 3001**
Narrated by Ibn Umar	**Narrated by Abdullah ibn Umar**
When the people of Khaibar dislocated Abdullah bin Umar's hands and feet, Umar got up delivering a sermon saying, "No doubt, Allah's Apostle made a contract with the Jews concerning their properties, and said to them, 'We allow you (to stand in your land) as long as Allah allows you.' Now Abdullah bin Umar went to his land and was attacked at night, and his hands and feet were dislocated, and as we have no enemies there except those Jews, they are our enemies and the only people whom we suspect, I have made up my mind to exile them." When Umar decided to carry out his decision, a son of Abu Al-Haqiq's came and addressed 'Umar, "O chief of the believers, will you exile us although Muhammad allowed us to stay at our places, and made a contract with us about our properties, and accepted the condition of our residence in our land?" 'Umar said, "Do you think that I have forgotten the statement of Allah's Apostle, i.e.: What will your condition be when you are expelled from Khaibar and your camel will be carrying you night after night?" The Jew replied, "That was joke from Abul-Qasim." 'Umar said, "O the enemy of Allah! You are telling a lie." 'Umar then drove them out and paid them the price of their properties in the form of fruits, money, camel saddles and ropes, etc.	Umar said: The Apostle of Allah (peace be upon him) had transaction with the Jews of Khaybar on condition that we should expel them when we wish. If anyone has property (with them), he should take it back, for I am going to expel the Jews. So he expelled them. Sahih Al-Bukhari Hadith 3.485 Narrated by Abdullah bin Umar Allah's Apostle gave the land of Khaibar to the Jews to work on and cultivate and take half of its yield. Ibn 'Umar added, "The land used to be rented for a certain portion (of its yield)." Nafi mentioned the amount of the portion but I forgot it. Rafi' bin Khadij said, "The Prophet forbade renting farms." Narrated 'Ubaidullah Nafi' said: Ibn 'Umar said: (The contract of Khaibar continued) till 'Umar evacuated the Jews (from Khaibar).

their last stronghold had fallen to the Muslims, or these might have been revealed when, seeing the fate of Khaiber, all the Jewish settlements of northern Hijaz had surrendered to the Islamic government...

The first section [of the Surah] was sent down at a time when all Jewish efforts to obstruct the message of Islam during the past six years had failed. First, in Madinah as many as three of their powerful tribes had done whatever they could to frustrate the mission of the Holy Prophet, with the result that one of the tribes was completely exterminated and the other two were exiled. Then by intrigue and conspiracy they brought many of the Arab tribes together to advance on Madinah, but in the Battle of the Trench they were all repulsed. After this, Khaiber had become their stronghold, where a large number of the Jews expelled from Madinah also had taken refuge. At the time these verses were revealed, that too was taken without any extraordinary effort, and the Jews at their own request agreed to live there as tenants of the Muslims. After this final defeat the Jewish power in Arabia came to an end. Then, Wad-il-Qura, Fadak Taima', Tabuk, all surrendered one after the other, so much so that all Arabian Jews became subdued to the same Islam which they were not prepared to tolerate before.

The fact that the Qur'an fails to mention this event in detail is surprising, since it effectively sealed Muhammad's control of much of Arabia, and crushed 'the Jewish threat' forever. This omission is even more surprising given the actions of a Jewess called Zaynab, who had lost her husband and father in the conflict. She attempted to assassinate Muhammad by food-poisoning, an event recorded in the Hadith, in which we encounter some ambiguity again, since one narration implies general complicity on the part of the Jews of Khaybar, rather than just individual guilt by Zaynab. There is also uncertainty as the fate of Zaynab, some narrations indicating she was executed, others implying she was left alive. Yet the Qur'an, amazingly, fails to mention the incident. Commentators often ascribe Muhammad's premature death to this incident. What is also significant is that the incident is so similar to the alleged assassination attempt by the Banu Nadir, and according to one of the narrations, the general body of the Jews of Khaybar were responsible for this action, which actually led to the death of one of Muhammad's companions. Yet, unlike the alleged incident with the Nadir, Muhammad did not order their deportation, or even their general punishment.

This becomes essential in considering the question of the exile of the People of the Book from Arabia. An examination of the table, listing some narrations pertinent to Khaybar demonstrates that there is no agreement between the traditions with regard to the permanence of the Jewish presence there. In some traditions, their presence seems to be conditional on sharing the produce of the land. Al-Muwatta Hadith 33.1 ambiguously states that the Jews would remain there as long as Allah willed it. The narrations in the second row imply that the Jews were only permitted temporary presence, the arbiter being the Muslim Ummah, although no doubt this is equated with the will of Allah, and no reference to the issue of produce is made. The second row bears all the hall-marks of special pleading, an attempt to justify the expulsion by asserting the existence of a prior determination to deport the Jews. Moreover, none of this is to be found in the Qur'an.

Sunan of Abu-Dawood Hadith 3000Narrated by Abdullah Ibn UmarThe Prophet fought with the people of Khaybar, and captured their palm-trees and land, and forced them to remain confined to their fortresses. So they concluded a treaty of peace providing that gold, silver and weapons would go to the Apostle of Allah (peace be upon him), and whatever they took away on their camels would belong to them, on condition that they would not hide and carry away anything. If they did (so), there would be no protection for them and no treaty (with Muslims).

They carried away a purse of Huyayy ibn Akhtab who was killed before (the battle of) Khaybar. He took away the ornaments of Banu an-Nadir when they were expelled. The Prophet (peace be upon him) asked Sa'yah: Where is the purse of Huyayy ibn Akhtab. He replied: The contents of this purse were spent on battles and other expenses. (Later on) they found the purse. So he killed Ibn AbulHuqayq, captured their women and children, and intended to deport them. They said: Muhammad, leave us to

you wish, and you will have half. The Apostle of Allah (peace be upon him) used to make a contribution of eighty wasqs of dates and twenty wasqs of wheat to each of his wives.

Shih Al-Bukhari Hadith 5.550Narrated by AbdullahThe Prophet gave (the land of) Khaibar to the Jews (of Khaibar) on condition that they would work on it and cultivate it and they would have half of its yield.Al-Muwatta Hadith 33.1 Yahya related to me from Malik from Ibn Shihab from Said ibn al-Musayyab that the Messenger of Allah, may Allah bless him and grant him peace, said to the Jews of Khaybar on the day of the conquest of Khaybar, "I confirm you in it as long as Allah, the Mighty, the Majestic, establishes you in it, provided that the fruits are divided between us and you." Said continued, "The Messenger of Allah, may Allah bless him and grant him peace, used to send Abdullah ibn Rawaha, to assess the division of the fruit crop between him and them, and he would say, 'If you wish, you can buy it back, and if you wish, it is mine.' They would take it."

Sahih Al-Bukhari Hadith 3.890Narrated by Ibn UmarWhen the people of Khaibar dislocated Abdullah bin Umar's hands and feet, Umar got up delivering a sermon saying, "No doubt, Allah's Apostle made a contract with the Jews concerning their properties, and said to them, 'We allow you (to stand in your land) as long as Allah allows you.' Now Abdullah bin Umar went to his land and was attacked at night, and his hands and feet were dislocated, and as we have no enemies there except those Jews, they are our enemies and the only people whom we suspect, I have made up my mind to exile them." When Umar decided to carry out his decision, a son of Abu Al-Haqiq's came and addressed 'Umar, "O chief of the believers, will you exile us although Muhammad allowed us to stay at our places, and made a contract with us about our properties, and accepted the condition of our residence in our land?" 'Umar said, "Do you think that I have forgotten the statement of Allah's Apostle, i.e.: What will your condition be when you are expelled from Khaibar and your camel will be carrying you night after night?" The Jew replied, "That was joke from Abul-Qasim." 'Umar said, "O the enemy of Allah! You are telling a lie." 'Umar then drove them out and paid them the price of their properties in the form of fruits, money, camel saddles and ropes, etc. Sunan of Abu-Dawood Hadith 3001Narrated by Abdullah ibn UmarUmar said: The Apostle of Allah (peace be upon him) had transaction with the Jews of Khaybar on condition that we should expel them when we wish. If anyone has property (with them), he should take it back, for I am going to expel the Jews. So he expelled them.Sahih Al-Bukhari Hadith 3.485Narrated by Abdullah bin UmarAllah's Apostle gave the land of Khaibar to the Jews to work on and cultivate and take half of its yield. Ibn 'Umar added, "The land used to be rented for a certain portion (of its yield)." Nafi mentioned the amount of the portion but I forgot it. Rafi' bin Khadij said, "The Prophet forbade renting farms." Narrated 'Ubaidullah Nafi' said: Ibn 'Umar said: (The contract of Khaibar continued) till 'Umar evacuated the Jews (from Khaibar).

HISTORY OR MUSLIM PROPAGANDA

This entire historical saga has been challenged in recent research. For example, a tradition unambiguously asserts that the exile of the Banu Qurayzah completed the expulsion of the Jews from Medina:

Sahih Al-Bukhari Hadith 5.362- Narrated by Ibn Umar

Bani An-Nadir and Bani Quraiza fought (against the Prophet violating their peace treaty), so the Prophet exiled Bani An-Nadir and allowed Bani Quraiza to remain at their places (in Medina) taking nothing from them till they fought against the Prophet again). He then killed their men and distributed their women, children and property among the Muslims, but some of them came to the Prophet and he granted them safety, and they embraced Islam. He exiled all the Jews from Medina. They were the Jews of Bani Qainuqa', the tribe of 'Abdullah bin Salam and the Jews of Bani Haritha and all the other Jews of Medina.

Despite what this narration states, it is clear that Jews continued to live in Medina, 'perhaps quite a number' according to Watt. One example was Abu sh'Shahm, a merchant, who actually bought some of the Qurayzah women and children. Haykal states that after the political/military collapse of the Jewish tribes, Jews began to return to Medina and resume their ordinary occupations. Muhammad guaranteed the religious rights of the returnees. Rodinson reports that after the Battle of Hunain, that is, two to three years after the supposed total expulsion of the Jews from Medina, 'Secret conclaves were held in the house of a Jewish resident of Medina and Muhammad had it burnt down.', demonstrating that Jews were still resident in the city. Watt asserts that there was no general campaign to 'cleanse' the Peninsula of Jews, but that Muhammad simply responded as and when the circumstances arose to attacks on his security. This in itself raises questions about the traditional Muslim saga of the Jews of Medina, since the clear impression of the Hadith and Sira literature is generally that then expulsion was total. An important challenge is found in an article by W. N. Arafat. He echoes Haykal's comment about Jews continuing to live in Medina:

For example, in his Jamharat al-ansab, Ibn Hazm occasionally refers to Jews still living in Medina. In two places al-Waqidi mentions Jews who were still in Medina when the Prophet prepared to march against Khaybar - i.e. after the supposed liquidation of all three tribes, including Qurayza. In one case ten Madanese Jews actually joined the Prophet in an excursion to Khaybar, and in the other the Jews who had made their peace with him in Medina were extremely worried when he prepared to attack Khaybar. Al-Waqadi explains that they tried to prevent the departure of any Muslim who owed them money.

What is so crucial both for an analysis of the historicity of the exile of the Jews from Medina and of the later more extensive expulsion of the People of the Book from Arabia is the reason for this scepticism - the unreliability of the Sira material:

The earliest work that we have, with the widest range of details, is Ibn Ishaq's Sira, his biography of the Prophet. It is also the longest and the most widely quoted. Later historians draw, and in most cases depend on him. But Ibn Ishaq died in 151 A.H., i.e. 145 years after the event in question. Later historians simply take his version of the story, omitting more or less of the detail, and overlooking his uncertain list of authorities. They generally abbreviate the story, which appears just as one more event to report. In most cases their interest seems to end there. Some of them indicate that they are not really convinced, but they are not prepared to take further trouble. One authority, Ibn Hajar, however, denounces this story and the other related ones as "odd tales". A contemporary of Ibn Ishaq, Malik, the jurist, denounces Ibn Ishaq outright as "a liar" and "an impostor" just for transmitting such stories.

It must be remembered that historians and authors of the Prophet's biography did not apply the strict rules of the "traditionists". They did not always provide a chain of authorities, each of whom had to be verified as trustworthy and as certain or likely to have transmitted his report directly from his informant, and so on. The attitude towards biographical details and towards the early events of Islam was far less meticulous than their attitude to the Prophet's traditions, or indeed to any material relevant to jurisprudence. Indeed Ibn Ishaq's account of the siege of Medina and the fall of the Banu Qurayza is pieced together by him from information given by a variety of persons he names, including Muslim descendants of the Jews of Qurayza.

Against these late and uncertain sources must be placed the only contemporary and entirely authentic source, the Qur'an. There, the reference in Sura XXXIII, 26 is very brief:

"He caused those of the People of the Book who helped them (i.e. the Quraysh) to come out of their forts. Some you killed, some you took prisoner." There is no reference to numbers.

Ibn Ishaq sets out his direct sources as he opens the relevant chapter on the siege of Medina. These were: a client of the family of al-Zubayr and others whom he "did not suspect". They told parts of the story on the authority of 'Abdullah b. Ka'b b. Malik, al Zuhri, 'Asim b. 'Umar b. Qatada, 'Abdullab b. Abi Bakr, Muhammad b. Ka'b of Qurayza, and "others among our men of learning", as he put it. Each of these contributed to the story, so that Ibn Ishaq's version is the sum total of the collective reports, pieced together. At a later stage Ibn Ishaq quotes another descendant of Qurayza, 'Attiyya by name, who had been spared, and, directly, a certain descendant of al-Zabir b. Bata, a prominent member of the tribe of Qurayza who figures in the narrative.

Of course, we must question Arafat's confident assertion of the reliability of the Qur'an, but he is right to assert preference for it as a purportedly earlier, possibly contemporary source as opposed to later Sira material. Hence, the consequence of this is that the Sira is not a dependable historical source. This is important, since so often scholars, especially Muslims, interpret the Qur'an and Hadith corpus in the light of the Sira literature. Simultaneously, having so interpreted the main authorities of Islamic belief in this way, they give credence to the presentation of history found in the works of Sira. Arafat continues his devastating critique as follows:

The attitude of scholars and historians to Ibn Ishaq's version of the story has been either one of complacency, sometimes mingled with uncertainty, or at least in two important cases, one of condemnatlon and outright rejection.

The complacent attitude is one of accepting the biography of the Prophet and the stories of the campaigns at they were received by later generations without the meticulous care or the application of the critical criteria which collectors of traditions or jurists employed. It was not necessary to check the veracity of authorities when transmitting or recording parts of the story of the Prophet's life. It was not essential to provide a continuous chain of authorities or even to give authorities at all. That is obvious in Ibn Ishaq's Sira. On the other hand reliable authority and a continuous line of transmission were essential when law was the issue. That is why Malik the jurist had no regard for Ibn Ishaq.

One finds, therefore, that later historians and even exegetes either repeat the very words of Ibn Ishaq or else abbreviate the whole story. Historians gave it, as it were, a cold reception. Even Tabari, nearly 150 years after Ibn Ishaq, does not try to find other versions of the story as he usually does. He casts doubt by his use of the words, "Waqidi alleged (za'ama) that the Prophet caused trenches to be dug." Ibn ai-Qayyim in Zad al-ma'ad makes only the briefest reference and he ignores altogether the crucial question of numbers. Ibn Kathir even seems to have general doubt in his mind because he takes the trouble to point out that the story was told on such "good authority" as that of 'A'isha.

Apart from mild complacency or doubtful acceptance of the story itself, Ibn Ishaq as an author was in fact subjected to devastating attacks by scholars, contemporary or later, on two particular accounts. One was his uncritical inclusion in his Sira of so much spurious or forged poetry; the other his unquestioning acceptance of just such a story as that of the slaughter of Banu Qurayza.

His contemporary, the early traditionist and jurist Malik, called him unequivocally "a liar" and "an impostor" "who transmits his stories from the Jews". In other words, applying his own criteria, Malik impugned the veracity of Ibn Ishaq's sources and rejected his approach. Indeed, neither Ibn Ishaq's list of informants nor his method of collecting and piecing together such a story would he acceptable to Malik the jurist.

In a later age Ibn Hajar further explained the point of Malik's condemnation of Ibn Ishaq. Malik, he said, condemned Ibn Ishaq because he made a point of seeking out descendants of the Jews of Medina in order to obtain from them accounts of the Prophet's campaigns as handed down by their forefathers. Ibn Hajar then rejected the stories in question in the strongest terms: "such odd tales as the story of Qurayza and al-Nadir". Nothing could be more damning than this outright rejection.

Against the late and uncertain sources on the one hand, and the condemning authorities on the other, must be set the only contemporary and entirely authentic source, the Qur'an. There the reference in Sura XXXIII, 26 is very brief: "He caused those of the People of the Book who helped them (i.e. the Quraysh) to come out of their forts. Some you killed, some you took prisoner."

Exegetes and traditionists tend simply to repeat Ibn Ishaq's tale, but in the Qur'an the reference can only be to those who were actually in the fighting. This is a statement about the battle. It concerns those who fought. Some of these were killed others were taken prisoner.

One would think that if 600 or 900 people were killed in this manner the significance of the event would have been greater. There would have been a clearer reference in the Qur'an, a conclusion to be drawn, and a lesson to be learnt. But when only the guilty leaders were executed, it would be normal to expect only a brief reference.

It appears therefore, that there has been an escalation in the reporting of the story, and we must ask ourselves why this would be so. It is of course possible that ibn Ishaq (or ibn Hisham's redaction of ibn Ishaq) was simply naïve, taking the word of supposed descendants of the Qurayzah or Nadir in Medina. It could also be the case that the story was attractive for polemical reasons. The revisionist school of Muslim history posits that much of the traditional presentation of the emergence of Islam is actually anachronistic reconstruction. Jay Smith, in a paper comparing the Bible and the Qur'an, argues that the cleavage between the Jews and Muslims was actually much later than the traditional Muslim depiction:

> The Qur'an implies that Muhammad severed his relationship with the Jews in 624 AD (or soon after the Hijra in 622 AD), and thus moved the direction of prayer, the Qibla at that time from Jerusalem to Mecca (Sura 2:144, 149-150). The early non-Muslim sources, however, depict a good relationship between the Muslims and Jews at the time of the first conquests (late 620s AD), and even later. Yet the Doctrina Iacobi warns of the 'Jews who mix with the Saracens,' and the danger to 'life and limb of falling into the hands of these Jews and Saracens' (Bonwetsch 1910:88; Cook 1983:75). In fact, this relationship seems to carry right on into the conquest as an early Armenian source mentions that the governor of Jerusalem in the aftermath of the conquest was a Jew (Patkanean 1879:111; Sebeos 1904:103).

What is significant here is the possibility that Jews and Arabs (Saracens) seem to be allies during the time of the conquest of Palestine and for a short time after (Crone-Cook 1977:6).

If these witnesses are correct than one must ask how is that the Jews and Saracens (Arabs) are allies as late as 640 AD, when, according to the Qur'an, Muhammad severed his ties with the Jews as early as 624 AD, more than 15 years earlier?

To answer that we need to refer to the earliest connected account of the career of the 'prophet,' that given in an Armenian chronicle from around 660 AD, which is ascribed by some to Bishop Sebeos (Sebeos 1904:94-96; Crone-Cook 1977:6). The chronicler describes how Muhammad established a community which comprised both Ishmaelites (i.e. Arabs) and Jews, and that their common platform was their common descent from Abraham; the Arabs via Ishmael, and the Jews via Isaac (Sebeos 1904:94-96; Crone-Cook 1977:8; Cook 1983:75). The chronicler believed Muhammad had endowed both communities with a birthright to the Holy Land, while simultaneously providing them with a monotheist genealogy (Crone-Cook 1977:8). This is not without precedent as the idea of an Ishmaelite birthright to the Holy Land was discussed and rejected earlier in the Genesis Rabbah (61:7), in the Babylonian Talmud and in the Book of Jubilees (Crone-Cook 1977:159).

Here we find a number of non-Muslim documentary sources contradicting the Qur'an, maintaining that there was a good relationship between the Arabs and Jews for at least a further 15 years beyond that which the Qur'an asserts.

Hence, Smith, with others, is arguing that the Muslim-Jewish breach was actually much later than claimed by Islamic sources, and thus the traditional presentation is an historical anachronism. He then goes further, examining the work of Wansbrough, which suggests that this was even a politically motivated polemical reconstruction from the ninth century:

...John Wansbrough, from SOAS (University of London)... uses an historical analysis similar to that of biblical criticism to arrive at his conclusions (Wansbrough

1977:9). Wansbrough maintains that the Qur'an, as we know it with all its literal and structural problems, could not have come into existence until 800 A.D. (Wansbrough 1977:160-163). The Qur'an, he suggests, is not a text which was handed to the world via one individual, but involved the work of various writers from about the ninth century (Wansbrough 1977:51).

Wansbrough expands on this claim by maintaining that the entire corpus of early Islamic documentation must be viewed as 'Salvation History', a history which 'is not an historical account of saving events open to the study of the historian, since salvation history did not happen, as it is a literary form which has its own historical context.' (Thompson 1974:328) In other words it was written with an agenda in mind. Thus, literary records of salvation history, although they present themselves as being contemporary with the events they describe, as we have mentioned earlier, actually belong to a period well after such events, which suggests that they have been written according to a later interpretation in order to fit the ethos of that later time. The actual 'history' in the sense of 'what really happened' has, therefore, become subsumed within later interpretation and is virtually, if not completely, inextricable from it (Crone 1987:213-215; Rippin 1985:156).

...Wansbrough contends that the Qur'an, the Tafsir, and Sira are all components of Islamic salvation history, which he suggests were written to point to God's role in directing the worldly affairs of humanity, especially during the time of Muhammad's life (Rippin 1985:154).

He argues that we do not know, and probably will never know what really happened. All we can know is what later people believed happened, as has been recorded in salvation history. The point of Islamic salvation history, he suggests, was to formulate a specifically Arab religious identity. This was accomplished by adopting and adapting ideas and stories from a well-established pool of Judeo-Christian religious themes, the inception of which could then be placed in seventh-century Arabia. Wansbrough refers to evidences within the Qur'an which point to their extrapolation from a Judeo-Christian context: for example, the prophetic line ending in the Seal of the prophets, the sequence of scriptures, the notion of the destroyed communities, and the common narrative motifs (Rippin 1985:157).

Wansbrough's point about 'adapting ideas and stories from a well-established pool of Judeo-Christian religious themes, the inception of which could then be placed in seventh-century Arabia' is vital here, because Arafat makes exactly the same point about the Qurayzah story:

> However, the story, in my view, has its origins in earlier events. It can be shown that it reproduces similar stories which survived from the account of the Jewish rebellion against the Romans, which ended in the destruction of the temple in the year AD. 73, the night of the Jewish zealots and sicarii to the rock fortress of Masada, and the final liquidation of the besieged. Stories of their experience were naturally transmitted by Jewish survivors who fled south. Indeed one of the more plausible theories of the origin of the Jews of Medina is that they came after the Jewish wars. This was the theory preferred by the late Professor Guillaume.
>
> As is well known, the source of the details of the Jewish wars is Flavius Josephus, himself a Jew and a contemporary witness who held office under the Romans, who disapproved of certain actions which some of the rebels committed, but who nevertheless never ceased to be a Jew at heart. It is in his writings that we read of details which are closely similar to those transmitted to us in the Sira about the actions and the resistance of the Jews, except that now we see the responsibility for the actions placed on the Muslims.
>
> In considering details of the story of Banu Qurayza as told by the descendants of that tribe, we may note the following similar details in the account of Josephus:
>
> According to Josephus, Alexander, who ruled in Jerusalem before Herod the Great, hung upon crosses 800 Jewish captives, and slaughtered their wives and children before their eyes?
>
> Similarly, large numbers were killed by others.

Important details of the two stories are remarkably similar, particularly the numbers of those killed. At Masada the number of those who died at the end was 960.35 The hot-headed sicarii who were eventually also killed numbered 600.36 We also read that when they reached the point of despair they were addressed by their leader Eleazar (precisely as Ka'b b. Asad addressed the Banu Qurayza), who suggested to them the killing of their women and children. At the ultimate point of complete despair the plan of killing each other to the last man was proposed.

Clearly the similarity of details is most striking. Not only are the suggestions of mass suicide similar but even the numbers are almost the same. Even the same names occur in both accounts. There is Phineas, and Azar b. Azar, just as Eleazar addressed the Jews besieged in Masada.

There is, indeed, more than a mere similarity. Here we have the prototype - indeed, that would suggest, the origin of the story of Banu Qurayza, preserved by descendants of the Jews who fled south to Arabia after the Jewish Wars, just as Josephus recorded the same story for the Classical world. A later generation of these descendants superimposed details of the siege of Masada on the story of the siege of Banu Qurayza, perhaps by confusing a tradition of their distant past with one from their less remote history. The mixture provided Ibn Ishaq's story. When Muslim historians ignored it or transmitted it without comment or with cold lack of interest, they only expressed lack of enthusiasm for a strange tale, as Ibn Hajar called it.

This escalating adaptation of a prior Jewish tradition is important. If we want to find a parallel with the expulsion of the people of the Book from Arabia, we need only look at the Book of Joshua and the expulsion of the Canaanites. Although the violence is not comparable, the raison d'être has some analogy. The Torah commands the People of God in the Holy Land (though not elsewhere) to and 'break down their altars, and dash in pieces their pillars, and burn their Asherim with fire; and you shall hew down the graven images of their gods; and you shall destroy their name out of that place.' (Deuteronomy 12:3), 'and you shall make no covenant with the inhabitants of this land; you shall break down their altars (Judges 2:2). Similarly, no covenant could exist with the infidels in the new Muslim holy land, so they had to be expelled, although the motives may have been somewhat different, as we shall see. Jay Smith has argued on the basis of archaeological evidence that the change of the Qibla from Jerusalem to Mecca occurred much later than the traditional Muslim historical presentation:

According to the Qur'an, the direction of prayer (the Qibla), was canonized (or finalized) towards Mecca for all Muslims soon after the Hijra. The date 624 A.D. is an educated guess for this occurrance (see Sura 2:144, 149-150).

Yet, the earliest evidence from outside Muslim tradition regarding the direction in which Muslims prayed, and by implication the location of their sanctuary, points to an area much further north than Mecca, in fact somewhere in north-west Arabia (Crone-Cook 1977:23)...

After giving examples from Iraq and Egypt, Smith concludes that the early mosques outside Arabia were still oriented towards Jerusalem:

If you take a map you will find where it is that these mosques were pointing. All four of the above instances position the Qibla not towards Mecca, but much further north, in fact closer to the vicinity of Jerusalem... We find further corroboration for this direction of prayer by the Christian writer and traveller Jacob of Edessa, who, writing as late as 705 A.D. was a contemporary eye-witness in Egypt. He maintained that the Mahgraye in Egypt prayed facing east which was towards the Ka'ba (Crone-Cook 1977:24). His letter (which can be found in the British Museum) is indeed revealing. Writing in Syriac, he refers to the Mahgraye, saying, "So from all this it is clear that it is not to the south that the Jews and the Mahgraye here in the regions of Syria pray, but towards Jerusalem or the Ka'ba, the patriarchal places of their races." (Wright 1870:604)... Both the Jews and Arabs (Mahgraye) maintained a common descent from Abraham who was known to have lived and died in Palestine... This common descent from Abraham is also corroborated by an Armenian

Chronicler as early as 660 A.D. (Sebeos 1904:94-96; Crone-Cook 1977:8; Cook 1983:75)...

Therefore, according to Jacob of Edessa, as late as 705 A.D. the direction of prayer towards Mecca had not yet been canonized.

Smith argues that this demonstrates that Jews and Muslims were still enjoying both good relations and a common sanctuary (and thus a common 'holy land') outside the Arabian Peninsula:

There was still a good relationship between the Muslims (referred to as Haggarenes, Saracens or Mahgrayes) and the Jews, and, consequently, there was no need to change the Qibla (which even the Qur'an admits was originally towards Jerusalem: Sura 2)

The point relevant to our consideration is that if the Qibla has been changed, the identity of 'the holy land' has been changed as well, from Palestine to Arabia, and linked to the breach with the Jews we have just examined; this indicates a later date for the expulsion of the Jews from the Hejaz. The 'ahadith of expulsion' only make any sense on the basis of the special position of Jazirat al-Arabi as the holy land of Islam; after all, the supposed 'idolatrous' practices of Jews and Christians were scarcely limited to the Arabian Peninsula, and neither do the ahadith in question make such a claim. The purported point is that the presence of mushrikun (idolaters/infidels) is inappropriate in the Islamic Holy Land, especially in and around the Qibla. Hence, if the Qibla and the Holy Land remained Jerusalem and Palestine for much longer than is claimed by traditional Muslim history, the likelihood is that the exile of the People of the Book from Arabia was likewise later than is presented in the Islamic sources. Conversely, historical evidence for the presence of the ahl-ul-Kitab two to three centuries after the supposed change of Qibla and exile under 'Umar calls into question the time of the change of Qibla.

Hence, if Palestine remained the Holy Land, and Muslims were still inclined to make use of Jewish traditions, the 'escalating adaptation of a prior Jewish tradition' which we examined becomes relevant for the whole issue about the exile of the Jews and Christians. A Qur'anic passage looks at the history of Bani Israil (note: not the Jews in Medina or the Arabian Peninsula) and states the following:

Surah Al-Maida 5:3030 the (selfish) soul of the other led him to the murder of his brother: he murdered him and became (himself) one of the lost ones. Then Allah sent a raven who scratched the ground to show him how to hide the shame of his brother. "Woe is me!" said he: "Was I not even able to be as this raven and to hide the shame of my brother?" Then he became full of regrets. On that account: We ordained for the Children of Israel that if anyone slew a person unless it be for murder or for spreading mischief in the land it would be as if he slew the whole people: and if anyone saved a life it would be as if he saved the life of the whole people. Then although there came to them our apostles with clear Signs yet even after that many of them continued to commit excesses in the land. The punishment of those who wage war against Allah and His Apostle and strive with might and main for mischief through the land is: execution or crucifixion or the cutting off of hands and feet from opposite sides or exile from the land: that is their disgrace in this world and a heavy punishment is theirs in the Hereafter.

Yusuf Ali comments on this passage as follows:

The story of Cain is referred to in a few graphic details in order to tell the story of Israel. Israel rebelled against Allah, slew and insulted righteous men who did them no harm but on the contrary came in all humility. When Allah withdrew His favour from Israel because of its sins and bestowed it on brother nation, the jealousy of Israel plunged it deeper into sin... For the double crime of treason against the State, combined with treason against Allah, as shown by overt crimes, four alternative punishments are mentioned, any one of which is to be applied according to the crime committed, viz., execution (cutting off of the head), crucifixion, maiming, or exile.

The references to the punishments of 'execution' or 'exile from the land' are related in some way to the prior history of Israel. However, it is significant that no reference is made in the passage to the Jewish tribe's resident in the Hejaz at the time of Muhammad, still less about Christian Arabs such as those at Najran. Yusuf Ali obviously draws lessons from the passage with respect to the behaviour of the Jews of Arabia, but does ascribe the setting of the passage to those Jews and their specific situation. Clearly, though, the fact that Yusuf Ali was able to draw this analogy is significant, and indicates that other Muslims could do likewise. When we relate this to Wansbrough's claims, we see an analogy with his idea of 'salvation history', especially that of 'the notion of the destroyed communities'. Such passages allowed the authors of Hadith and Sira literature to create narrations justifying the exile of the ahl-ul-Kitab. Even then, Sira literature does not present a united front. About Khaybar, Arafat states the following:

Indeed Ibn Kathir takes the trouble to point out that 'Umar expelled only those Jews of Khaybar who had not made a peace agreement with the Prophet. Ibn Kathir then proceeds to explain that at a much later date, i.e. after the year 300 A.H., the Jews of Khaybar claimed that they had in their possession a document allegedly given them by the Prophet which exempted them from poll-tax. He said that some scholars were taken in by this document so that they ruled that the Jews of Khaybar should be exempted. However, that was a forged letter and had been refuted in detail. It quoted persons who were already dead, it used technical terms which came into being at a later time, it claimed that Mu'awiya b. Abi Sufyan witnessed it, when in fact he had not even been converted to Islam at that time, and so on.

This point is crucial with regard to our theme. Arafat quotes ibn Kathir as holding that the Khaybar Jews were still in residence about three hundred years after their supposed general expulsion. The Encyclopaedia of Islam also holds that Jews were still present in Khaybar at this time. If this is the case, the ahadith that claim that all Jews were 'cleansed' from the region at the time of 'Umar are historically inaccurate and represent a politically motivated innovation centuries later. If 'Umar only expelled a minority of Jews lacking a peace treaty with Muhammad, then later regimes and their apologists manufactured these narrations to justify a contemporary policy of sectarian exclusion. Further, we see a common patter – the later 'magnification' of a policy based upon an earlier event - 'Umar expels a few Jews in his time, later regimes expel them all. Moreover, this calls into question the veracity of the supposed narration about 'two religions not co-existing in the Arabian Peninsula', since if 'Umar only expelled those Jews not enjoying dhimmah status, it must mean that either he disobeyed the Prophet's last injunction, or that this supposed imperative did not actually exist. The evidence points to the latter. As we shall see, there is also evidence that the purported evacuation of the Christians from the Arabian Peninsula, especially Najran, bears uncanny resemblance to this historical reconstruction.

MUHAMMAD AND THE CHRISTIANS

THE NAJRAN TREATY

According to Muslim sources, as the power of Islam increased in Arabia, the political entities within the Peninsula, essentially tribal zones or city-states, naturally oriented their foreign policy towards the new power in the region. There is no reason to doubt this, and indeed, it is quite likely that this occurred. One of these entities was Najran, where the majority of the people were Christians, and which was famous for its cathedral-like building. Mawdudi, in his introduction to the surahs in Yusuf Ali's translation, observes that a number of the ayat (verses) of Surah Al-i-Imran, were purportedly revealed to Muhammad at this time: 'The second discourse (vv. 33-63) was revealed in 9 A.H. on the occasion of the visit of the deputation from the Christians of Najran' He repeats this in his commentary.

Like others, he also claims that Najran was fabulously rich, event to the point of being able to raise an army 100,000 strong, which is almost certainly an exaggeration. An entity so rich would be a tempting goal for conquest. Further, if it were somehow allied to the Byzantines, Muhammad would naturally be concerned about having a potential threat as neighbours. On this basis, it can be understood that Najran would be concerned about the intentions of the new Islamic political entity arising in Arabia.

According to Muslim traditional history, concerned both for religious dialogue with a faith professing Abrahamic origins like itself, and also for regular diplomatic relations, a delegation of Najrani Christians visited Muhammad. Yusuf Ali refers to this visit:

In the year of Deputations, 10th of the Hijra, came a Christian embassy from Najran (towards Yaman, about 150 miles north of Sanaa). They were much impressed on hearing this passage of the Qur'an explaining the true position of Christ, and they entered into tributary relations with the new Muslim State. But ingrained habits and customs prevented them from accepting Islam as a body.

The Holy Prophet, firm in his faith, proposed a Mubahala, i.e., a solemn meeting, in which both sides should summon not only their men, but their women and children, earnestly pray to Allah, and invoke the curse of Allah on those who should lie. Those who had a pure and sincere faith would not hesitate. The Christians declined, and they were dismissed in a spirit of tolerance with a promise of protection from the State in return for tribute.

This event is recorded in the Hadith. The latter presents the aim of the visit as an attempt to curse Muhammad, although how any Muslim would know this is not revealed. More likely as an explanation is an attempt by Muslim sources to make the supposed history conform to the Qur'anic reference to cursing. The Sira of Ibn Ishaq states that the group was sixty strong, and included the political leader of Najran, Abdu'l-Masih, an administrator called al-Ayham, and a distinguished bishop-theologian, Abu Haritha. It is claimed that Abu Haritha was funded by the Byzantine Emperor, and the delegation were said to be '...Christians according to the Byzantine rite...'

A modern Christian writer suggests that they were Nestorians.The Syrian Orthodox Church ('Monophysite'), perhaps implausibly, claims they belonged to their confession.

It is much more likely that they were Abyssinian-influenced Monophysites, rather than Chalcedonian Orthodox of Byzantium. The Encyclopaedia of Islam holds that Monophysitism was the dominant sect in Najran. It is not impossible that if the bishop restricted his oversight to the Monophysite Christians of the Arabian Peninsula, he may have had some sort of political arrangement with the Byzantine ruler. Mawdudi, in his introduction to S. 105, refers to Abyssinian-Byzantine collaboration against Dhu Nuwas, the fanatical anti-Christian Jewish King of Yemen, but which implies that the primary religious influence was indeed Abyssinian:

> ... in retaliation for the persecution of the followers of the Prophet Jesus Christ (peace be on him) in Najran by the Jewish ruler Dhu-Nuwas of Yaman, the Christian kingdom of Abyssinia invaded Yaman and put an end to the Himyarite rule there, and in 525 A.D. this whole land passed under Abyssinian control. This happened, in fact, through collaboration between the Byzantine empire of Constantinople and the Abyssinian kingdom, for the Abyssinians at that time had no naval fleet. The fleet was provided by Byzantium and Abyssinia sent 70,000 of its troops by it across the Red Sea to Yaman.

It is interesting in this regard that Yusuf Ali suggests Abyssinia as responsible the origins of Christianity in Najran:

> Yemen had easy access to Mesopotamia and the Persian Gulf by way of the sea, as well as with Abyssinia. That accounts for the Christians of Najran and the Jewish dynasty of kings (e.g. Zu-Nuwas, d. 525 A.D.) who persecuted them in the century before Islam, - also for the Christian Abyssinian Governor Abraha and his discomfiture in the year of the Prophet's birth (S.cv.), say 570 A.D. Jewish-Christian influences were powerful in Arabia in the sixth century of the Christian era.

However, a probable resolution to the problem is that Muslim writers like ibn Hisham and ibn Ishaq, who often found it difficult to distinguish the various Christian sects (as often remains true today), and writing years after the event, were guilty of an inaccurate anachronism. Another unlikely point is Mawdudi's claim, referring to a tradition by Ibn Abbas, that the Christian delegation, like pagan questioners, asked about the 'substance' of Allah, something that Christians, believing in the spirituality of God, were unlikely to raise, and it should be remembered that the delegation included a theologian, raising questions about the historicity of the tradition:

> Ibn Abbas has reported that a deputation of the Christians of Najran along with seven priests visited the Holy Prophet (upon whom be peace), and they said: "O Muhammad, tell us what is your Lord like and of what substance He is made." The Holy Prophet replied: "My Lord is not made from any substance: He is unique and exalted above everything." Thereupon Allah sent down this Surah.

This question is more likely to be the anachronistic reading of a later anti-Trinitarian Muslim polemic than any genuine query. Interestingly, according to the Sira, when the delegation reached Medina, Muhammad allowed them to pray in his mosque. Even today the Saudis forbid non-Muslims access to the Two Holy Cities because of 'Umar's action, yet the latter clearly violate Muhammad's own practice as presented here. This in itself raises questions about the exile. If the issue is that the ahl-ul-Kitab, because of their supposed 'idolatrous' practices, should not be resident in the Holy Land of Islam, especially in the Holy Cities of the Hejaz, why did Muhammad allow such 'idolatrous' practices in his own mosque?

According to ibn Ishaq/ibn Hisham, the Christians informed the Muslims that Jesus was God; the son of God; the third person of the Trinity '...which is the doctrine of Christianity.' Specifically, they argued that Jesus is '...the third of three in that God says: We have done, We have commanded... if He were one he would have said I have done... but He is He and Jesus and Mary.'

The Christian delegation supported their claims by pointing to his miracles. These apparently included making '..Clay birds and breathe into them so that they flew away; and all this was by the command of God Almighty, "We will make him a sign unto men."' The delegation pointed out Jesus had no human father, and that He '...spoke in the cradle...' The text goes on to say that the Qur'an (i.e. Surah 3 Al-i-Imran) came down in answer to these assertions. Muhammad replied by reciting S. 3:64:

Say: "O People of the Book! Come to common terms as between us and you: that we worship none but Allah; that we associate no partners with Him; that we erect not from among ourselves Lords and patrons other than Allah." If then they turn back say: "Bear witness that we (at least) are Muslims (bowing to Allah's will)."

At this point Muhammad proposed, in similar terms to those of Elijah on Mount Carmel, that both sides invoke the curse of God on the other, and the identity of the victim of divine judgement would demonstrate the veracity of the claims of the contesting parties. According to ibn Ishaq, the Christians hesitated at this point, and retired for mutual consultation. The 'Aqib, the Najran political leader, purportedly affirmed that Muhammad was indeed a Prophet and cautioned about the potential consequences of cursing such a divine emissary - namely, the death of the elders and the youth - i.e. the destruction of the society and its people.

How the Muslims would know this is not revealed, still less is it clear how someone writing generations after the event would be aware of it in the absence of any reference in the Qur'an or Hadith. It is often the case that a story loses nothing in the telling, and it is likely this should be understood as an anachronistic reconstruction to serve a contemporary anti-Christian polemic.

There is further evidence of historical anachronism and even fabrication in the Sira material. It is well-known that Christians object to the picture of Jesus and the Trinity in the Qur'an as being unrepresentative of orthodox, Biblical Christianity. The references to 'clay birds' and speaking while still in the cradle are not found in the canonical gospels, a point Yusuf Ali recognises. Rather, the story derives from the apocryphal Gospel of Thomas and the 'cradle' story is taken from the so-called Gospel of the Infancy which itself derives from the Gospel of Thomas:

Gospel of Thomas the Israelite First Greek Form	**Gospel of the Infancy**
And having made some soft clay, He fashioned out of it twelve sparrows... And Jesus clapped His hands, and cried out to the sparrows, and said to them: Off you go! And the sparrows flew, and went off crying. *Gospel of Thomas the Israelite Second Greek Form* And Jesus made of that clay twelve sparrows, and ...looked upon the sparrows, and said: Go away, fly, and live, and remember me. And at this word they flew, and went up into the air...	1. We find (1) what follows in the book of Joseph the high priest, who lived in the time of Christ. Some say that he is Caiaphas. (2) He has said that Jesus spoke, and, indeed, when He was lying in His cradle said to Mary His mother: I am Jesus, the Son of God, the Logos, whom thou hast brought forth, as the Angel Gabriel announced to thee; and my Father has sent me for the salvation of the world. 36. Now, when the Lord Jesus had completed seven years from His birth, on a certain day He was occupied with boys of His own age. For they were playing among clay, from which they were making images of asses, oxen, birds, and other animals; and each one boasting of his skill, was praising his own work. Then the Lord Jesus said to the boys: The images that I have made I will order to walk. The boys asked Him whether then he were the son of the Creator; and the Lord Jesus bade them walk. And they immediately began to leap; and then, when He had given them leave, they again stood still. And He had made figures of birds and sparrows, which flew when He told them to fly, and stood still when He told them to stand, and ate and drank when He handed them food and drink.

GOSPEL OF THOMAS THE ISRAELITE FIRST GREEK FORM GOSPEL OF THE INFANCY

And having made some soft clay, He fashioned out of it twelve sparrows... And Jesus clapped His hands, and cried out to the sparrows, and said to them: Off you go! And the sparrows flew, and went off crying.*Gospel of Thomas the IsraeliteSecond Greek Form*And Jesus made of that clay twelve sparrows, and ...looked upon the sparrows, and said: Go away, fly, and live, and remember me. And at this word they flew, and went up into the air... 1. We find (1) what follows in the book of Joseph the high priest, who lived in the time of Christ. Some say that he is Caiaphas. (2) He has said that Jesus spoke, and, indeed, when He was lying in His cradle said to Mary His mother: I am Jesus, the Son of God, the Logos, whom thou hast brought forth, as the Angel Gabriel announced to thee; and my Father has sent me for the salvation of the world.36. Now, when the Lord Jesus had completed seven years from His birth, on a certain day He was occupied with boys of His own age. For they were playing among clay, from which they were making images of asses, oxen, birds, and other animals; and each one boasting of his skill, was praising his own work. Then the Lord Jesus said to the boys: The images that I have made I will order to walk. The boys asked Him whether then he were the son of the Creator; and the Lord Jesus bade them walk. And they immediately began to leap; and then, when He had given them leave, they again stood still. And He had made figures of birds and sparrows, which flew when He told them to fly, and stood still when He told them to stand, and ate and drank when He handed them food and drink.

Apart from Muslims, few would seriously doubt that these apocryphal pseudo-gospels were the sources for the heterodox Christology of the Qur'an, but many Christians and Orientalists have assumed that Muhammad must have encountered a group of heretical Christians from where he gained these ideas, and because of the Sira and Hadith material, put the blame on the Najran Christians. However, whether the Najran Christians were Byzantine Chalcedonians, Nestorians, or more likely Abyssinian-linked Monophysites, they would not have held to such a Christology. A cursory examination of J.N.D Kelly's Early Christian Doctrines reveals that much of the dispute between these groups was based on semantics, rather than substantial issues. None of them, however, believed that Jesus was the 'third of three', as presented in the Qur'an and Sira. Based on Matthew 28:19, the historic formula has always been that Jesus was the Second Person of the Trinity; still less did they believe in three gods. All groups agreed on the presentation about the Trinity in the Creed of the Council of Nicaea (325):

> We believe in one God, the Father Almighty, maker of all things visible and invisible; and in one Lord Jesus Christ, the Son of God, the only-begotten of his Father, of the substance of the Father, God of God, Light of Light, very God of very God, begotten, not made, being of one substance with the Father. By whom all things were made, both which be in heaven and in earth. Who for us men and for our salvation came down and was incarnate and was made man. He suffered and the third day he rose again, and ascended into heaven. And he shall come again to judge both the living and the dead and in the Holy Spirt.

There is no evidence that Monophysites diverged from this position. In fact the Ethiopian Orthodox Church, whose liturgy remains in its ancient Geez language, asserts its Biblical orthodoxy on the question of the Trinity, and this is important since it is likely that Najran Christians were linked to Abyssinia:

> The formula for the Trinity is this, "Worship we the Father, worship we the Son, worship we the Holy Spirit, three in one and one in three".
>
> God is one in Godhead, Three in Persons, in the name of Father, Son and Holy Spirit. The Holy Trinity has no beginning and will exist for ever without end. In the Trinity there is none that precedes and none that follows; none that is elder and none that is younger, none that is ruler and none that is subject; the Three are One, in all things equal (Jn. 10: 30; 1 Jn. 5: 7.). In nature, in authority, in Lordship, in Godhead, in Divinity, in creating, in saving, in giving, in taking away, in breadth, in fulness, in length, they are one.

The eternal and immutable God has been revealed in three co-eternal Persons. The Father is the first Person, i.e. the first hypostasis of the one God, the Son is the second Person begotten of the only Father, the Spirit is the third hypostasis who proceeds from the only Father whom He has as the cause of his own eternal existence. The Spirit is called

Spirit because he breathes and is moved of the Father and rests in the Son. He is wholly pure, shining, undefiled, holy, purifying and illuminating and sanctifying the other intellectual and spiritual beings. The dogma of the three separate Persons is inseparable from the dogma of the one God. "There are three that bear witness in the Heaven, the Father, the Logos, and the Holy Spirit, and these three agree in one." (1 John 5:7). "The grace of the Lord Jesus Christ, and the love of God and the communion of the Holy Spirit be with you all, Amen", (2 Cor. 13:13).

The position of the Eastern ('Byzantine') Orthodox Church on the Trinity is well-represented by John of Damascus, who engaged in debates with Muslims:

(We believe) in Father and Son and Holy Spirit whereinto also we have been baptized. For so our Lord commanded the Apostles to baptize, saying, baptizing them in the name of the Father, Son, and Holy Spirit. Further we say that each of the three has a perfect subsistence that we may understand not one compound perfect nature made up of three imperfect elements, but one simple essence, surpassing and preceding perfection, existing in three perfect subsistences.

The Greek Orthodox Church presents its position as follows:Still another wrong doctrine is that the Father is one God, the Son is another God, and the Holy Spirit still another God. There cannot be "three gods," says the Church, and certainly not "gods" who are created or made. Still less can there be "three gods" of whom the Father is "higher" and the others "lower." For there to be more than one God, or "degrees of divinity" are both contradictions which cannot be defended, either by divine revelation or by logical thinking?

Thus, the Church teaches that while there is only One God, yet there are three who are God - the Father, the Son, and the Holy Spirit - perfectly united and never divided yet not merged into one with no proper distinction.

As for the so-called Nestorian position, the Assyrian Church of the East makes clear its position by referring to an early Confession of Faith:

Synod of Mar Sabrisho AD 596

It seemed good to his fatherhood and to all the metropolitans and bishops to write this composition of the faith... which accurately and plainly teaches us the confession which is in one glorious nature of the Holy Trinity of Father, Son, and Holy Spirit, ...by which the heathen are conquered who acknowledge a multitude of gods, and Judaism is judged which does not acknowledge a Trinity of qnome, and all heresy is convicted and condemned which denies the Godhead and manhood of our Life-giver, Jesus Christ, accepting it with the exact meaning of the holy fathers, which the illustrious among the orthodox, the blessed Theodore the Antiochian, bishop of the city of Mopsuestia, "the Interpreter of the Divine Scriptures," explained, with which all the orthodox in all regions have agreed and do agree, as also all the venerable fathers who have governed this apostolic and patriarchal see of our administration have held, while we anathematize and alienate from all contact with us everyone who denies the nature of the Godhead and the nature of the manhood of our Lord Jesus Christ, whether through mixture and commingling, or compounding or confusing, introducing, with regard to the union of the Son of God ...He is, in his eternal Godhead and in his manhood from Mary, one true Son of God...

Hence, the Christological/Theological presentation of Christian doctrine in ibn Ishaq/ibn Hisham cannot have originated either with 'Byzantine', Monophysite or Nestorian Christians. None would have presented Jesus as 'third of three' whether in terms of the Biblical Trinity or in the Qur'anic misconception of three gods. Neither would they have presented the Trinity implied by ibn Ishaq/ibn Hisham, God, Mary and Jesus (presenting the Trinity in this way would explain Jesus being portrayed as 'third of three'); they clearly would have believed in a Trinity of Father, Son and Spirit. Nor is there any evidence in either the canonical gospels or even in the pseudo-gospels of Thomas and Infancy for the reference to the use of the first person plural by God, and also absent is any reference to God making Jesus a 'sign unto men'.

Moreover, it can be seen from the quotes given from the three Eastern Orthodox strands we have examined that they all used essentially the same canon as the Church in the West. One of the greatest academic Biblical scholars of the modern era was Professor F. F. Bruce of Manchester University, among whose many works was one entitled The Canon of Scripture.

He notes that by 508 A.D. the Syrian Jacobite (Monophysite) Church held the same canon as found in the West, whilst the Nestorians accepted a canon of only twenty-two books. The Greek Orthodox Church accepts all twenty-seven books. The Ethiopian Orthodox canon is slightly different, accepting the same canon as the wider Church plus eight books addressing Church order. However – and this point is crucial – no canon whatsoever includes either the pseudo-gospel of Thomas or that of the Infancy, nor any supposed 'gospel' teaching these ideas. This being the case, the Najran delegation, whether they were indeed 'Byzantine-rite', Monophysites or Nestorians, could not have quoted the material about 'clay birds' and Jesus 'speaking in the cradle', since the material appears in literature regarded by all as non-canonical. The heterodox Trinitarian/Christological picture that ibn Ishaq/ ibn Hisham records as presented by the Najran Christians to Muhammad cannot be genuine, which means the incident itself – or at least the particulars presented in the Sira – cannot be authentic.

The Sira material is therefore unreliable and unsound – to put it in Muslim terms, it is not sahih. From whence then did ibn Ishaq/ibn Hisham derive this story? It is noteworthy that it is not even present in the Hadith. Rather than speculating about the possible existence of supposed heretical Christians using apocryphal gospels, the obvious place to look for the origin of this material is the very source ibn Ishaq/ibn Hisham and Muslims of the period would want to defend – the Qur'an. In other words, we must reverse ibn Ishaq's picture; rather than the verses in Al-i-Imran descending at the time of the Najran visit to answer Christian apologetic, the Sira of ibn Ishaq/ibn Hisham has invented a myth of Christians upholding the heterodox Christology that the Qur'an attacks, in order to justify the Qur'an's polemic against such teaching, and protect the Qur'an from accusations of inaccuracy, which undermined its claim to be divine revelation. We can establish this by examining relevant Qur'anic material.

For example, the reference to Jesus being '...the third of three' is found in Surah 5:73. Maida 'They surely disbelieve who say: Lo! Allah is the third of three; when there is no God save the One God.' Even the comments about Jesus being God and the son of God should be understood, not as in their Biblical concepts, but rather as the Qur'an understands those terms – that God could be 'lowered' by being metamorphosed into a man, and that God could have physical offspring, and in the words of Watt, that '...Jesus is a deity apart from God...' . For example, Surah Maida 5:17 states 'In blasphemy indeed are those that say that Allah is Christ the son of Mary'. Again, Watt comments that 'What is denied here is the assertion of complete identity between Jesus and God... generally regarded as the heresy of confusing the hypostases.' Surah. Maryam 19:88ff states 'They say: "(Allah) Most Gracious has begotten a son!" ... For it is not consonant with the majesty of (Allah) Most Gracious that He should beget a son.' Surah Tauba 9:30 '...the Christians call Christ the son of Allah. ...Allah's curse be on them: how they are deluded away from the truth! 9:31 They take their priests and their anchorites to be their lords in derogation of Allah and (they take as their Lord) Christ the son of Mary; Yet they were commanded to worship but one Allah: there is no god but He. Praise and glory to him: (far is He) from having the parents they associate (with him).' Watt comments:

In the light of the Qur'anic attack on tritheism, it seems certain that the denial that the Messiah was the son of God was a denial that he was a deity separate from God; and this is confirmed by the later part of 9:30 which identifies what is denied with the views of 'former unbelievers'... that is presumably of the pagans.

The use of the first person plural for God and of Jesus being made a 'sign' is found in Surah 23 Al-Muminun 50 – 'And We made the son of Mary and his mother as a Sign'. The claim that Jesus spoke in the cradle is present in Surah 19 Maryam 29 But she pointed to the babe. They said: "How can we talk to one who is a child in the cradle?" S. Ali-i-Imran 3:46 'He will speak unto mankind in his cradle...' The reference to clay birds is discovered in Surah Al-i-Imran 3:45ff: '"He shall speak to the people in childhood... I make for you out of clay as it were the figure of a bird and breathe into it and it becomes a bird by Allah's leave' The same text also deals with the issue of Christ performing miracles by 'the command of God'. Verse 59 addresses the point about Jesus having no human father 'This similitude of Jesus before Allah is as that of Adam: He created him from dust then said to him: "Be" and he was.' Yusuf Ali comments in this regard:

After a description of the high position which Jesus occupies as a prophet, we have a repudiation of the dogma that he was Allah, or the son of Allah, or anything more than a man. If it is said that he was born without a human father, Adam was also so born. Indeed Adam was born without either a human father or mother. As far as our physical bodies are concerned they are mere dust. In Allah's sight Jesus was as dust just as Adam was or humanity is. The greatness of Jesus arose from the divine command "Be": for after that he was-more than dust - a great Prophet and teacher. (3.59)

It can be seen that ibn Ishaq/ibn Hisham have placed the Christology attacked in the Qur'an into the mouths of the Najran Deputation. The question is why? The answer to this is essential for understanding the actual reason for the expulsion of the ahl-ul-Kitab from the Jazirat-al-Arabi, and also its genuine dating. According to the picture presented by the revisionist school of Islamic origins as represented by people such as Cook, Crone and Wansbrough, etc., Islam did not really emerge as the settled religious entity we now understand until about two centuries after the death of Muhammad. Jay Smith

The sources also seem to suggest that the Qur'an was put together rather hurriedly "the book is strikingly lacking in overall structure, frequently obscure and inconsequential in both language and content, perfunctory in its linking of disparate materials, and given to the repetition of whole passages in variant versions. On this basis it can plausibly be argued that the book is the product of the belated and imperfect editing of materials from a plurality of traditions." (Quoted in Hagarism, Crone-Cook 1977:18,167) Thus Crone and Cook believe that because of the imperfection of the editing, the emergence of the Qur'an must have been a sudden and late event (Crone-Cook 1977:18,167).

As to when that event took place we are not altogether sure, but we can make an educated guess. From the earlier discussion concerning the dating of the earliest manuscripts we can conclude that there was no Qur'anic documentation in existence in the mid-late seventh century. The earliest reference from outside Islamic literary traditions to the book called the 'Qur'an' occurs in the mid-eighth century between an Arab and a monk of Bet Hale (Nau 1915:6f), but no-one knows whether it may have differed considerably in content from the Qur'an which we have today. Both Crone and Cook conclude that except for this small reference there is no indication of the existence of the Qur'an before the end of the seventh century (Crone-Cook 1977:18).

Crone and Cook in their research go on to maintain that it was under the governor Hajjaj of Iraq in 705 A.D. that we have a logical historical context in which the 'Qur'an' (or a nascent body of literature which would later become the Qur'an) was first compiled as Muhammad's scripture (Crone-Cook 1977:18). In an account attributed to Leo by Levond, the governor Hajjaj is shown to have collected all the old Hagarene writings and replaced them with others 'according to his own taste, and disseminated them everywhere among [his] nation.' (Jeffrey 1944:298) The natural conclusion is that it was during this period that the Qur'an began its evolution, possibly beginning to be written down, until it was finally canonized in the mid to late eighth century as the Qur'an which we now know.

Smith points out this late dating are also true of other source material for Islam:

1. The Sira are accounts concerning the traditional life of the prophet (including his battles). The most comprehensive Sira was written by Ibn Ishaq (died 765 A.D.), though none of his manuscripts exist today. Consequently, we are dependent on the Sira of Ibn Hisham (died 833 A.D.), which was supposedly taken from that of Ibn Ishaq, though, by his own admission (according to the research of Patricia Crone) he omitted those areas which might have caused offense (such as anything which he felt was repugnant, poems not attested elsewhere, as well as matters which he could not accept as trustworthy) (Crone 1980:6).
2. The Hadith are thousands of short reports or narratives (akhbar) on the sayings and deeds of the prophet which were collected by Muslims in the ninth and tenth centuries. Of the six most famous collections of Hadith, those of al-Bukhari (died 870 A.D.) are considered by many Muslims as the most authoritative.
3. The Ta'rikh are histories or chronologies of the prophet's life, the most famous written by al-Tabari (died 923 A.D.) early in the tenth century.
4. The Tafsir are commentaries and exegesis on the Qur'an, its grammar and its context; the best known also written by al-Tabari (died 923 A.D.).

It can be seen that the dating for all these sources is quite late, and very late in some cases. This being so, we cannot rely on any of them for concrete evidence in regard to historical events in the early years of Islam, a point to which we will return later, but that is not our primary concern at this juncture. The point to make is to examine what occurred after the conquest of the Levant and Iraq, and later Egypt. The Arabs came into contact with more advanced cultures which were predominantly Christian. Although the Qur'an was not yet codified, the 'Hagarenes' would have brought certain religious traditions with them which found their way into their later holy scripture. Among these were several assertions about Jews and Christians. These are the same issues which have proved embarrassing to Muslims today – the idea that Jews hold that Ezra was the son of God, that Mary was the sister of Aaron, and the very points about Christian doctrine we have examined – such as Jesus creating clay birds, and the Trinity being God, Mary and Jesus. Watt notes in connection with the traditional Muslim charge of tahrif, 'corruption', against the Bible, that the idea does not occur in the Qur'an itself, but 'after the conquest of Iraq, Syria and Egypt, however, the doctrine of tahrif, of "corruption" was elaborated in various ways to give the Muslim Arabs a defence against the better-educated Christians with whom they were now mixing.'

Once the Arabs began to be literate, and especially after they began to proselytise, these gaffes became obvious obstacles, both to the consolidation of the Ummah and the conversion of the Christian masses. After all, the Christians would immediately object that Islam's presentation of Christian doctrine was not commensurate with the facts, and if this was the case, it naturally followed that the Qur'an could not be a genuine divine revelation. Hence, the Muslims were faced with a major problem – how to explain away these problems? The most obvious way was to assert that the Qur'an was responding to what Christians who encountered Muhammad presented as Christian doctrine, and this is what ibn Ishaq/ibn Hisham did – to argue that, at least as far as the Najran delegation were concerned, these ideas were indeed genuine Christian dogmas. Hence, it would not matter what Christians elsewhere objected.

This would not only answer the Christians, but also any Muslim troubled by Christian objections to the Qur'anic depiction of Christian doctrine. The cat is somewhat let out of the bag by the Sira's 'report' of the Najran Christians asserting that Christ is Allah, 'the third of three', and then stating the redundant (and false) comment 'which is the doctrine of Christianity'. The Sira adds this point because it is patently untrue – such a Christology was not 'the doctrine of Christianity', as the Christians of Syria and Iraq would have emphasised. In this respect, Sira material such as that of ibn Ishaq/ibn Hisham is not history, but rather propaganda, seeking to defend Islam against Christian detractors and Muslim doubters, whose concerns could have been raised by the Christians emphasising that the Qur'an's presentation of Christian Trinitarianism and Christology was inaccurate.

In this respect, the Sira material was a product of its time. It is well-known that at the time of Bukhari there were literally thousands of false ahadith, and that he sifted through 600,000 of them, reducing them to about 7000, many of these parallel narrations, reducing the actual number to about 3000. Hence, fabricated historical records of the Prophet and his Companions were a feature of the era, the same epoch in which, according to the revisionist school, Islam actually became established as a settled religious system. Many of these narrations served a definite polemical purpose, and not always against Jews and Christians. For example, the Sunni-Shi'ite breach partly revolves around competing claims about the Qur'an and Hadith. The Shi'ite Encyclopedia states the following about their difference with the Sunnis:

"We say that so much of revelation has come down which is not embodied in the present Quran that if it were to be collected, its extent would undoubtedly be 17000 verses ... Although all of them were revelation but they (the extra ones) are not a part of Quran. If they would be a part of Quran, it would surely have been included in the Quran we have." Shi'i reference: Shi'ite Creed (al-I'tiqadat al-Imamiyyah), by Shaykh Saduq, English version, pp 78-79.

The transcript of the Quran that Imam Ali wrote contained commentary and hermeneutic interpretation (Tafsir and Ta'wil) from the Holy Prophet some of which had been sent down as revelation but NOT as a part of the text of Quran. A small amount of such texts can be found in some traditions in Usul al-Kafi and else. These pieces of information were Divine commentary of the text of Quran which was revealed along with Quranic verses but were NOT parts of Quran. Thus the commentary verses and Quranic verses could sum up to 17000 verses. As Sunnis know, Hadith Qudsi is also revelation, but they are not a part of Quran.

Hence, the Shi'ite position is that there was extra divine revelation apart from the Qur'an, and this remains a major distinction from the Sunnis, since the Shi'ite Hadith collections are believed to derive from this literature, via their Twelve Imams. Thus, the Sunnis and Shi'ites do not have an identical Hadith corpus, which in itself raises questions about the reliability of such material. A clear example of a polemical Sunni hadith, in which the narration is actually placed on the lips of Ali, revered as the first Imam by Shi'ites, denies the existence of this special addition to the Qur'an:

Sahih Al-Bukhari Hadith 4.283- Narrated by Abu Juhaifa

I asked Ali, "Do you have the knowledge of any Divine Inspiration besides what is in Allah's Book?" 'Ali replied, "No ...I don't think we have such knowledge, but we have the ability of understanding which Allah may endow a person with, so that he may understand the Qur'an, and we have what is written in this paper as well." I asked, "What is written in this paper?" He replied, "(The regulations of) blood-money, the freeing of captives, and the judgment that no Muslim should be killed for killing an infidel."

A similar idea is put forward in another narration:

Sahih Al-Bukhari Hadith 8.747- Narrated by Ali

We have no Book to recite except the Book of Allah (Qur'an) and this paper. Then 'Ali took out the paper, and behold! There was written in it, legal verdicts about the retaliation for wounds, the ages of the camels (to be paid as Zakat or as blood money). In it was also written: -Medina is a sanctuary from Air (mountain) to Thaur (mountain)..."

However, another narration presents a similar notion about literature apart from the Qur'an but does not mention Ali:

Sahih Al-Bukhari Hadith 6.537- Narrated by Abdul Aziz in Rufai Shaddad bin Ma'qil and I entered upon Ibn 'Abbas. Shaddad bin Ma'qil asked him, "Did the Prophet leave anything (besides the Qur'an)?" He replied. "He did not leave anything except what is between the two bindings (of the Qur'an)." Then we visited Muhammad bin Al-Hanafiyya and asked him (the same question). He replied, "The Prophet did not leave except what is between the bindings (of the Qur'an)."

It can be seen, not least from the divergence within these narrations, that the Sunni ahadith served a polemical, propagandistic purpose. The aim was to refute Shi'ite theology, and accusations against Sunni distinctives, and for this purpose, 'history' was reconstructed, a 'history' that obviously the Shi'ites could not accept, anymore than Sunnis could accept Shi'ite narrations which undermined Sunni distinctives. If this occurred within Islam, we should not be surprised that the more substantial objections of Jews and especially Christians demanded similar and even more far-reaching historical reconstruction. This can be seen in various narrations. For example, one hadith, regarded as sahih, insists that Jews do indeed regard Ezra as the son of Allah, as do Christians with regard to Jesus, according to the Muslim idea of what is involved in divine sonship. [89] More substantially, the famous gaffe about Mary being the 'sister' of Aaron is anachronistically placed on the lips of Muhammad specifically in answer to the query of Najran Christians:

Sahih Muslim Hadith 5326- Narrated by Mughirah ibn Shu'bah

When I came to Najran, they (the Christians of Najran) asked me: You read "O sister of Harun" (i.e. Maryam) in the Qur'an, whereas Moses was born much before Jesus. When I came back to Allah's Messenger (peace be upon him) I asked him about that, whereupon he said: The (people of the old age) used to give names (to their persons) after the names of Apostle and pious persons who had gone before them.

Clearly, the answer given is not supported by either the Bible or by Hebrew history in general, a point that would have been made by both Jews and especially Christians, the biggest community in the conquered territories of the Fertile Crescent and North Africa. It is significant that the answer is supposedly given in response to the question of the Christians of Najran, as we shall see. Essentially, what we witness in the Sira and Hadith literature is a polemical creation of national myth. Many nations possess such myths, seeing their origins often in some special divine act. Even when religion is absent, national mythologies abound, and in many cases, conscious fabrication is a feature. We need only consider Stalin's famous fabricated photographs, removing Bolshevik rivals like Trotsky from revolutionary prints and thereafter doctoring the history of the Russian Revolution to enhance Stalin's rather secondary role therein. After all, this is the mutual accusation Sunnis and Shi'ites hurl against each other in regard to both Hadith and Sira, especially with respect to the succession to Muhammad. Shi'ites hold it should have gone to Ali, as, they believe, divinely revealed to Muhammad, whereas it actually went to Abu Bakr, and Sunni ahadith attempt to present history in accord with their distinctives. For example, the following narration, supposedly from Ali himself, the hero of the Shi'ites, presents Muhammad as indicating that it was unlikely that Ali would be appointed by the people as Amir:

AL-TIRMIDHI HADITH 6124- NARRATED BY ALI IBN ABUTALIB

When Allah's Messenger (peace be upon him) was asked whom they should appoint commander after he had gone, he replied, "If you appoint AbuBakr as commander you will find him trustworthy, with little desire for worldly goods but eager for the next world; if you appoint Umar as commander you will find him trustworthy and strong, fearing for Allah's sake no one's blame; and if you appoint Ali as commander, but I cannot see you doing so, you will find him a guide who is rightly guided who will lead you in the straight way."

Ahmad transmitted it.

This is clearly an anachronistic narration from a later time, serving an anti-Shi'ite polemic. These examples demonstrate that the historical picture presented by the Hadith literature is essentially subjective propaganda serving a political / theological polemical purpose, and thus unreliable as an historical source. This can also be seen in Sira and Hadith material emphasising the prophethood of Muhammad observable from an early age. According to Islamic history, Muhammad as a child once accompanied his Uncle Abu Talib and grandfather during a trading journey to the Syrian town of Bostra. This was an important Christian centre, being the official residence of the Bishop of the Monophysite Christians, and possessing a Cathedral. The caravan passed the cell of a hermit monk called Bahira who usually paid such caravans no attention.

However, on this occasion he invited the party to a meal. They left the camels in the care of the youngest member of the group, but then Bahira demanded the attendance of everyone in the party. According to the story, Bahira possessed an ancient book predicting the advent of a great prophet. It was supernaturally revealed to him that this person was in the caravan, seeing a cloud and a tree protecting him from the glaring sun. When the boy was brought to him, he saw a mark between his shoulders, a definite sign of prophethood. Of course, the boy was Muhammad. The monk warned Abu Talib to take special care of him since the Jews would seek to harm him. Sira material, such as that dealing with the Companions, refers to this monk. There is also a narration in the Hadith. However, despite a feeble attempt by Yusuf Ali to relate S. 10:94 to the incident, there is nothing about this supposed grand supernatural event in the Qur'an, an incredible omission. Neither are we are informed as to the identity of this 'ancient book' Bahira possessed.

As to the cause of the invention of the story, there is an obvious and ironic parallel in the 'childhood miracle' stories about Jesus found in Thomas and Infancy. However, there is a deeper, theological/political reason for its genesis. The Qur'an, as it is well known, claims that the advent of Muhammad was predicted in the Torah and the Gospel. Obviously, this was not the case. There is nothing in Biblical Eschatology to suggest the advent of a new prophet, and it is clear from what we have examined about the canon of Scripture that the latter was considered firmly closed by the time of Muhammad. Therefore, especially after the Muslim conquests of Christian lands like Iraq and Syria, it was important for Muslims to demonstrate that some Christians at least, perhaps from some ancient literature now lost, were looking for a new prophet. A comment from von Denffer helps to demonstrate this:

...some sort of authentication of the future prophet's message is here given by a Christian authority in religious matters... this episode lends support to the view that some earlier Christians understood the role and message of Muhammad differently from their contemporaries... This view is also met with in the Qur'an...

The narration also betrays its polemical nature by its reference to the Jewish opposition to Muhammad. Interestingly, von Denffer indicates some reserve in his regard of the story's authenticity. We should also view the story of Waraqa, the Christian relative of Khadijah, who, according to the Muslim tradition, translated the gospels and authenticated the prophethood of Muhammad, again a story found in the Sira and Hadith. Again, we find an example of a vaticinia ex eventu (prophecy after the event), in this case predicting the effective exile of Muhammad from his home. von Denffer repeats the important aspect of this story: 'Once again a learned Christian recognizes the prophet in Muhammad and gives some kind of authentication on the basis of the previously-revealed scriptures.' Another link in the chain is found in the treatment of the Messages to the Rulers, 628-9, found in the Sira and Hadith.

This story betrays an anachronism even by traditional Muslim dating, since Muslim scholars such as Mawdudi and von Denffer hold that verses 33-120 of Al-i-Imran were revealed at the time of the Najran delegation in 631, yet the letter to the Byzantine Emperor Heraclius, sent two or three years previously, actually quotes from these verses! This demonstrates yet again why the traditional sources are unreliable. Both the Sira and Hadith implausibly imply that Heraclius was inclined to accept Islam, but held back because of public opposition, which would have course have cost him his throne, and with it power and luxury. von Denffer notes an even more unlikely story, from ibn Hisham that one Byzantine bishop who actually 'pleaded for accepting Muhammad as the expected prophet, was beaten to death.' It is noteworthy that both these stories are absent from the Qur'an, and there seems to be no objective historical evidence for them. We find similar implications in the story of the letter to the Coptic leader. In this respect, the story of the Najran delegation is the last link in the chain. As can be seen from Bukhari 5:663, there is the implication that one of the delegation may have recognised Muhammad as a prophet, and ibn Ishaq/ibn Hisham present the bishop confiding his belief in Muhammad's prophethood to a colleague who later became a Muslim:

> Abu Haritha's mule stumbled and Kùz said, 'May So-and-so stumble [i.e. Curse him!], meaning the apostle. Abu Haritha said 'Nay but may you stumble.' 'But why, brother?' he asked. 'Because by God he is the prophet we have been waiting for.' Kùz said, 'Then if you know that, what stops you from accepting him?' He replied, 'The way these people have treated us. They have given us titles, paid us subsidies, and honoured us. But they are absolutely opposed to him, and if I were to accept him they would take from us all that you see.' Kùz pondered over the matter until later he adopted Islam, and used to tell this story, so I have heard.

In other words, love of position and luxury, rather than genuine conviction, prevented the bishop from converting, as with Heraclius. The origin of this story should be found in the accusation in the Qur'an, Surah Tauba 9:34, against priests and monks that they are financially avaricious. Again, the Qur'an was validated by a story which presents the priests as possessing the character of which the Qur'an accuses them. Similarly, we should read these texts in the light of the situation the Arabs faced in the conquered lands; they had to prove that the Christians were indeed expecting another prophet, and the objections of Christian leaders to this were met in part by accusing them of ulterior motives for rejecting the prophethood of Muhammad. It is perhaps in this light we should understand the narrations about Najran needing an 'honest man'. von Denffer refers to ibn Hisham, and states that 'there were certain financial matters in dispute among the people from Najran, and they therefore wanted the prophet to nominate a trustworthy person as arbitrator for them.' This should perhaps be linked to the narration forbidding the Najran Christians from charging usury. The message of the Qur'an, Hadith and Sira is the same – the Christian leaders are dishonest, and thus should not be believed, the Muslims are honest, and are reliable, and therefore so is their message. Essentially, this is a polemical message to potential Muslim doubters and to Christian objectors.

This issue of deceit is further emphasised with regard to the Najran delegation. von Denffer also quotes the Muslim commentator Nisaburi, who presents Muhammad as urging the Najran monks 'Surrender (to Islam)!', to which they reply that they have surrendered. Muhammad accuses them of lying, on the basis of their 'calling Allah a son, your worshipping the cross, and your eating pork.' They then argue about Christological matters, with Muhammad pointing to human characteristics of Jesus, which silence the Christians, surely a most unlikely event, and at this point the verses from Al-i-Imran are revealed. Another commentary from Nisaburi substitutes 'drinking wine' for 'eating pork'. Again, these are actually words from the Qur'an, from the text which supposedly came into existence with respect to the Najran visit, and which is here anachronistically placed on the lips of the Najran Christians to serve a polemical purpose:

Surah Al-i'Imran

19 Lo! Religion with Allah (is) The Surrender (to His will and guidance). Those who (formerly) received the Scripture differed only after knowledge came unto them, through transgression among themselves. Whoso disbelieveth the revelations of Allah (will find that) Lo! Allah is swift at reckoning.

20 And if they argue with thee, (O Muhammad), say: I have surrendered my purpose to Allah and (so have) those who follow me. And say unto those who have received the Scripture and those who read not: Have ye (too) surrendered? If they surrender, then truly they are rightly guided, and if they turn away, then it is thy duty only to convey the message (unto them). Allah is Seer of (His) bondmen. (Pickthall Translation) Hence, when we come to consider ahadith relating to the exclusion of the People of the Book from Arabia, we cannot regard such traditions as possessing historical credence. Rather, they serve a political/propaganda purpose, reminding us of Wansbrough's assertion that the literary authorities and traditions of Islam were created years after their supposed time-setting to serve a contemporary agenda. This is not simply true of the Hadith; it is also true of the Sira. Even Watt, considering the issue of conversion to Islam,

mentions that the Sira of ibn Hisham contains some stories of such, 'but these, even though true in general, may have had details modified to bring them into line with later ideas.' This is, we suggest, what has occurred with the Sira's treatment of the Najran deputation. Jay Smith, in an article examining biographies of Muhammad, notes the late dating of source material:

The majority of these titles no doubt, especially those written by Muslims, will reiterate much of the material passed down through the centuries about Muhammad, which had their "origins" in the classical period of Islam; between 750-950 A.D. (the approximate dates attributed to the four genres of compilations concerning the prophet's life and teachings, compiled by notable individuals such as Ibn Ishaq=d.765, Ibn Hisham=d.833, al-Bukhari=d.870, and al-Tabari=d.923).

Yet because of their late dates, there is a growing concern in the West that much of the data which we possess on the life of Muhammad is perhaps erroneous, or has at least been embellished (Cook 1983:63). There simply are no documents which were written from the period of the prophet himself with which we can corroborate the historicity of the classical compilations. In fact the "oldest texts we have concerning the life of the Prophet go back to about 125 years after his death" (Rodinson 1996: xi).

Smith later examines Rodinson's approach to historical sources about Muhammad:

Of concern to him was what actually happened, rather than what the later compilers would like us to believe happened. He made it quite plain in his foreword that the biography of Muhammad would always be built on speculation, that the information we possessed on Muhammad "are far from being certain historical fact...that there is nothing of which we can say for certain that it incontestably dates back to the time of the Prophet" (Rodinson 1996:xi). And so, to accentuate this concern Rodinson would commence almost every story with phrases like, "seemingly," or "it was said," or "as was recounted later," and so on (Rodinson 1996: xii).

Having recognised the unreliability of Hadith and Sira material, we can approach the story of the Najran delegation with proper scepticism. According to the traditional presentation, the following hadith established the nature of the political relationship of the Najran Christians to Muhammad:

Abdullah ibn Abbas Abu dawud 3035

The Apostle of Allah (peace be upon him) concluded peace with the people of Najran on condition that they would pay to Muslims two thousand suits of garments, half of Safar, and the rest in Rajab, and they would lend (Muslims) thirty coats of mail, thirty horses, thirty camels, and thirty weapons of each type used in battle. Muslims will stand surely for them until they return them in case there is any plot or treachery in the Yemen. No church of theirs will be demolished and no clergyman of theirs will be turned out. There will be no interruption in their religion until they bring something new or take usury. Isma'il said: They took usury. The full text of this treaty assures the Najran Christians of their lives, properties, lands, creed, etc. No hardships or humiliation shall be imposed on them nor shall their land be occupied by [our] army...there will be no oppressors or oppressed. Those who practice usury shall seek no protection from me. No one shall be taken as responsible for the fault of another.

A Muslim site presents the story as follows, although one should question whether in fact the leader of the Najran Christians actually described himself as 'Pope', in the absolute sense that later characterised the leader of the Copts and Roman Catholics: ...The letter that the Prophet ...wrote to the Pope of Najran, Abul Harith, clearly outlines the contours of Christian religious freedom. ...The Prophet's letter to the Pope of Najran stated: "In the name of Allah Most Gracious, Most Merciful". From Muhammad ...the Apostle of Allah to the Pope of Najran and other Bishops, "Be it known to the Pope and other Christian elders that to run the administration of the Churches is their own responsibility; Allah and his Apostle bestow kindness to these people. Through this letter the Apostle of Allah announces that no bishop or religious head would not be removed from his status, nor would his powers be curtailed. In addition, no interference would be made in their religious rites as long as the scholars of Christianity would execute their religious obligations with honesty and devotion, their dignity would be preserved, and they (the Christians) as well should not raise difficulties for others". ...In the Ninth Hijrah year, a party representing the Christians of Najran reached Medina to meet the Prophet... This delegation included the leading people of Christianity. It included among the notables Pope of Najran - Abul Harith, the Bishop Abdul Maseih the leader of the party Ileahm...

Khadduri's version of the text guarantees protection until the Najran Christians breach the terms '...by giving support to oppression' (the nature of which is undefined). Watt's version states that the first reference to usury is associated with blood-revenge and concerns the pre-Islamic period. This indicates that Muhammad was cancelling debts that led to strife. The next reference to usury clearly concerns individuals, who violate the treaty, and should any do so; the dhimmah (protection) of the Prophet is withdrawn from that particular person. In other words, the offending individual becomes liable to punishment. It should be noted that Muhammad's farewell sermon made similar points. von Denffer comments on the treaty 'In the time of 'Umar the people of Najran started charging interest, which, according to ibn Sa'd, gave 'Umar the right to expel them...' On this basis, it is obvious that the purported statement of Ismail concerning usury was a later gloss, even by traditional standards. If the Najran Christians only violated the treaty during the reign of 'Umar (634-644), the alleged comment of Ismail could only have come years after the treaty, so either this tradition is composite, or it is totally anachronistic. Most likely, this accusation was invented to justify the policy of exile, and it is noteworthy that the hadith is found in Abu Dawud, a less reliable corpus even by Islamic standards, and one of the latest at that. Moreover, it is found nowhere else.

In fact, it can be seen that the purported historical accounts are mutually contradictory on several counts. The hadith claims the Najran Christians were expelled because they violated the prohibition on usury. In fact, the Abu Dawud text is even self-contradictory, since it affirms that the Najran Christians were given a compact of security dependent upon tribute, essentially in the sense of military aid. This in itself makes it likely that the reference to usury is an interpolation. The second text does not make usury the basis of transgression, but rather 'oppression'. The final text simply insists upon 'honesty and devotion' and respect for others. The various texts about the sectarian cleansing by Umar justify the exclusion not because of transgression of any kind but simply because the Prophet ordered the expulsion on the grounds of their faith. In other words, the command was absolute, rather than conditional, yet the reference to usury implies that the fate of the Najran Christians was indeed conditional. The three positions cannot be reconciled.

THE CONSEQUENCE OF THE TABUK EXPEDITION

After performing the final pilgrimage, Muhammad purposed to attack the Byzantine Empire. Watt holds that it was probably after the conquest of Mecca at the beginning of 630 and especially after the expedition to Tabuk towards the end of that year that Muhammad recognised that he would face military opposition from the Christian tribes on the periphery of the Byzantine Empire. He claims that at the time of Tabuk expedition the 'sword verse' concerning the killing of infidels, the original reference being to Jews and Pagans, was expanded to include the Christians, clearly an explicit reference to the Byzantines and the satellite entities on the periphery:

Surah 9. Tauba

Fight those who believe not in Allah or the Last Day nor hold that forbidden which hath been forbidden by Allah and His apostle nor acknowledge the religion of truth (even if they are) of the People of the Book until they pay the Jizya with willing submission and feel themselves subdued. The subsequent verse explicitly includes Christians in its denunciation: The Jews call Uzair a son of Allah and the Christians call Christ the son of Allah. That is a saying from their mouths; (in this) they but imitate what the unbelievers of old used to say. Allah's curse be on them: how they are deluded away from the truth! This verse is interesting as much for what it does not say as what it does enjoin. Although ordering war against the People of the Book unless they pay Jizya, it nowhere demands their exile. Likewise, although it imprecates a curse on the ahl-ul-Kitab, it is not for turning the graves of the prophets into places of worship, but for holding to the divine sonship of respectively, Ezra and Christ, however misconceived the Qur'anic notion may be. At the time of the Tabuk expedition against the Byzantines a similar arrangement to that imposed upon the Christian state of Najran was made with the Christian kingdom of Aila (modern Aqaba in Jordan), after Muhammad wrote them an invitation to accept Islam or pay the Jizya, and pledging their security. Similar pacts were made with Jewish communities in the region. Likewise, the pact with the Zoroastrian entity of Bahrain, the dhimmah extended to them assumes some people will retain their old religion, whether they are Jews or 'Magians' (Zoroastrians), and those choosing to do so will pay the Jizya tax. The timing of the pact with Aila is important for our theme, for it was after the Tabuk expedition against the Byzantine Christians that Muhammad is held to have made the statement of expulsion, as found in parallel ahadith:

Sahih Muslim Hadith 4366	**Al-Muwatta Ha Hadith 4**
Narrated by Umar ibn Khattab Umar heard the Messenger Allah (peace be upon him) sa will expel the Jews and Christ from the Arabian Peninsula will not leave any but Muslims	**The Expulsion of the Jews f Madina** Yahya related to me from M from Ismail ibn Abi Hakim tha heard Umar ibn Abd al-Aziz "One of the last things that Messenger of Allah, may A bless him and grant him pe said was, 'May Allah fight Jews and the Christians. They the graves of their Prophets places of prostration. Two d shall not co-exist in the land o Arabs.'"

Sahih Muslim Hadith 4366 Narrated by Umar ibn al-Khattab Umar heard the Messnoger of Allah (peace be upon him) say: I will expel the jews and Christians from the Arabian peninsula and will not leave any but Muslims...	Al-Muwatta Hadith The expulsion of the Jews from Madina Yahya related to me from Malik from Ismail ibn Abi Hakim that he heard Umar ibn Abd al-Aziz say, "One of the last things that the Messenger of Allah, may Allah bless him and grant him peace, said was, 'May Allah fight the Jews and the Christians. They took the graves of their Prophets as places of prostration. Two deens shall not co-exist in the land of the Arabs.'"
Sahih Al-Bukhari Hadith 1.427 Narrated by Aisha and Abdullah bin Abbas When the last moment of the life of Allah's Apostle came he started puttion his 'Khamisa' on his face and when he felt hot and short of breath he took it off his face and said, "May Allah cyrse the Jews and Christians for they bult the places of worship at the graves of their Prophets."The Prophet was warning (Muslims) of what those had done.	Al-Muwatta Hadith Hadith 45.08 The Expulsion of the Jews from Madina Yahya related to me from Malik from Ibn Shihab that the Messenger of Allah, may Allah bless him grant him peace, said,"Two deens ahall not co-exist in the Arabian Peninsula." Malik said that ibn Shihab said, "Umar ibn al-Khattab searched for information about that until he was absolutely convinced that the Messenger of Allah, mayAllah bless him and grant him peace, had said, "Two deens shall not co-exist in the Arabian peninsula,' and he therefore expelled the Jews from Khaybar."

It is by no means clear even among Muslims that the exile of the People of the Book was the last words of Muhammad. A Shi'ite narration, for example, holds that Muhammad's last words were on a completely different subject to any supposed intent to expel the People of the Book. According to the Hadith, a large number of revelations 'descended' upon Muhammad immediately prior his death. The Hadith states that Surah 9 Tauba was the last Surah revealed in full and the last verse was S. 4:176. There is some ambiguity as to the identity of the last revelation, and von Denffer writes about this uncertainty:

> The Last Revelation Many Muslim scholars agree that the last revelation was Sura 2, verse 281: 'And fear the day when ye shall be brought back to God. Then shall every soul be paid what it earned and none shall be dealt with unjustly.' Some also say that it was 2:282 or 2:278. It has also been suggested that all three verses were revealed on one occasion. The Prophet died nine nights after the last revelation. Others hold that Sura 5:4 was the last to be revealed: 'This day I have perfected your religion for you, completed my favour upon you and have chosen for you Islam as your religion.'
>
> The opinion that this verse was the last revelation is not sound according to many scholars, since it was revealed during the last pilgrimage of the Prophet. This information is based upon a hadith from 'Umar. Suyuti explains concerning the verse in Sura 5 that after it nothing concerning ahkam and hal'al and haram was revealed, and in this sense it is the 'completion' of religion. However, revelation reminding man of the coming day of judgement continued and the last such revelation is the above verse.

Moreover, there are narrations which state that Muhammad's last words, and indeed the threat of exile, concerned not the ahl-ul-Kitab, but rather the pagans. In some ways, this would be more in keeping with Muhammad's religious policy, although there appears to be no evidence for such an expulsion; the pagans either converted naturally, or under pressure after the victory of Muhammad in Mecca. At any rate, they were subjugated. There is some parallel in the Qur'an itself for spatial restrictions on pagans; the last revealed surah says nothing about restricting the Jews or Christians, but forbids entry to the Sacred Mosque to the pagans.

Sahih Al Bukhari Hadith 4.288	Sahih Al-Bukhari Hadith 4.393
Narrated by Said bin Jubair Ibn Abbas said Thursday What (great thing) took place on Thursday!" Then he started weeping till his tears wetted the gravels of the ground. Then he said, "On Thursday the illness of Allah Apostle was aggravated and he said, 'Fetch me writing materials so that I may have something written to you after which you will never go astray.' The people (present there) differed in this matter and people should not differ befor a prophet. They said, 'Allah Apostle in seriously sick.' The prophet said, Let' me alone, as the state in which I am now, is better than what you are calling me for.The prophet on his death-bed gave three orders saying, 'Expel the pagans from the Arabian Peninsula, respect and give gifts to the foreign delegates as you have seen me dealing with them.' I forgot the third (order)." (Ya qub bin Muhammad said, "I asked Al-Mughira bin Abdur-Rahman about the Arabian Peninsula and he said, 'It compreses Mecca, Medena, Al-Yama-ma and Yemen." Ya'qub added, "And Al-Arj, the beaginning of Tihama.")	Narrated by Said bin Jubair that he heard Ibn 'Abbas saying, "Thursday! And you know not what Thursday is? After that Ibn 'Abbas wept till the stones on the ground were soaked with his tears. On that I asked Ibn 'Abbas, "What is (about) Thursday?" He said, "When the condition (i.e helth)of Allah's Apostle deteriorated he said, 'Bring me a bone of scapula, so thay I may write something for you after which you will never go astray. the people differed in their opinions although it was improper to differ in front of a prophet. They said, What is wrong with him? Do you think he is delirious? Ask him (to understand).' The Prophet replied, Leave me as I am in a better state than what you are asking me to do.'Then the Prophet ordered them to do three things saying, Turn out all the pagans from the Arabian Peninsula, show respect to all foreign delegates by giving them gifts as I used to do.'" The sub-narrator added, "The third order was something beneficial which either Ibn 'Abbas did not mention or he mentioned but I forgot."

SAHIH AL-BUKHARI HADITH 5.716- NARRATED BY IBN ABBAS

Thursday! And how great that Thursday was! The ailment of Allah's Apostle became worse (on Thursday) and he said, fetches me something so that I may write to you something after which you will never goes astray." The people (present there) differed in this matter, and it was not right to differ before a prophet. Some said, "What is wrong with him? (Do you think) he is delirious (seriously ill)? Ask him (to understand his state)." So they went to the Prophet and asked him again. The Prophet said, "Leave me, for my present state is better than what you call me for." Then he ordered them to do three things. He said, "Turn the pagans out of the Arabian Peninsula; respect and give gifts to the foreign delegations as you have seen me dealing with them." (Said bin Jubair, the sub-narrator said that Ibn Abbas kept quiet as rewards the third order, or he said, "I forgot it.") (See Hadith No. 116 Vol. 1)

In the Qur'an, there is no call for the general expulsion of the pagans, anymore than there is with respect to the People of the Book. The specific texts pertinent to our theme are:

Surah 2 Al-Baqara

191 And slay them wherever ye catch them and turn them out from where they have turned you out...

Surah 5 Al-Maida

33 The only reward of those who make war upon Allah and His messenger and strive after corruption in the land will be that they will be killed or crucified, or have their hands and feet on alternate sides cut off, or will be expelled out of the land...

34 Save those who repent before ye overpower them. For know that Allah is Forgiving, Merciful.

S. 2:191 has reference to the pagans at Mecca who had caused the migration of the Muslims through persecution.

However, it only applies to those pagans individually guilty of such oppression. Similarly, S. 5:33-34 prescribes banishment as one possible punishment for engaging in war against the Muslims, clearly in regard to those offending against the law. It applies to no specific religious confession, and neither is it justification for the exile of a religious community simply because of their theological differences with Islam.

There seems a certain incongruity about Muhammad giving pledges to Jews, Christians and Zoroastrians in the region and then immediately overturning them by ordering their expulsion, in the case of Najran only about two years after issuing the dhimmah. Is it likely he would utter such a command so soon after negotiating arrangements with the Najran Christians? Another very revealing problem concerns the purported justification for the expulsion - namely, that Jews and Christians turned the graves of the prophets into places of worship. Leaving aside the fact that many Muslims around the world have done exactly this with their own saints, and also ignoring the question as to whether the accusation against 'the People of the Book' was accurate (cf. Qur'anic gaffes on Mary's deity or Ezra's divine sonship), and whether even if it were true of some, was it general, one obvious query arises: why did Muhammad only invoke this prohibition at the end of his life? Why not sooner, if the same conditions prevailed? Why was this command not found in the Qur'an, or even in Hadith Qudsi? Why is there no hint of it in Muhammad's Last Sermon?

According to traditional Muslim history, caliph Umar later justified the exile of the ahl-ul-Kitab from the Arabian Peninsula in 640 on the basis of Muhammad's last command. However, the reference in the narration to his investigations about the subject questions about its authenticity, since it demonstrates that there was at least some uncertainty about it. Surely, as these were the last words of Muhammad, everyone would have been both hanging on his every word and repeating it? Why then the uncertainty? Further, since there are a number of parallel ahadith on the subject, why the need to investigate the narration, since it was so well attested?

Moreover, it should be noted that there is no agreement about the particulars in the various parallel ahadith about the subject, which surely raises further questions about authenticity.

THE REIGN OF ABU BAKR

One of the most telling arguments against the authenticity of the narrations of expulsion is the failure of the first caliph, Abu Bakr, to implement the supposed command of the Prophet to exile the People of the Book from the Arabian Peninsula. In fact, von Denffer notes that the treaty guaranteeing the security of the Najran Christians was upheld by Abu Bakr. Indeed, he not only upheld the treaty, he renewed it, impressed by the loyalty of the Najran Christians during the Riddah (apostasy) rebellions, when some tribes refused to pay zakat and apparently reverted to paganism. Why did he not take action against the Jews of the Hijaz at this time? If Muhammad had indeed actually intended to exile the People of the Book from the Peninsula, why did not the first Caliph implement the dying command of the Prophet?

Courbage and Fargues make this very point about Umar's violation of Muhammad's treaties with the Jews of Hijaz and Christians of Najran on the basis of Muhammad's supposed death-bed command: 'If the Prophet had actually ordered the expulsion of the Christians and the Jews, why was it not implemented by Abu Bakr, his immediate successor, and why did Umar wait until the end of his caliphate to execute it?' Equally, John Bagot Glubb observes about the supposed death-bed order by Muhammad: 'Had he really given such an order, it was curious that Abu Bekr made no attempt to enforce it... he was conscientious... in executing, to the least detail, everything which Muhammad during his lifetime had enjoined.' Indeed, this omission is completely incongruous, especially if Abu Bakr was conscientious enough to collate the Qur'an, as Muslim history holds. Such disobedience would be quite out of character and totally inexplicable in any of the Khulafah Rashidoon, unless it was never actually ordered in the first place.

THE REIGN OF UMAR

As we have seen, it was caliph Umar who was credited with enacting the exile of the People of Book in obedience to the supposed last words of Muhammad. Perhaps because

Muslim sources are often characterised by confusion and variant traditions, Umar emerges as a complicated personality in such sources. For example, in the Hadith, he is shown to be concerned for the welfare of the dhimmis (Jews, Christians and Zoroastrians). He advised whoever would be his successor to treat them kindly:

Amr ibn Maimun

Sahih Al-Bukhari Hadith 5:50

... I also recommend him concerning Allah's and His Apostle's protectees (i.e. Dhimmis) to fulfill their contracts and to fight for them and not to overburden them with what is beyond their ability...

Equally, he was insistent that when a Christian or Jew died, the relative holding to that faith were his or her heirs. He was not antagonistic to Muslims praying in church buildings according to one tradition. The Christian Arabs of the Taghlib tribe objected to paying the Jizya on the basis of their being Arabs and because of its humiliating nature. On these grounds, they threatened to emigrate unless they were released from this, and to avert this, Umar substituted the sadaqah tax paid by Muslims. He did the same for the Christians of Tanukh. Umar's terms for the surrender of Damascus were generous. He ordered that the people should keep possessions of their lands, and that they should only pay Jizya in accordance with their ability. If they were too poor to pay this, his policy was again generous:

...require no more of them... never to take them as prisoners, nor to do any injustice or harm to them or to take any of their property unless you have a claim to it. You must fulfil the obligations you accepted in accordance with your agreement with them.

As to the request of taking out their crosses during their holidays once a year, you should not prevent them from so doing outside the city, provided they agree not to take with them their banners and standards.

This good-will to the People of the Book is further indicated by the text of Umar's treaty with the Palestinians, after the conquest of Jerusalem by the Arabs in 637 A.D. The Orthodox Christian Patriarch of the city, Sophronius, ceremonially handed the keys of the city to Umar, recognising his rule. The Caliph pledged freedom of religion and access to the holy places, and gave assurance to the Christians of...the safety of their persons, their goods, their churches, their crosses - whether they be in good or bad shape - and their worship in general. Their churches will neither be touched nor destroyed; they and their dependants will not undergo any damage and it will be the same for their crosses and their processions.

Palestinian Christians were exempted from paying the head-tax. Further, Umar, rejecting the objections of the Palestinian Christians, guaranteed the same rights to the Jews of Palestine. At one point, during the time for salat, Umar was strolling with Sophronius in the Church of the Holy Sepulchre. The latter invited him to pray on the premises, but the Caliph declined, on the grounds that later Muslims would transform the Church into a mosque. He went outside to pray, and Muslims later did build a Mosque on the place where he performed salat. These examples do not sit well with the traditional picture of the man who 'cleansed' the Arabian Peninsula of Jews and Christians.

As we have stated, the problem is that the sources dealing with Umar often reveal contradictory tendencies. For example, the purported 'Code of Umar', allegedly imposed by the Muslim commander Abu Ubaid, is extremely sectarian and repressive. It is often alleged that this pact has been subjected to later emendations. It is noteworthy that there are several versions of the text. One version, from a Muslim source, renders it as follows:

When thou camest into our land we asked of thee safety for our lives and the people of our religion, and we imposed these terms on ourselves: not to build in Damascus and its environs church, convent, chapel, monk's hermitage; not to repair what is dilapidated of our churches nor any of them that are in Muslim quarters; not to withhold our churches from Muslims stopping there by night or day; to open their doors to the traveller and wayfarer; not to shelter there nor in our houses a spy, not to hide one who is a traitor to the Muslims; to beat the naqus only gently in our churches; not to display a cross on them; not to raise our voices in prayer or chanting in our churches; not to carry in procession a cross or our book; not to take out Easter or Palm Sunday processions; not to raise our voices over our dead...not to sell wine nor parade idolatry in companies of Muslims; not to entice a Muslim to our religion not to invite him to it; ...to keep our religion wherever we are; not to resemble the Muslims in wearing the Qalansuwa, the turban, shoes, nor in the parting of the hair, nor in their way of riding, not to use their language nor be called by their names; to cut the hair in front and divide our forelock; to tie the zunnar round our waists; not to engrave Arabic on our seals; not to ride on saddles; not to keep arms nor put them in our houses nor wear swords to honour Muslims in their gatherings; to guide them on the road, to stand up in public meetings when they wish it; not to make our houses higher than theirs; not to teach our children the Koran; not to be partners with a Muslim except in business; to entertain every Muslim traveller in our customary style and feed him in it three days. We will not abuse a Muslim, and he who strikes a Muslim has forfeited his rights.

The text contains clear anachronisms revealing its emended character. For example, at the time of the conquest of Syria, there were clearly no 'Muslim quarters'. The servile tone of the code as well as its questionable declaration that its conditions were self-imposed undermines its authenticity. What is significant is the actual dating of the code. It is usually held that it emerged in the ninth century, two centuries after the reign of Umar. We will see the significance of this dating in our next section.

According to traditional Islamic history, the exile of the Jews from Khaybar took place on the basis of the following traditions:

Sahih Al-Bukhari Hadith 3.890

Narrated by Ibn Umar

When the people of Khaibar dislocated Abdullah bin Umar's hands and feet, 'Umar got up delivering a sermon saying, "No doubt, Allah's Apostle made a contract with the Jews concerning their properties, and said to them, 'We allow you (to stand in your land) as long as Allah allows you.' Now Abdullah bin Umar went to his land and was attacked at night, and his hands and feet were dislocated, and as we have no enemies there except those Jews, they are our enemies and the only people whom we suspect, I have made up my mind to exile them." When 'Umar decided to carry out his decision, a son of Abu Al-Haqiq's came and addressed 'Umar, "O chief of the believers, will you exile us although Muhammad allowed us to stay at our places, and made a contract with us about our properties, and accepted the condition of our residence in our land?" 'Umar said, "Do you think that I have forgotten the statement of Allah's Apostle, i.e.: What will your condition be when you are expelled from Khaibar and your camel will be carrying you night after night?"

Sahih Al-Bukhari Hadith 3.531

Narrated by Ibn Umar

Umar expelled the Jews and the Christians from Hijaz. When Allah's Apostle had conquered Khaibar, he wanted to expel the Jews from it as its land became the property of Allah, His Apostle, and the Muslims. Allah's Apostle intended to expel the Jews but they requested him to let them stay there on the condition that they would do the labour and get half of the fruits. Allah's Apostle told them, "We will let you stay on thus condition, as long as we wish." So, they (i.e. Jews) kept on living there until 'Umar forced them to go towards Taima' and Ariha'.
Sahih Al-Bukhari Hadith 4.380

Narrated by Ibn Umar

Umar bin Al-Khattab expelled all the Jews and Christians from the land of Hijaz. Allah's Apostle after conquering Khaibar, thought of expelling the Jews from the land which, after he conquered it belonged to Allah, Allah's Apostle and the Muslims. But the Jews requested Allah's Apostle to leave them there on the condition that they would do the labour and get half of the fruits (the land would

The Jew replied, "That was joke from Abul-Qasim." 'Umar said, "O the enemy of Allah! You are telling a lie." 'Umar then drove them out and paid them the price of their properties in the form of fruits, money,
camel saddles and ropes, etc. Sunan of Abu-Dawood Hadith 3001

Narrated by Abdullah ibn Umar

Umar said: The Apostle of Allah (peace be upon him) had transaction with the Jews of Khaybar on condition that we should expel them when we wish. If anyone has property (with them), he should take it back, for I am going to expel the Jews. So he expelled them.

yield). Allah's Apostle said, "We shall keep you on these terms as long as we wish." Thus they stayed till the time of 'Umar's Caliphate when he expelled them to Taima and Ariha.

Malik ibn Anas

Al-Muwatta Hadith

Hadith 45.19

The Expulsion of the Jews from Madina
Malik said, "Umar ibn al-Khattab expelled the Jews from Najran (a Jewish settlement in the Yemen) and Fadak (a Jewish settlement thirty miles from Madina). When the Jews of Khaybar left, they did not take any fruit or land. The Jews of Fadak took half the fruit and half the land, because the Messenger of Allah, may Allah bless him and grant him peace, had made a settlement with them for that. So Umar entrusted to them the value in gold, silver, camels, ropes and saddle bags of half the fruit and half the land, and handed the value over to them and expelled them."

The tone of the traditions sounds like special pleading, reflecting the nature of an anachronistic vaticinia ex eventu (prophecy after the fact). Probably Muhammad did indeed guarantee the permanent presence of the Jews, but later traditions emended the edicts. Hence the invention of the gloss that the Jews could stay for as long as the Muslims wished, to justify the violation of the rights of the Jews of Hijaz. If Muhammad ordered the expulsion of the ahl-ul-Kitab despite his previous guarantees, why the need to establish that either the Jews or Christians had violated their compacts (e.g. by taking usury)? Again, the Muslim historical sources cannot reconcile the absolute imperative in the narration of Muhammad's last command with the conditional nature of the reports of 'Umar's actions. The conditional element attached to these ahadith contradicting the absolute character of Muhammad's command suggests that both Jews and Christians were originally given absolute guarantees, conditional only on loyalty to the state, i.e. not aiding the enemies of the state. We have seen that whilst some Muslim tribes rebelled during the reign of Abu Bakr, the Najran Christians remained loyal, and no-one suggests that the Jews of the Hijaz rebelled. Hence, new 'conditions' had to be invented to circumvent the guarantees Muhammad gave. The tone of Bukhari Hadith 3.890 suggests this was the case, and that the People of the Book protested their rights according to the dhimmah Muhammad gave them.

WHEN DID THE EXILE OCCUR AND WHY

As well as exiling the Jews, both secular historians and Islamic sources assert that Umar also expelled the Najran Christians to Kufa in Iraq. On the other hand, Trimingham claims that it may have been only some doctrinally aberrant Christians who were expelled, and states that there is evidence of the Najran Christians in Arabia as late as 897 AD. The Encyclopaedia of Islam records the presence of a bishop in Najran as late as the ninth and tenth centuries. It also notes the existence of Christians in Yamama and Bahrain in 893 and 899 and in Sana and Yemen in 837 and 850. Equally, Courbage and Fargues state about the supposed dating of the exile in the time of Umar:

Two centuries later, the great chroniclers of Islam believed that the whole of Central Arabia was emptied of Christians and Jews in the wake of Umar's action. But there are pieces of evidence to suggest that this was not quite the case. For example, it was a Christian of Medina, admittedly a slave, who assassinated Umar. During the reign of Mu'awiya, the founder of the Umayyad dynasty, a force of 200 Christians formed the police of Medina and in Mecca a'cemetery for the infidels' existed for a long time.

Yet if non-Muslims did remain in the peninsula their numbers in the central region were small. It is almost certain that, three centuries after the revelation, only a tiny group of Christians remained in Najran. The Jews were confined to the periphery.

Small numbers or no, the very fact that Christians remained in central Arabia surely questions the authenticity of the ahadith in question, since the narrations of expulsion indicate no exceptions. For example, according to Bukhari Hadith 4.288, identifying the borders of the Arabian Peninsula, Yemen is included in its bounds. Yet even today, there are still Jews living in Yemen, which at least points to some tensions and confusion among the traditions, if not outright contradictions. Of course, it is quite likely by the ninth and tenth centuries, the number of Christians in central Arabia was indeed small, as the process observable elsewhere in Muslim-ruled lands would have prevailed - gradual conversion to Islam.

It is the dating that is so significant. The actual exile probably happened in the ninth century. Up to the ninth century, a number of Transjordanian Christian towns remained self-governing. It was also when the so-called 'Pact of Umar' emerged, anachronistically read back into the time of the second caliph, just as, we suggest, was the general evacuation of the ahl-ul-Kitab. Jay Smith notes '... the earliest documents which we can refer to today are those compiled by Ibn Hisham (the Sira of the prophet), and the large Hadith compilations of al-Bukhari, Muslim and others, all written in the ninth century, and thus 200 to 250 years after the fact.' When we consider the suggestions of historical revisionists like Crone, etc., and what Jay Smith has advocated, a common theme arises: that the real origins of Islam, as the faith is now understood, only occurred in some two hundred years after Muhammad. It is then that both the Qur'an and the Hadith receive their final redactions, and only thereafter that Sira literature emerges in its final redaction. In short, what occurs is the construction of a historical national mythology, in this case, as has occurred in so many cases of the formation of a national identity down the centuries, a polemical assertion against a rival ideology - in this case, Judaism and Christianity.

To return to Watt's comments about the consequence of Muslim conquest of Iraq, Syria and Egypt with their 'better-educated Christians', he notes that 'From this period onwards Islam and Christianity have been rivals...' Naturally, the presence of Jews and Christians in the Muslim heartland with historical traditions of what actually occurred could have 'blown the whistle' on this propagandistic historical revision. This would be especially true of the Jews near Mecca and Medina which had only lately been transformed into the leading shrines of Islam in place of Jerusalem. Hence the evacuation of the People of the Book at this time, which would naturally entail their eventual assimilation by the larger Christian and Jewish communities to which they were forcibly removed, or their eventual conversion to Islam. The timing of the exile is significant in this regard. It is also significant that the Najran Christians were exiled to a place near Kufa, a leading city of the Muslims by this time, and a garrison settlement at that. Kufa had only been founded in 638, and the Christians were purportedly evacuated to this garrison city in 642, only four years later. Why were the Christians exiled to this place, where they would be isolated from other Christians, rather to the major centres of Christian presence in the Levant, like the Jews, who were removed to Jericho (Ariha)?

The answer to that is to examine the nature of forced evacuations. This was not an act of chauvinism, such as the ethnic cleansing of people from the former Yugoslavia; nor was it a supposed 'security' act, such as Stalin's uprooting of Caucasus peoples at the Second World War because of supposed collaboration with the Germans. Rather, it should be compared to the story of Mordechai Vanunu, the Israeli scientist and Christian convert who blew the whistle on the Israeli nuclear programme. He was not a traitor - he did not spy for Syria, etc. He simply opposed nuclear weapons. He was not only imprisoned, but also isolated from all contact. The reason for this draconian, repressive treatment can be found in the argument of the trial prosecutor - 'the security damage already done by Vanunu's disclosures, and the further damage threatened by allowing Vanunu access to the media.' This single individual had revelations damaging to the regime. Obviously, he was no military threat to them.

Similarly, the Muslims, defending their beliefs about Qur'anic Christology, would be concerned to protect the integrity of their beliefs. The Najran Christians, being blamed for holding the heretical Christology that the Qur'an attacks, would have to be isolated and removed, to prevent the truth from being known. Their position was worse than that of the Jews, since the latter were a minority, and were disliked by the Christians because of the Crucifixion and because of the persecutions recorded in the Acts of the Apostles, for the massacre of Palestinian Christians during the Persian occupation of Jerusalem in the seventh century, and for the earlier persecution of Arab Christians by the Jewish king of Yemen Dhu Nuwas. No Christian would take seriously their comments. Moreover, their objections, apart from the gaffe about Ezra, would be merely theological in the sense of objecting to a Gentile prophet, rather than objections to the presentation of their historical religion in the Qur'an. The Christians, however, were the majority in the conquered territories, and their objections to Qur'anic Christology were more far-reaching and dangerous. If the Najran Christians were blamed for the presentation of the distorted Christology of the Qur'an, as in the Sira, measures would have to be taken to prevent them from objecting. Isolated, they would either eventually convert to Islam, because of the Jizya, or individuals would, if possible, migrate to other Christian communities where their offspring would inter-marry. Either way, the truth would die out.

The point Arafat made about the magnification of Biblical and Qur'anic stories is relevant here. The Qur'anic texts referring to 'expelling the pagans' who had previously expelled Muslims, and of banishing those People of the Book who engaged in conflict with the Muslims, were 'magnified' by the Hadith and Sira stories about the Jews of Arabia, and by reference to the Biblical traditions of the slaughter of the Canaanites, and applied to the 'infidels' in the new Islamic Holy Land. After all, even a conservative Orientalist commentator like Watt accepts that both Hadith and Sira are, to some degree, 'expansions' of the Qur'anic material. No doubt, as Trimingham accepts, Umar did indeed remove some Christians from Najran for some reason, and probably did the same to some Jews, as Arafat suggests. Later Muslim commentators would then magnify the story to conceal what actually occurred to the People of the Book in Arabia in the ninth century. It would be anachronistically read back to suggest that the exile was total, rather than individual. The fact that objective historical sources contradict the traditional Muslim presentation of the exile of the People of the Book from Arabia is the greatest clue to the inauthentic nature of the entirety of Islamic claims.

Both Christianity and Islam claim to be revealed religions based in historical events. One cannot be a Christian and deny the historical event of the Crucifixion, even if one would wish to preserve elements of the theology associated with the event. Equally, Islam demands belief in the historicity of what supposedly occurred in the cave at Hira; denying it renders one apostate. Either these events actually happened, or, except in some Feuerbachian sense, the religions are not true. Denying or disproving any of the historical events in the Bible for any conservative believer would demolish his faith. This is also true of Muslims. After all, the Sunni-Shia split partly revolves around competing views of early Islamic history. Likewise, if the narrations of exile only existed in the collection of Abu Dawud, they would have little import, but they also occur in sahih material. The same is also true of the story of the Najran deputation. What makes it especially important is that many verses of the Qur'an are supposedly based on the visit of this delegation; if the Najran Christians did not, and could not have said what the Sira claims they stated, and then the accusations of Qur'anic Christology are disproved, and Muslims are left explaining their origin. The authenticity of the Qur'an would be demolished.

Were the Najran Christians still around we could settle the issue once for all, and possibly still could if Saudi Arabia allowed free archaeological access to investigate. However, all reports from that country about archaeology suggest that this will not be forthcoming, since the authorities are notorious for covering-up evidence of the former Jewish and Christian presence in the country. Since the Saudi regime employs Islam, rather than ethnic identity, nationalism or ideology as its basis, it cannot allow the foundations of the religion to be challenged. In that respect, the Saudi regime has much in common with the Muslims who actually fabricated the story of Umar's ejection of the ahl-ul-Kitab, and indeed implemented the exile, over two hundred years after it supposedly occurred.

Bibliography

Abbott, Nabia. *Aishah: The Beloved of Mohammad.* London: Al-Saqi, 1998.

Andrae, Tor. *Mohammed: The Man and His Faith.* London: George Allen & Unwin, 1936.

Armstrong, Karen. *Islam: A Short History.* New York: Modern Library, revised ed., 2002.

Asad, Muhammad. *The Message of the Qur'an.* Gibraltar: Dar al-Andalus, 1980.

Asani, Ali, et al. *Celebrating Muhammad: Images of the Prophet in Popular Muslim Poetry.* Columbia, Ashgate/Variorum, 2000.

Azam Malik, trans.). Houston, TX: The Institute of Islamic Knowledge, 1997.

Baljon, Jon M.S. *Modern Muslim Koran Interpretation (1880-1960).* Leiden: E.J. Brill, 1961.

Barlas, Asma. *"Believing Women" in Islam: Unreading Patriarchal Interpretations of the Qur'an.*

Bell, Richard. *Introduction to the Qur'an.* Edinburgh: Edinburgh University Press, 1963.

Bell, Richard. *The Qur'an Translated,* 2 Vols. Edinburgh: T. & T. Clark, 1960.

Bowker, John. *What Muslims Believe.* Oxford, UK: Onewworld, 1999.

Burton, John. *The Collection of the Quran.* Cambridge, UK: Cambridge University Press, 1977.

Cook, Michael. *Muhammad.* New York: Oxford University Press, 1983.

Cragg, Kenneth. *The Mind of the Quran: Chapters in Reflection.* London: George Allen & Unwin, CT: Yale University Press, 2002.

Dawood, N.J. *The Koran.* Harmondsworth: Penguin, 1956.

Denny, Frederick Mathewson. *An Introduction to Islam.* New York: Macmillan, 1994.

Elias, Jamal J. *Islam.* Upper Saddle River, NJ: Prentice Hall, 1999.

Esack, Farid. *Qur'an, Liberation and Pluralism.* Oxford, England: Oneworld, 1997.

Esack, Farid. *The Qur'an: A Short Introduction.* Oxford, England: Oneworld, 2002.

Gilsenan, Michael. *Recognising Islam: an anthropologist's introduction.* London: Croom Helm, 1982.

Hawting, G.R. et al., eds. *Approaches to the Quran.* London: Routledge, 1993.

Hodgson, Marshall G.S. *The Venture of Islam,* 3 Vols. Chicago, IL: University of Chicago International, 1983.

Izutsu, Toshihiko. *God and Man in the Koran.* Salem, NH: Ayer Co. Publ., 1980.

Jansen, J.J.G. *The Interpretation of the Koran in Modern Egypt.* Leiden: E.J. Brill, 1974.

Kahn, Muhammad Zafrulla. *Muhammad, Seal of the Prophets.* New York: Viking Press, 1981.

Khalifa, Rashad. *Quran, Hadith, and Islam.* Fremont, CA: Universal Unity, 2000.

Lings, Martin. *Muhammad: his life based on the earliest sources.* New York: Inner Traditions London: Oxford University Press, 1955.

McAuliffe, Jane Dammen, ed. *The Encyclopedia of the Qur'an,* Vol. 1. Leiden: E.J. Brill, 2001.

Mir, Mustansir. *Dictionary of Qur'anic Terms and Concepts.* New York: Garland, 1987.

Motzki, Harald, ed. *The Biography of Muhammad: The Issue of the Sources.* Leiden: E.J. Brill, 2000.,

Nasr, Seyyed Hossein. *Ideals and Realities of Islam.* London: Allen & Unwin, 1966.

Nasr, Seyyed Hossein. *Islamic Spirituality I: Foundations.* New York: Crossroad, 1987.

Nasr, Seyyed Hossein. *Islamic Spirituality II: Manifestations.* New York: Crossroad, 1991.

Nasr, Seyyed Hossein. *Muhammad: Man of God.* Chicago, IL: Kazi Publ., 1995.

Nasr, Seyyed Hossein. *The Heart of Islam: Enduring Values for Humanity.* San Francisco, CA: New York Press, 1984.

Newby, Gordon D. *A Concise Encyclopedia of Islam.* Oxford, UK: Oneworld, 2002.

Peters, F.E. *A Reader on Classical Islam.* Princeton, NJ: Princeton University Press, 1994.

Peters, Francis E. *Muhammad and the Origins of Islam.* Albany, NY: State University of New Press, 1961.

Rahman, Fazlur. *Islam.* Chicago, IL: University of Chicago Press, 2nd ed., 1979.

Rahman, Fazlur. *Major Themes of the Qur'an.* Minneapolis, MN: Bibliotheca Islamica, 1980.

Rippin, Andrew, ed. *The Qur'an: Style and Contents.* Aldershot, UK: Ashgate, 2001.

Rippin, Andrew. *Muslims: Their Religious Beliefs and Practices.* London: Routledge, 2nd ed., 2001.

Rippin, Andrew. *The Qur'an and Its Interpretive Tradition.* Aldershot, UK: Ashgate, 2002.

Robinson, Francis. *Atlas of the Islamic World since 1500.* New York: Facts on File, 1982.

Rubin, Uri, ed. *The Life of Muhammad.* Aldershot: Ashgate, 1998.

Ruthven, Malise. *Islam in the World.* New York: Oxford University Press, 2nd ed., 2000.

Schuon, Frithjof. *Islam and the Perennial Philosophy.* London: World of Islam Festival Publ. Co., SCM Press, 1996.

Sells, Michael. *Approaching the Qur'an: The Early Revelations.* Ashland, OR: White Cloud Press, Society, 1996.

Stowasser, Barbara Freyer. *Women in the Qur'an: Traditions and Interpretations.* New York: T. & T. Clark, 1939.

Tayob, Abdulkader. *Islam: A Short Introduction.* Oxford, England: Oneworld, 1999.

The Koran Interpreted. Arthur J. Arberry, trans. New York: Macmillan, 1955.

The Koran. J.M. Rodwell, trans. London: J.M. Dent & Sons, 1909 (reprint ed., 1974).

Wadud-Muhsin, Amina. *Qur'an and Woman: Reading the Sacred Text from a Woman's Perspective.*

Waines, David. *An Introduction to Islam.* Cambridge, UK: Cambridge University Press, 1995.

Watt, William Montgomery. *Muhammad at Mecca.* Oxford, UK: Clarendon Press, 1953.

Watt, William Montgomery. *Muhammad at Medina.* Oxford, UK: Clarendon Press, 1956.

Watt, William Montgomery. *What is Islam?* London: Longman, 1970.

Wild, S., ed. *The Qur'an as Text: Islamic Philosophy, Theology, and Science.* Leiden: E.J. Brill, 1997.

Williams, John Alden, ed. *The Word of Islam.* Austin, TX: University of Texas Press, 1994.

Index

H

I

J

L

M

N

O

P

R